WHAT OTHERS ARE SAYING...

Jim Howard's story is so remarkable that it testifies to the kind of full circle story writing only God can do with fully surrendered people! I hope elders, pastors and overseers everywhere read this book and never stop believing that God can take any situation and turn it into something beautiful!

Johnny Scott
Lead Pastor, Generation Christian Church, Trinity, FL

If you ever felt you were not worthy of God's forgiveness, I encourage you to read this book. Before your eyes you will see a true story unfold that demonstrates that God has a plan, though unseen, for everyone. This story of Jim Howard's life, experiences, and how God continually intervened and engineered his circumstances will reveal to you that God does love us and has a plan and purpose for your life regardless of your past. You too can make a difference, as Jim has, and fulfill the purpose God has planned for your life.

Mark Graham
CEO and President Planning Advisors

Thank you Jim for sharing *God's Unseen Plan*. The authenticity as a man and transparency are refreshing. Your heart for the Lord as you testify to God's providence in every experience is such an encouragement. *God's Unseen Plan* prayerfully will be used mightily in spurring other men on about sharing their journeys and come to know Christ intimately.

James J. Sutherlin, Jr.
Connect4 Executive Connections

I have known and been friends with Jim Howard since we were partners in a police patrol car in the mid-1970s and have long been aware of some of what he has documented in his book. I found his autobiography to be a fascinating read about his sometimes difficult life, in some ways due to the life path he sadly chose for himself and in other ways due to the obstacles placed before him by others. Despite the reasons for his life journey he has finally returned to his Lord and seems happy and at peace with himself. This is something we all strive for. I wish Jim and his family the very best as he continues on this path.

Bruce R. Hierstein
Assistance Chief, Norfolk Police Department, Retired

Hard to put the book down. You never can tell how intriguing a person's life is until you read Jim's story. Powerful and God driven.

Bill Pressel
Elder at Generations Christian Church, Trinity, FL

God's Unseen Plan charts Jim's adversity, self-discovery, and realization that God was walking alongside him at every step of his journey. Reading this book provides you the inspiration that with the right mindset, faithfulness and openness to listen, God's plan is revealed to all of us. If you are a young man seeking inspiration in your life you should read this book!

Simon Osamoh
Former British Police Detective & Founder Kingswood Security

June & John,

To two true warriors of God!
Let us rejoice in God's
Perfect Plan He has for us!

Your brother in
Christ,

Jim
Jeremiah
29:11

GOD'S
UNSEEN PLAN

FINDING PERFECTION
ONLY IN GOD'S GRACE

JIM HOWARD

HigherLife Publishing

Oviedo, Florida

HigherLife Publishing & Marketing
 PO Box 623307
 Oviedo, FL 32762
 AHigherLife.com

God's Unseen Plan / James Howard. – 1st ed.
ISBN 978-1-951492-68-7 (paperback)
ISBN 978-1-951492-69-4 (ebook)
ISBN 978-1-954533-08-0 (hardback)

10 9 8 7 6 5 4 3 2 1

Dedication

I dedicate this book to my wife Wendy.
Without your encouragement, this book would
never have been written.

Contents

Foreword

It's quite an honor when someone asks you to write a foreword, especially when the book's title is *God's Unseen Plan*. However, the greater honor is having a friend that is always there for you. A friend that always has your best interest at heart. A friend that has seen you through some of the toughest times in your life and celebrated the best with you too. That friend came into my life in 2002 when he, his wife, and eighteen-month-old daughter rented the house across the street. Initially, it was just nice to have someone in that empty house. We introduced ourselves and waved and smiled as we saw each other in the neighborhood. At that time, I was married to my second wife and we were very active in our church. And then it happened: We did what we were supposed to do as Christians. We invited the Howards to our church. That's how it all began. An eighteen-year friendship in which we grew from just neighbors to the best of friends and truly kindred souls. Now we may see each other three or four times a month, or three or four times a year, but we talk often. Jim Howard is the first person I call when I need true Christian counsel. He isn't going to tell me what I want to hear. He's going to tell me what I *need* to hear.

Back in those early days, Jim and I jogged together. One day after one of our runs, we were cooling down in my driveway and he told me this: "I'm not sure I believe in the existence of God or Jesus or the Holy Spirit." I told him to stay open-minded and gave my stock answer. I said I was not a Bible scholar, but I knew that

I most definitely had a relationship with God—a relationship I knew was real, even though I couldn't explain it. Over the years, Jim had shared some pretty shocking details about his life with me, and I understood why he doubted. However, I could see that he was feeling a tap from his heavenly Father, who was saying, "I'm here. Just let Me know when you're ready."

As I mentioned, Jim and I had both been through some ups and downs. He'd seen me through divorce, the loss of my parents, many moves and changes in careers and churches, my daughter's wedding, and my son's music career, all the way to where I am today at a very content and fulfilling time in my life. Jim and Wendy were our guests at First Christian Church of Tarpon Springs and they never left. They are still there in its new location under its new name, Generations Christian Church. Jim's faith and ministry have exploded. He is a leader in that church now; and after retiring from law enforcement for the second time, he started a non-profit organization to help churches with their safety and security plans and teams. I was honored to serve on his board of directors for several years and have watched Jim continue to grow in his faith, extending his undying love and passion to everyone around him.

God's Unseen Plan is Jim's journey through life and his inner battle with his faith. When asked why he decided to write it, his answer surprised me. He said he hadn't really wanted to, but others around him had encouraged him so he had. It took a while to take shape and he gives credit to God for revealing some things to him in 2018 that he needed to know in order to finish it. He said, "It's God's timing, not mine."

This is not just Jim's journey, it's every Christian's in one way or another. Jim's complete transparency reveals how he struggled with his faith and his purpose, and even his existence at times. This book shows us that we are all God's creations, flawed and full of sin, but loved unconditionally and eternally, nonetheless. May Jim's courage to write give others the courage to never give up.

This book is for everyone: every man, woman, father, mother, son, or daughter that has ever asked themselves if God or Jesus or the Holy Spirit really exists. Jim proves that nobody needs to look too far for that clarity. It's right here, or right over there, or just around the corner, or in a new neighborhood in Trinity, Florida. I take no credit for anything in Jim's life. Not for turning him around or making him change in any way. I simply did what Christians are told to do: Love your fellow man and invite them to your church to let them hear about the love and grace and redemption that are found only in a relationship with God. Jim did that and we all get to benefit from his decision. All glory to God for Jim and this amazing autobiography. *God's Unseen Plan* is a must-read for any Christian. As these pages and Jim's life tell us: "We are not always aware that we are living God's will for our lives, but we sure know when we're not."

Jim, thank you for this honor,

Steve Plummer
Friend of the prophetic warrior and his brother in Christ—always

JIM HOWARD

Preface

Every time I told my story, someone urged me to write this book, but in my heart, I always wondered about it. Who would really be interested in my life? I guess we will find out. I am no movie star (even though I did have a small part in a TV series called the "FBI Files" a few times). I am not a professional athlete, but I will never forget the time I got a clean sack on a quarterback when his team was beating us by twenty points. I will also never forget the triple I got on opening day of Pony League baseball in the summer of 1969. However, an event in 1970 left me broken. It was only after I came back to the Lord in 2002—thirty-two long years later—that I realized that even as an average guy, I had overcome a great deal. Now I know where I am going. That is because of Jesus' promise never to leave me and His unseen plan in my life.

It has not been easy. I have had to swallow my pride, leave my ego at the door, trust Him with everything, and appreciate the fact that every day is a blessing from God. I am a child of God and He has an incredible journey planned for me. He has a home for me in His kingdom.

I have four little rules I live by and teach to anyone that will listen. Every morning before I start my day, I pull up my YouVersion app and read the verse of the day. Then I thank the Lord for giving me another day and ask him to lead me in His will, not mine. At the end of the day, I have a talk with my Father—just as God used to talk to Adam in the cool of the day in Genesis 3:8. I thank Him for the good parts of the day and complain about the bad.

He is my Father. I am always looking for His advice, the direction and help every loving Father shares with His son. The forth rule is the last thing I need to do before I close down for the night. I read some sort of daily devotion. I use David Jeremiah's daily bible study "Today's Turning Point." You can sign up for it online at davidjeremiah.org.

Our Father, Son, and Holy Spirit should be the last thing on our mind when we call it a day. That way we put the world behind us and fall asleep in our Father's arms. I cannot explain the difference it has made in my life and my sleep. To understand the power of Christ you need to do these daily four things, you will see the difference.

I finally realized that He had given me a gift, the gift of a storyteller, and you are about to read my story in my own words. My one request is that after you read it, please honor Jesus by sharing His Word with a friend or a family member. Tell them that we can all be forgiven and saved. If it were not for Him, I would not be here today telling you my story.

Acknowledgments

I f God had not had a plan for me, this book would not have been possible. He placed people in my life that helped mold me and bring me to where I am today. I give all glory and praise to Him for that process.

I want to thank HigherLife Publishing for helping me get this book to my readers. I am not the easiest person to work with, and I truly appreciate your patience.

I am thankful for my parents for teaching me the Golden Rule and the concept that if you work hard it will pay off. I want to thank my brothers, John, Joel, and Jeff. I am so proud of you. Through all we have gone through, we never lost sight that we were the "Howard Boys."

I wish I could list all of those that helped me in my career in the Norfolk Police Department. I am afraid I would forget someone, and I really don't want to do that. The department taught me about family, even though it was sometimes dysfunctional. They also taught me how to fight hard for the things I believed in. Thanks so much.

I want to thank my church family. You took me in and didn't see me as a sinner. Instead you looked at my heart and trusted that God had a plan for me. Mike Smith, Bill Pressel, and Greg Johnson showed me that I could still keep my man card and be a Christian. I also want to thank Johnny Scott for his constant support in my ministry and in writing this.

I want to thank my running buddy for fifteen years, Chris, and my Grand Canyon buddies, Mike, Doug, and Ed, for listening to me about one day writing this book. I guess we will have to find something else to talk about now.

I want to thank my daughters, Jessica and Jaycee. You taught me about unconditional love—which saved me. You have grown into beautiful, strong women, and have made me so proud.

A special thanks goes to my beautiful wife, Wendy. She saw the goodness in my heart from the first day we met. She never gave up on me, even in the darkest hours of our marriage. I am still amazed and thankful that she didn't leave me. Without her encouragement, this would never have been written. She understood the importance of telling my story to help others that have been in situations like mine. She knows there is always hope, no matter how bad the situation. She is the inspiration in all I do.

Introduction

In September 1970, an event occurred that changed many lives in my little town. Each one of those affected has their own story to tell. I have always felt that theirs were more important than mine, and I pray that one day they will share theirs too.

In 2002, a few Christians pulled me aside and told me that I needed to write about it. At that time, I was the prodigal son of Luke 11:15-31 just returned home. Yet even after my Father celebrated my return, I still had doubts about His unconditional love for me. Because of those doubts, I didn't want to write. In order to write such a tale, I would have to bare all, and I wasn't ready to do that.

Later, when we started Trinity Security Allies (TSA), a church security ministry, I still didn't want to do it. When I finished each training session, I explained to the participants that church violence could happen anywhere—even a small town in Texas as in my story. People told me I needed to share what happened and how it affected me *at the beginning* of training because it gave me greater credibility as a teacher. People like Steve Hopper and my wife, Wendy, and many others kept pushing me to write, and so in 2018 I began to "write" this book just to appease them.

In 2020 the COVID-19 pandemic hit and shut down TSA's live training schedule. As I prayed about God's plan, I finally felt His call to write. In three months, with His strength and the support of others, I had it done.

When I finished, Bill Pressel, who had been one of the first to encourage me to do this called me just to talk. I told him I had finished, and he begged to read it. I sent him my first draft. He called me three days later to say how much he enjoyed it. It was a great book. These were words of encouragement that my earthly father had never given me. Bill told me my book would help men who thought God could not love them because of all the sins they had committed. If this is true and I help one person come to Christ, the time and effort it took to write will be worth it. To that one person I say this: God's grace is amazing. Surrender to it, accept it, and enjoy it.

Jim Howard

I didn't understand why this was happening to us. What had we done that was so wrong that God would punish us like this?

It had started on a Sunday night right after church and here we were three days later, feeling like we were fleeing for our lives. We hadn't even had enough time to say goodbye to our friends. We had packed all our belongings in a trailer and bolted to Florida. All I could think was: *God, wasn't I good enough? Didn't I pray enough? Was I not Christian enough? What did I do that was so terrible that You would punish us like this?*

I couldn't wrap my head around what was happening. Less than a month ago I was living the dream of every farm boy in Texas. I was two months away from turning sixteen and having the time of my life. I played football on Thursday nights and marched in the band on Fridays. Soon I would get my driver's license and be able to drive my dad's Dodge truck around the farm to help with chores. Then I'd ask him to drive it on a Saturday to take my girlfriend out on a date. I was even planning to run for student council the next year.

I was a big man on campus, but in a span of three days my whole life had changed. Less than a week ago my life was perfect, but now we were running from tiny Glen Rose, Texas to Pensacola, Florida, and my dreams had turned to nightmares.

God could have easily stopped all this from happening. He could have stopped the killing of one father and the incarceration of the other. Neither family deserved this. That was all I could think about as my mother drove our Buick towing the trailer, speeding away from the place I used to call home.

Howards in Fort Worth, TX
(notice the guns)

For the first eight years of my life, I lived in Fort Worth, Texas. I was the oldest of four boys—all with names starting with J. There was only a two-year gap between my brothers John and Joel. My brother Jeff wasn't born until I was thirteen. I had a half-sister named Joy from my dad's first marriage, but because she lived with her mom, we only got to see her on weekends. John, Joel, and I were so close in age and in appearance that my parents bought us all the same clothes. To avoid confusion, most of the time people just referred to us as "The Boys" or "The Howard Boys."

When I was eight, my parents bought a one-hundred-and-eight-acre farm six miles outside the small town of Glen Rose, Texas. The farm had everything young boys could ever want—woods, animals, a creek, and all sorts of places to explore. The house was built in the 1920s and had been unoccupied for over fifteen years. It had never been painted, the electrical wiring was ancient, and there were holes in the floors, ceilings, and walls. The whole house was built on a rock foundation that we were always too scared to crawl under as kids.

Farm House in Glen Rose, TX 1962, side view below

Windmill and Tank at Farm

Pool Hall - Grandfather's "office" next to bank where my mother worked

The farm had its own windmill that fed water into a tank that was the only water source for the entire property. There was no running water in the house. If you wanted water, you had to pump it at the windmill and carry it back to the house. If you had to use the bathroom, you went to the outhouse. The property was a fixer upper, but our family packed up everything and moved there from the relatively large city of Fort Worth.

Living in Glen Rose required a completely different frame of mind. At the time, the population was around fifteen hundred people, including my dad's father, mother, and one of his brothers. Living in a town that small took some getting used to. There were no Ben Franklin five-and-dime stores where you could find any toy you wanted. There were no drive-in theaters, A&W Root Beer Restaurants, and no large grocery stores. On top of that, Glen Rose was in a "dry county" meaning there was no alcohol sold there. This was because of its reputation for moonshine during Prohibition. That really didn't matter to our family because my parents didn't drink.

Even though Glen Rose didn't have all the things we were accustomed to in Fort Worth, it did have something that Fort Worth was lacking—and that was character. You could walk all over the downtown area in less than two minutes. If our grandpa, Pops, wasn't at his house, you could count on him being in his "office," the domino room in the back of the pool hall right next to the bank where Mom would eventually work. It was impossible to walk around without running into someone you knew, meaning we always had to be on our best behavior. Town Hall sat right in the middle of the town with a real honest-to-goodness *Acrocanthosaurus* (dinosaur footprint or dinosaur track).

If you wanted to take a vacation away from downtown, you went to Oakdale Park and stayed in the cottages there. Next to it was Oakdale Plunge which hosted the town swimming pool. I learned how to swim there. During the summer, Oakdale Plunge was the place to be. They had a jukebox, fast food, and fountain Dr. Pepper, and you could always ask for shot of cherry syrup in it. In those months, Mom would drop us off at the pool during her lunch hour and Dad would pick us up when he got off work. Sometimes we got bored at the pool and went across the street to the Paluxy River to climb on the boulders for a little while.

The town's movie theater (open only on Friday and Saturday nights) ran movies for two weeks and put up the poster for the next week's movie every other Thursday. To get in cost fifty cents, popcorn was a nickel, and a drink was a dime. For a dollar you could have a pretty good time in Glen Rose.

My father was always quick on punishment at home. If one of us just looked at him the wrong way, he abruptly pounced on us with his huge hands and whacked our backsides. No warning. No words. We never dared to speak. If you said something wrong in front of him, he'd immediately lash out. His favorite form of punishment was his belt, and for the longest time just hearing someone take off a belt made us cringe. Whenever we were out for the evening and did something wrong, he would say "wait till we get home" and we knew that no matter how good we were after the infraction, there was no escaping his wrath. And not just one of us most of the time, but *all* of us. He was an equal opportunity punisher. If one of us transgressed, we all got it. He'd line us up and punish each one of us. Sometimes my mom stepped in and defended us, but she was afraid of him too.

The sad thing about our situation was that at the time, we thought this kind of punishment was universal. Friends of mine at school spoke about the beatings they received from their fathers, some of which were so bad that they weren't sure if they could sit down for the rest of the day. No one ever died from spankings, but we still all talked about them at school the next day. They were all part of the normal daily routines in Glen Rose.

Though I never thought about it until later in life, my dad was not only violent, but also racist against Hispanics and Blacks, often calling them "Mexicans" or the "N" word. Once I was invited to a Hispanic classmate's birthday party. The entire class was talking about how much fun it was going to be. I went home with my invitation and my dad told me that the Howards did not go to parties with "Mexicans." They were not like us; therefore, they were not welcome.

Even the small town of Glen Rose had its dark secrets. I once heard my dad talking to some of the other men of the town. They were talking about an African American truck driver. They referred to him using the "N" word. As I listened, I learned that his truck had broken down on Highway 67 and he'd asked about some place to stay in Glen Rose. He was told that he had better be out of town when the sun went down.

The physical abuse from my Father didn't stop once we moved to the farm, but overall life wasn't bad at all. As long as we stayed out of our father's way, we grew up like any other boys in Texas. I'm not sure what the magic about growing up in Texas was. The first game I remembered playing with my brothers or friends was Cowboys and Indians. We always had an arsenal of toy guns. We had six shooters, repeating rifles, plastic machine guns, and Colt 45s. We all wanted to be outlaws or the sheriff of a small town. *Gunsmoke, Have Gun-Will Travel, Maverick, The Rifleman,* and of course, *Rawhide,* were TV favorites at the Howard house. If it wasn't Cowboys, it was Army. We were always searching for that hidden enemy that was lurking in the bushes and needed to be flushed out and destroyed. TV shows like *Combat, The Rat Patrol, McHale's Navy, Twelve O'Clock High,* and *Hogan's Heroes* planted dreams of being war heroes deep within us. Cowboys or the military, we didn't care, as long as we were outside and chasing each other around. Long hours of battling the Nazis or the Japs or chasing outlaws—but always fighting for what was good—filled our days. Texas was this great big frontier that was waiting to be conquered.

The first time we were given a tour of the farm, it was by a real estate guy—a tall and lanky cowboy with a legitimate cowboy hat and boots. While he was pointing out the different amenities of the place, he walked over to a pile of tin. He told my dad how good the tin still was and that it could be used to either replace the roof or build a barn. He lifted up a sheet of it, and underneath lay a rattlesnake. My mom immediately grabbed us boys and moved us away, but once we got to a safe distance, I watched that cowboy pick up two rocks. He threw one at the snake to hit it and then threw the second rock at the snake while leaning over and picking up the first rock he had thrown. Two rocks: one he threw and then picked up while throwing again. I saw him do this for about thirty seconds, and then he leaned down, picked up the snake by its tail and whipped its head against a tree a couple times just to make sure it was dead. He took the snake and tossed it into the field. In that moment I knew I wanted to be a cowboy too—just like him.

This was, in part, due to the patriotism inherent in being a Texan. We learned at an early age about the history of Texas and the six flags that had flown over our grand state: Spain, France, Mexico, the Republic of Texas, the Confederate States of America, and now, the United States of America. We knew all about the history of the Alamo and its heroes. We all said the Pledge of Allegiance, knew the Star-Spangled Banner by heart, and went to church on Sunday. We also believed that Nazis were still a threat. The war had ended less than twenty-three years ago, and we were certain that a group of them had escaped, made friends with the Russians, and still planned to use their advanced technology against us in some way. On top of the usual fire and tornado drills at school, we also had bomb drills in which we were trained to get under our desks and put our hands over our heads in case of a nuclear threat.

Patriotism even extended to our comic book preferences. I didn't grow up on Batman. I grew up on "Sgt. Rock and Easy Company" or "G.I. Combat" featuring guys like Johnny Cloud, the American Ace, or the Haunted Tank with the ghost of J.E.B. Stuart watching over the tank commander. There was the modern Captain Ahab, Captain Storm, a PT boat commander whose ship was destroyed by a Japanese submarine. He lost his crew and one of his legs in the attack and spent the rest of his days searching the Pacific for the sub that cost him so much. It didn't hurt either that the Confederate Air Force Base (now called the Commemorative Air Force) was down in Harlingen, Texas, only seven hours away. My dad had been in the army during WWII, stationed in Hawaii after the attack on Pearl Harbor. He had been a prison guard for captured

Doctor English's office where we first met him

enemy soldiers. After the war, he started working for General Dynamics. He was big into old planes and we were always looking out for air shows that flew propeller planes and some of the new jets. I never heard my parents talk about politics, but they taught us to love our country and respect first responders and the military.

On one of our first visits to the farm before we had officially moved in, my dad shut the car door on one of my fingers and it took the tip of my finger off. It happened on a Sunday, meaning they had to take me to the local doctor's office and contact the on-call doctor to treat me. This was our family's first encounter with Doctor Bob English. He came into the room and immediately started asking questions, first to my parents about our family and then to me to keep my mind off my missing fingertip. After he fixed up my finger the best he could, he went back to talking to my parents—this time about our move to Glen Rose. He told us about his wife, Carla, and that they had eight children of their own. He talked to us about Glen Rose, saying that we would come to love it here. He told us to call him if there was ever anything we needed. He talked about the local school and the local church of which he was a part and invited us to attend too.

As we drove back to Fort Worth, all I could think about was how different Doctor English was compared to my dad. While my dad had looked at my injury as nothing but an inconvenience, Doctor English had showed me compassion. He had wanted to help me with the pain. After meeting the doctor, my dad told me that my mom quickly changed her mind about moving to Glen Rose. At first, she had been hesitant but now she seemed excited to move. I didn't realize at the time how that chance meeting with Doctor English (and later his family) would change our lives.

That first summer at the farm, we focused on making the house more livable. We put carpet down to cover the holes in the floor, ignoring the fact that a strong breeze lifted it because of the holes. My dad put paneling on the walls to keep the winter wind from ripping through the house. We were able to put plumbing in, or rather my dad was. He dug trenches, laid the pipes, put in the fixtures; and before we knew it, our house had all the amenities that most people these days take for granted. We were moving up. We now had running water in the kitchen and one bathroom.

We started to improve the farm area as well. We fixed the fences and started looking for livestock. We turned it into a ranch, purchasing baby calves and raising them until we could sell them for

Me and our horse Candi in front of the barn Dad built

meat. We had chickens, dogs, cats, and at one time even a pet rac-
coon. Dad bought a used tractor and soon we had a large garden
where we grew corn, black-eyed and snap peas, okra, tomatoes, cu-
cumbers, and all sorts of melons. Even though things in the house
were still tense because of my dad, once I experienced life on a
farm, I never wanted to leave it.

Then it was time for school. I was shocked when I walked in for
the first time. The whole fifth grade class fit into one classroom! In
Fort Worth, each grade required several classrooms. Not here! In
Glen Rose the entire fifth grade was comprised of thirty-four students. The first week of school we played sports. Not just kickball
or messing around on the playground, but legitimate team sports.
We played baseball, football, track, soccer, basketball, and others.
In Glen Rose, if you could walk and chew gum at the same time,
they placed you on a sports team. School life in Glen Rose was all
about sports. During all this, I continued to play music. I switched

from violin to French horn and was soon playing beyond anyone's expectations.

At a very early age my mother realized I had an ear for music. I could pick up a song and sing it with perfect pitch. While still in Fort Worth, the school sent home letters about the choice of instruments we could play—either brass instruments like trumpets, trombones, and horns or stringed instruments. My parents were sure that I was going to come home with a brass instrument, it being the more "manly" of the two. They were surprised when I came home, saying I wanted to learn to play the violin. My father was disappointed. He thought the school had made the choice for me. I think my father was concerned about our masculinity. He often accused us boys of being sissies because we always ran to our mother. My father sat me down and asked me why I chose the violin over the brass instruments. I explained to him that I noticed all the boys went for the brass instruments, but the girls were doing the strings. I liked girls and wanted to be around them. That was one of the only times I remember seeing my father laugh without calling me stupid. Later in life, I found out that he still wished that I had learned a brass instrument instead of violin.

My mom, on the other hand, had dreams for me. She had visions that I would grow up and be a minister of music at a church. Pushing this dream, she got me an audition for the Texas Boys' Choir. My dad was sure they would not accept me, but I was accepted and spent a year learning how to sing.

My parents were Baptists and I always went to church as a kid. We used to go on Sunday morning for Sunday school and after that, big church. I remember looking forward to Wednesday nights because that was chili night at the church, and we had a choice between two chilis: with beans or without beans. I didn't care which chili I got, as long as I got to crush saltine crackers in mine. I was careful not to crush too many or make a mess though, so I did not get a look from my dad. While we were in church, we had to sit still and act like gentlemen. If we did not, we got "that look" from our dad, which meant there would be punishment waiting at home. People used to comment about how polite and neat we were, but we were just afraid of our dad. Even my youngest brother would be on his best behavior; dad didn't show any slack because he was the youngest. No, if one of us messed up, chances were all of us were going to get it.

I never went to my dad about issues or questions about life. In fact, I didn't talk to my dad about much of anything. He wasn't supportive of the activities we were involved in, and he didn't want to know about them. We were a commodity. He was waiting until we could pull our weight and work the farm. By the time I was a teen, I could see that. He was giving me more and more responsibilities with the livestock and around the house. I learned how to cook, iron, and do most of the household chores at a young age. Because I was the oldest, more was expected of me. It didn't bother me much then. As long as I got my chores done, I was still allowed to go out and do the activities I loved. I could play football and stay in the band. If I worked extra hard, my dad would take me into town on Saturday nights to go to the movie theater.

My dad didn't put up with anything that might cause him stress or discomfort. When we were still living in Fort Worth, I went through a phase when I started sleepwalking and having nightmares. I would run through the house screaming and crying about things chasing me. My mom would wrap me up in her arms and tell me that everything was okay, that nothing was chasing me. After this happened a few times, my parents decided to take me to the doctor. The doctor reassured them that it was natural for children my age to experience this, something called night terrors. He explained that it was not uncommon, that his child had gone through them for a while, and that they could last until I was eleven. He directed my mom to keep doing what she was doing: hold me tight, tell me everything was okay, and when I calmed down, take me back to bed. However, my dad did not want to wait until I was eleven for me to grow out of the night terrors. The next time I had one, instead of letting my mother take care of it, he cornered me in the bathroom and threw a bucket of cold water on me. I don't recommend it, but the fear of drowning and my dad caused me not to have another night terror. I guess my dad did find the cure for night terrors after all.

We all used to talk about how hard our dads worked. I can't think of a single friend of mine that had a deadbeat dad. Some of my friends had dads that drank too much, but the overall opinion about all of our dads was that they worked hard and provided for their families. During the week, my dad got up at four in the morning. Thirty minutes later he got us boys up to help him. We helped him feed the livestock, and sometimes that meant holding up big bottles so baby calves could nurse. If we fell asleep while the calf nursed, we got a rude awakening when the calf butted the bottle and it hit us in the head, spraying us with slime. It wasn't a great way to start the morning, but Dad would let us go back to bed till six-thirty once the chores were done. It was the best sleep of the day. He then drove to meet his carpool to Fort Worth where

First Baptist Church today

County Courthouse

he worked for General Dynamics. He got home at five in the afternoon, had dinner with us, worked the farm till ten, and then did the same thing the next day. Over and over again. I used to think that my dad was the hardest working man in the entire town.

Around my second year in Glen Rose, I found Christ. Once we started going to the First Baptist Church, the church that Doctor English had recommended, I felt God's presence for the first time. Doctor Robert English was one of two doctors of the town and after the incident with my finger, our families became close friends fast. He and his wife had eight children of their own, two sets of twins, four boys and four girls. The twin boys were my brother John's age and Howie English was the same age as my brother Joel. First Baptist Church was where I first felt God's hand on me and a place where I felt comfort. I accepted Christ as my Lord and Savior at age ten or eleven, and Doctor English played a large part in that decision. I still loved my dad because of how he provided for us, but Doctor English became my spiritual mentor. He was also a deacon at the church and the leader of the Royal Ambassadors (RAs), the boy scouts of the Baptist Church. He instilled in us the importance of not only memorizing the Bible, but also having a personal relationship with Jesus Christ. I looked forward to this time away from home when I could study the Bible. Doctor English not only helped me with my walk with God, but he also made it fun.

In 1967, Doctor English put together a contest to see who could recite all of the books in the Bible while standing in front of him and the congregation. The winners would get an all-expense paid trip to see the Houston Astrodome and a Houston Astro baseball game. This was a big deal at the time because the Astrodome had just opened that year. To think I had a chance to go to what some people were calling "the eighth wonder of the world" was beyond anything I could imagine. I put a lot of work into memorizing the books and ended up being one of the winners.

I got to leave the small town of Glen Rose to go to Houston, Texas and stay at the Rice Hotel. We saw the Houston Astros play the St. Louis Cardinals. I watched Rusty Staub hit two home runs during the game that night. It was the first time I had ever seen an animated scoreboard light up. While I watched the game, all I could think about was whether or not my dad could ever change to be more like Doctor English. If there was a chance that my dad and I could connect like I could with the doctor, it would be wonderful. In fact, the doctor was able to connect with anyone he met. Doctor English saw something in me, and I knew it. Over time, his affirmation became important to me.

On February 11, 1967, my dad's birthday, my youngest brother Jeff was born. The fact that God has a sense of humor was never more evident than on that day. We all wanted a baby sister; in fact, the whole county had been hoping that the Howards would finally get that daughter they wanted, but God said no. Mom decided that four boys was enough. It was different having a little brother around. Being the oldest, I was responsible for all of the babysitting in the house. My life didn't change that much, but having a baby in the house made the tension between my mom and dad even worse than it was before.

In the summer of 1969, the RAs had an opportunity to go to a summer camp near Glen Rose, but our group of young men did not have a counselor. I was fifteen at the time so Doctor English approached my parents and asked if they would allow me to be the counselor. He explained that there would be older counselors there and he would come out in the evenings and check on me to make sure everything was okay. My group was only six young guys between the ages of twelve and thirteen, but to be given that opportunity was monumental in my mind. When I got there and went to the first counselor's meeting, I learned that I was the youngest counselor they had ever had. The four days went off without a hitch and I got accolades from the older counselors on my maturity and my ability to handle my group. I found myself looking forward to Doctor English's visits in the afternoon, seeking and getting his approval for a job well done. While I can't remember a single time when my dad told me he was proud of me, Doctor English was always quick to pay a compliment. I was hoping that in time, my dad would change to be like Doctor English. Then everything would be perfect.

It was when I got back from summer camp that the whispers began. Mom was spending a lot of time at the church and at the hospital. There were rumors that Dad was seeing a doctor, but not a regular doctor. Doctor English's name was thrown around a lot at home. Mom urged Dad to talk to him and Dad accused her of spending too much time with him. One day Doctor English came over with his twin sons to go shooting with us boys. As some point, Dad and Doctor English started talking, a conversation we were not privileged to hear. At the time, I was praying that Doctor English was counseling Mom and Dad and that things were finally going to get better at home.

The summer of 1969 had the first man on the moon and was my first year as a camp counselor. I was doing more with the church, the RAs, the choir and band, and football. I was also learning more about girls. While things were going well on the outside, at home they were only getting worse. My dad wasn't involved in my life outside of the home as long as I got my chores done, but he was becoming more distant and his fights with my mom more frequent. The arguments sometimes sounded like they got physical, but they never fought in front of us. I remember my mom having bruises that she claimed were caused from clumsiness, but when she appeared one day with a black eye, we knew it was something more. At night we heard them arguing and hoped that Dad wouldn't come in and take his anger out on us.

That summer, I took driver's education. Our football coach, Coach Schuelke, was the driver's ed. teacher, the swimming teacher at Oak Plunge that taught me how to swim, and the baseball, track, and basketball coach. Sometimes I saw Coach Schuelke more than my own parents. I would meet him in downtown Glen Rose and we would take the driver's ed. car and just drive. One time I drove all the way to Cleburne, which was thirty miles away. Always in a baseball cap, he sat in the passenger seat and read a paper, sometimes even falling asleep. However, there were times when you thought he was asleep, and you'd see him peeking over to check how fast you were going. We'd talk about current events, football, and the upcoming season. It was in Cleburne that I bought my first forty-five record.

In 1968, I really found music. My dad had forced us to listen to country, western, and classical music. I ended up really enjoying classical music, even learning the names of the composers. In music appreciation class, I could match the composer to the piece with ease which caused me to catch a lot of flak for my "uppity"

Dinosaur Track on Downtown Band Stand

music choices. To be honest, we were in Texas and if there wasn't a fiddle it in, it was "uppity" music. Also, in '68 I bought a small handheld AM transistor radio and started listening to some of the rock stations from Fort Worth. It was pocket-sized and had a white earpiece, a precursor to the later Walkman's, I guess. I carried it around the farm so I could listen while I worked. That music opened my eyes up to a whole new world. We didn't have Christian rock back then, so all this music was new to me. Sure, I had heard people talk about Elvis and seen his movies, but I had never had the opportunity to actually *listen* to his music. My first album was from Blood, Sweat and Tears with David Clayton-Thomas.

As soon as I heard that, I wanted to be a famous rock and roll performer. I was already in the school band, which led me to want to be in a brass-heavy band like Blood, Sweat and Tears. David Clayton-Thomas had that raspy voice that I couldn't copy, but I could play my French horn, and knew that, with practice, I'd play other instruments too. I was hooked on the sounds of the Beatles, the Doors, Creedence Clearwater Revival, and yes even, the

Monkees. Everyone at that time listened to "I'm a Believer" and "Last Train to Clarksville." My parents didn't believe in "that kind" of music, so the radio and our musical choices became a secret between me and my brother John.

In the summer of 1970, I stayed with Joy for a week. She and her husband lived near Fort Worth. They both worked during the day, so for most of my stay I had total run of their house. Her husband had an incredible stereo and showed me how to operate it. He also had Playboy magazines, which led to my first time seeing a girl in the nude. My dad had detective magazines, but nothing quite like this. I wasn't interested in the magazines, but I was interested in the music.

They had a copy of Simon and Garfunkel's "Bridge Over Troubled Water." As I listened, I felt like I had finally found something I could imitate. My voice was similar to Paul Simon's or Art Garfunkel's and the brass section in "Keep the Customer Satisfied" didn't

Summer of 1970 in Glen Rose, TX

disappoint my brass-playing dreams. I played that album until I could belt out every single one of the songs. I had to have it, but first I needed a record player. That year I saved up all my money and purchased a small turntable and speakers.

My freshmen year in school was one of the best years of my life. I was finally really accepted at my small school. I was set to play my first year in JV football. It didn't matter what position I was playing; I was just excited to participate in such a heavy tradition in Texas. Football games were on Thursday nights, so I was able to participate in the marching band on Friday nights at all the varsity games. I had me my first real girlfriend, along with my first real kiss. I felt like life couldn't get any better.

Church was still an important part of my life. We went to church on Sunday morning as well as Sunday and Wednesday nights. Around the middle of the year, the church put together a folk music fest for the youth. It was radical—a musical called "Good News: A Christian Folk Musical." I was excited because it was something more than the traditional hymns. It was a way for me to finally express myself in the "semi-rock" world. It had drums, piano, and even an electric guitar. I auditioned, got a lead role; and after doing several shows at First Baptist, we were asked to perform at other local churches. My mom was seeing her dream of me as a music minister coming true. It was the best year of my life, but it was also the year that everything began to fall apart.

I was really looking forward to my sophomore year in high school. Between football, band, school, my girlfriend, and my soon-to-be driver's license, my life was perfect. It was my second year of JV football and I finally felt like I was getting the hang of it. The

JV Football 1970

coaches were putting me in all sorts of different positions: running back, tight end, and defensive end. My week was full of outside activities.

Wednesday nights I went to church for choir practice with my mother and Thursday nights was JV football. If my parents were ever too busy to take me back to school for the games, I just stayed in town and waited till the game started. That became the highlight of my week—hanging around downtown before the game. There was a little restaurant in town that offered a discount to the football players if they wore their jerseys. I would get country-fried steak and mashed potatoes.

On Friday nights, I played in the marching band for the varsity football games. When we had to travel for away games, there was always this senior majorette that fell asleep on my shoulder during the long bus rides because she felt I was "safe." I was safe. I didn't even think about doing something because most of these girls had senior football-playing boyfriends, and I didn't want to get my butt kicked. Once the girl's boyfriend pulled me aside at school and pushed me up against a locker. He asked if I was the kid that his girlfriend always fell asleep on, and in a cracked voice I said, "Yeah." Thinking I was about to get beaten up, I was surprised when he leaned in and shook my hand in thanks, saying he knew he could trust me.

From that point on, I was a friend of all the varsity football players. I was always out now, and mostly out of my father's reach. But it didn't keep me completely away. At home it was only getting worse. Now instead of using his hand or his belt to hit us, he was using the first thing he could get his hands on.

When I was changing into my football uniform once, Coach Schuelke approached me, pointing at my legs, and asking me if there was anything I wanted to talk about. I looked down and there were welts on my leg where my dad had beaten me with a half-broken water hose. We had a horse on the farm and sometimes we let her wander around the farm. Someone had left the water hose out and she had stepped on it and cut it in two. When my dad found out, he blamed me and started hitting me with it.

My mom stepped outside and said she was the one that had left it uncoiled, but my dad simply said that he was punishing me for something I had done but he hadn't found out about yet. There was no apology, only the welts. When Coach asked me about them, I just responded that I had done something wrong and been punished. He told me that if I ever wanted to talk that I could come to him and then went back into his office. That was just how it was in the 1960s in Texas. Injuries as a result of punishment were the norm and nothing was ever said about them.

I remember when my dad finally came to a baseball game to watch me play. It was the first time he had ever come to one of my games. During the summer, I played Pony League Baseball. The only sport my dad and I ever played was baseball. He would throw balls for us to hit. We spent hours around the farm playing games like that. He would hit the baseball and if we caught it in the air, it was a hundred points and if it bounded seventy-five.

My dad was known around town for his baseball skills. Friends would talk about his throwing arm. He could stand in the back of center field and throw a baseball over the fence behind the catcher. He told us that one time when he was playing, a line drive was hit right out to him in center field. Fielding the ball, he fired that ball at home plate only to have it sail over the backstop fence. He learned how to control his arm and became sort of a legend on the field for his throwing capability. He was known for being able to throw people out at bases after a long hard drive to field.

Having him come to the first baseball game of the season to watch me play was a big deal to me. He pulled our pickup truck right up to the field. As he got out of the truck, I thought he was going to come down to the bleachers and actually watch me play. Instead, he got in the bed of the truck, unfolded a lawn chair, pulled out a book, and started to read. I just looked at him. He said he would be here till I finished playing. I was first at bat that night and with the first pitch I hit a triple. He never saw it.

He only came once to watch me play football too. I found out later that the only reason he came to my football game was because he and my mom had gotten into an argument about how he was never interested in what I was doing. He had gone to prove my mom wrong, and to get back at her. After the game was over I asked him if he saw me sack the quarterback. His only response was, "Oh, that was you?" He didn't even know my number. He thought it was someone else.

Things at the house kept getting worse. The verbal arguments were getting louder; there was no more trying to hide them from us. The physical confrontations escalated to the point that my mom was beginning to get physical back at my dad. In the past I had never seen her stand up to him in this way. It was like she was almost daring him to hit her in front of us. I had heard somewhere that my parents were being counselled by Doctor English. I found out later that Doctor English was only counseling my mom. Dad had come to the conclusion that there was nothing wrong with him. Mom was saying the doctors disagreed with him and that he needed medication. He kept telling her that this was his house, and that this was the way it was going to be and there was nothing she could do about it. He even quoted the verse in which Paul said that it was the wife's job to submit to her husband. Their arguments continued to escalate until one fateful Sunday when it all erupted.

I was snapped back to reality when one of the moon-shaped hubcaps on the trailer scraped the side barrier on a Mississippi River bridge. It woke everyone in the car and there was a brief second of panic. I looked at my mom, obviously still in shock, and wondered if she was about to lose it. Through my anger at her for making us leave Glen Rose, I knew that this was as hard on her as it was on the rest of us and I felt sorry for her, partially because I felt that what had happened was somehow my fault.

If I had been a better son, and more obedient to my dad, then maybe none of this would have happened. I could have stopped this insanity. I watched her take control of the situation, something I had seen her do many times. She gripped the steering wheel with white knuckles and assured us that she had just driven a little too close to the curb for the big hubcaps on the trailer. She told us that everything was fine, and I watched as her face changed from scared to determined. As she kept on driving, I kept on asking God why. Why He had let this happen?

saw my dad go after my mother and she screamed for help. I rushed in between the two of them and caught a couple of my father's blows. I turned and pushed him away. As he came toward us, I thought that this was going to be the end of me. Mom was shouting, I was shouting, and next thing I knew, all my brothers were in the room, crying and shouting. My dad stepped back and stormed out of the house. We didn't know where he was going, but we felt that when he got back, he'd have some sort of plan. Thirty minutes later he came back and calmly asked if he could speak to Mom. She told us to go into our room and they began talking. We felt like it was finally over—that all this would end. It had to be. A few minutes later my mom told me to get ready to drive her to the church.

As I drove, Mom didn't say anything. We sat through the church service in complete silence. The only time we spoke was during the singing of the hymns. On our way home, she drove, and when we got about a mile from the house, she stopped the car. She looked at me and told me she wasn't coming home. She told me I needed to walk back and tell my dad. I started crying. Without her, he might kill me. I begged her not to leave us. I didn't know what he would do if I came home without her. Getting out of the car, I watched as she turned around and drove back toward town.

I found out later that my dad had told her that if I ever stepped in between the two of them again, he would kill me. Mom didn't tell me that then, and as I walked home all I could think about was how little she cared about us.

During that long mile back to the house, I comforted my two closest brothers who were with me. It was the only way I made it home that night. I told my mother this later, and she insists that they were not there, and I made that walk alone. Perhaps God sent two angels to walk home with me that night. I don't know. What I did know was that when I got home my dad was going to kill me. I prayed the entire walk home that Mom would come back and get me, promising that everything was going to be okay.

She didn't come back and when I got home, my dad was waiting for me. I walked in, holding back the tears, and told him that Mom wasn't coming home. I saw his jaw tighten in the way it does before a fight and was ready for him to attack me. Instead he told me to get my chores done and go to bed. I wasn't sure why he wasn't reacting the way I thought he would, but I just did exactly as I was told. Later, I explained to my brothers what happened, and we were all in shock. None of us could believe that not only had Mom left, but Dad hadn't killed us. If we had only known what was about to happen, we would have known that wasn't far from the truth.

My mom left on August 16, 1970. I can't remember if school had started or if we just stayed home, hoping she would walk through the front door and things would go back to normal. Maybe Dad would realize he couldn't live without her and apologize. We went to school eventually, but we didn't talk about it. Divorce was not discussed in Glen Rose. In all my days there, I never heard of a single family getting a divorce. In 1968, Tammy Wynette had a hit single on the radio called "D.I.V.O.R.C.E." but, to be honest, I didn't really know what it meant.

Eventually, I got it in my mind that I would not let this happen. I would pray to God and He would take care of it. Doctor English would counsel my mom, and then she and my dad would make up and things would go back to normal. If this whole argument had been my fault for stepping between them, maybe I could talk to them and apologize. Maybe that would help.

I came home from school, hoping that she would be there, but she wasn't. Not that day or the next. I heard whispers around town of moms that disappeared and never came back. I lay in bed, not knowing where my mom was. It was almost too much for me to handle.

Nights turned into days, which became a week. Another week passed and there was still no sign of her. In my mind, she had just abandoned us. Dad had been too much for her, so she just packed up and left. What was odd to us was that Dad didn't seem angry about it at all. In fact, he acted as if nothing was wrong. He would get up early, take care of the farm, and go to work. We saw him in the afternoon, but he never spoke about Mom's absence.

I thought maybe my dad had simply made up his mind that she was gone, and that was that. I saw no grief, pain, anger, or any other emotion in him. I didn't know if he was in communication with Mom, if he had made a missing person report with the police, or if anyone was even looking for her. I didn't know anything, and it was splitting me apart. I didn't even talk about her with my brothers. Suddenly it was as if she never existed.

On August 27, she came to the house while Dad was at work. I could hardly believe she was back. She told us to get as much stuff as we could and come with her. We were leaving Dad and moving in with Doctor English and his family. She said she had lived in fear of our lives for the last ten days, and now we would finally be safe.

The English family welcomed us with open arms and told us that we were going to be okay. Doctor English and my dad were friends. They were going to sit down together and talk everything out. We didn't know then that the talking was over by that point. In my head though, it still felt like I was leaving Dad.

Later, Mom pulled me aside and told me that she didn't feel that she and Dad were ever going to be together again. She told me that Dad had been to the doctors and been diagnosed with paranoid schizophrenia. I had never heard of that before. Mom explained that it meant that Dad was overly paranoid and felt like everyone was against him. I thought back to all of the friendships my dad had with the members of our town and our church. What Mom was saying didn't make sense to me. She said the reason he was more violent recently was because he believed that she was having an affair with Doctor English, but he didn't have any proof. She went on to say that people had told Dad that she and Doctor English were trying to get him committed to a mental institution. Dad had stopped taking his medicine, and that's why she left him. What she didn't tell me was that in a few days she was going to serve him with divorce papers, which would send him over the edge.

I still had not told anyone at school what was happening. In all honesty, I didn't know what to say about the whole situation. It seemed a lot of people already knew what was happening, or at least I felt like they did. The looks I got and the way people stopped talking whenever I entered a room fueled my thoughts even more. I wondered if maybe I was the paranoid one now. Despite all this,

I was still holding out hope that Mom and Dad would be able to make things work and my life would resume its normal pace.

A few days after my mom came and took us, she told me that she was going to officially divorce my dad. We would be staying with the English family until she could afford a place of our own. She reassured me that we would stay in Glen Rose, so that we could continue to have a relationship with our dad and be close to all our friends. She continued talking, but all of it went in one ear and out the other.

I didn't see the divorce papers until the death of my dad years later. They were served September 11, 1970. Less than two weeks later, our lives drastically changed in a way that none of us saw coming.

The rest of our time in Glen Rose was somewhat of blur. I remember we took a church trip to Six Flags Over Texas, the brand-new amusement park. It was there that I told my girlfriend my parents were getting a divorce. It didn't seem real to me. I still believed that something would change. I thought that if I could be a better son, my dad would start taking his medication and Mom would take him back. Even through my hope, reality was starting to sink in that there was no fixing my parents' relationship.

Mom wanted out, and she was doing everything in her power to accomplish that. Still I kept praying. I prayed that Doctor English would be able to take care of everything. Because of his faith, I believed God would listen to him and take care of everything.

I remember seeing my dad's car parked right across the street from our school when he carpooled to Fort Worth. When I did, I wondered what he was doing after work. I hoped that he missed his family and was working to get us back—and to win Mom back.

During all this though, I felt a huge weight lifted off my shoulders. I knew that I would never have to face my dad's erratic punishments again. If he couldn't change his ways, Mom would not take us back there. We were finally safe from him.

Even though it was chaotic at the English house, I had never felt this safe before. My dad could not get me here. I could concentrate fully on school, football, band, and my girlfriend. Even so, it was hard to take my mind off my parents. The whispers about our situation kept getting louder and louder. I didn't believe any of them, but the lies became even more intense.

Whispers about my mom and Doctor English. About how the two of them were conspiring together to get my dad sent to an asylum. About how the two of them were having an affair, and how during the ten days my mom went missing, she had really been in a motel with him in Fort Worth. People around town were pointing at me. I'd hear them talking, only to go silent as I approached. Even my football team was talking about it, asking me about my parents and Doctor English. Coach Schuelke (whom I saw more than my own parents) pulled me aside and asked if I wanted to talk about anything. I couldn't shake the feeling that he knew something and wanted to tell me but couldn't. He could see I was hurting.

On September 20, my two oldest brothers and I were dropped off at the farm to see our dad. I didn't understand the concept of visitation at that time; all I knew was that I was finally seeing my dad. He didn't give us a hug or tell us that he missed us, but we did notice a change. He asked how we were and spoke to us pleasantly. He let us talk about school and our lives, and we could see he was listening. The only time he mentioned Mom was when he asked us if we knew where she had gone when she was away.

Out of the blue, he asked us if we wanted to go shooting. Every young boy in Texas wanted to go shooting, but this suggestion was unusual coming from my dad. He had never wanted to do anything with us, so we were surprised. We excitedly agreed. He took us to the back of our property where we had buried an old car in the woods. We set up objects around the area and on the car to shoot—cans, dish soap bottles, and boards. Dad had a Smith and Wesson .22 caliber revolver. It looked like a police gun, but it was just a .22 he carried around the farm in case of snakes. He was proud of it, but I rarely saw it. That afternoon, we shot at all the things we had set up, and sometimes even the old car.

He was so different. I wondered if he was trying to win us back. At the time I thought that if he even mentioned trying to get Mom back, I would go home and beg her to give him a second chance. We would go back to being a family again.

But he never did. After we finished, we went back to the house and had to get ready to go back to Doctor English's house. We had church that night and we didn't want to miss it.

Before the split, we always sat together as a family in church. This night was different. I remember being very uncomfortable. Mom and I sat to the left of the church, Dad sat alone in the middle, and Doctor English, one of his sons, and my brother Joel sat on the right. I can't remember where John or Jeff were. All I remember from that night was that right before service ended, Mom asked me to drive her home early because she didn't feel well. We went back to the English's and sat together in her temporary bedroom. I was playing Simon and Garfunkel on my small stereo, singing under my breath to "The Boxer."

She asked me to sing for her and all I could do was smile and say no. She asked why I didn't sing for her. If anyone else asked me to sing for them, I would, but never for her. I realized I couldn't answer that question. Maybe it was because she left me to face my dad alone, or maybe I was mad at her for not giving Dad another chance. It could have been that I was sick of all the rumors and wanted to hear the truth from her.

I didn't know why, so I just went back to my music. I just wanted to listen in peace and enjoy this moment of quiet. I had this nagging feeling that this was the calm before the storm, that this was the moment right before my life fell apart. I didn't know how right I was.

My whole life changed with a phone call. I don't remember who answered the phone, I just remember it ringing and then all hell breaking loose.

My mom started screaming "No, no, Carlie, tell me this isn't true." She kept repeating it over and over again. All of us knew something bad had happened, but I just stayed in my room with the music, praying that it was nothing too serious. Conjectures raced around in my head: One of my brothers got hurt, maybe one of Doctor English's kids. Someone got hit by a car or something. At one point I considered getting up and locking my door so no one could tell me what happened, so I could stay in doubt.

But then I heard it: "James just shot Doctor English." I thought my mom was just telling a bad joke, but after she collapsed on the floor and kept repeating it, I was forced to face reality. The other English children that were home started to cry. I fell to the floor in disbelief.

I couldn't believe this was happening. We were just shooting with my dad. We had just seen him. All I could think was that one of us had done something wrong, something that caused him to act out like this. It was later that I learned that victims of domestic violence tend to think that everything is their fault. I just kept reviewing that afternoon, trying to think of anything we might have done.

Then I got angry. My dad was a monster for doing this to us! He just shot my Christian mentor, someone I could talk to about my problems, my only confidante. He had taken him away from me and my brothers. It seemed like forever that I lay there, crying, pounding my hands on the floor. This had to be some sort of lie. This couldn't happen.

Things started happening at the house. We learned that my dad had not been arrested. Everyone feared he was going to come to the English house and kill us all next. It dawned on me that my brother Joel and Doctor English's son, Howie, had been with Doctor English at the church. I asked Mom about Joel and Howie. She told me they were okay, but that they had been in Doctor English's car when my dad had walked up and shot Doctor English in the back. They had run into the church to get help. After the shooting, Dad just got back in his truck and fled. No one knew where he was. We heard a car door shut outside and we huddled together, scared that it was my dad, but it was only a deputy, sent to the house in case my dad decided to show up here.

We were only getting bits and pieces of information. We were told to stay at the house because my dad was still at large. I was told that Doctor English didn't die at the scene, that he had been taken to the hospital for surgery. I was told that even if he did survive, he wouldn't be the same because of the damage done to his brain. People were saying that it was only a matter of time before Doctor English passed, but I was still praying for a miracle. He was on life support, but with no brain activity. Joel and Howie were safe and being looked after. All we could do was wait.

Word came to us that Dad had been found and surrendered to the deputies. Dad had broken into his friend Buck Bridwell's house on the other side of town. He had used his phone to call Buck, telling him that he would surrender to the police only if Buck was there. Law enforcement surrounded the house, Buck talked my dad into coming outside, and my dad was arrested. Soon after we heard that, we were told that Doctor English had passed.

They say that when you go through a tragic event, you shut down. Sometimes it takes years for you to remember everything that happened. After hearing that Doctor English had passed, I don't remember anything else from that night.

The next day my mom sent all of us boys to school. I think they wanted us out of the house, so they could decide on the next course of action for both families. I never heard it come out of her mouth, but I was sure that Carlie English wanted us out of her house.

We started hearing stories of what happened at the church. One version was that my dad just walked up to the car and started shooting Doctor English. Another was that my dad shot at Joel and Howie. People said that he was looking for my mother and wanted to kill her but found Doctor English instead and decided to kill him. One story went that Doctor English reached for his gun under the seat when my dad approached the car, but that my dad had already started shooting. The rumors were suffocating, and going to school seemed the best way to get away from them.

Most of the teachers were surprised and shocked that I was at school. I walked from class to class in a trance. The week after the incident seemed to run together, and to this day I still can't remember what happened. I think it was the day after the shooting that I was approached by Doctor English's oldest daughter and her husband. They showed up at school to pick me up while I was getting ready for football practice. I could tell that something was wrong just by looking at their faces. My dad had posted bail. He was out of jail and everyone was afraid he was dangerous. I couldn't believe what I was hearing. The father I had feared, who had killed my mentor, was now out walking on the streets? We quickly drove to the English's where we found my mother in a panic.

She was talking in circles, scared out of her mind that my father could show up at the house at any moment. I tried to stay strong for my mom and the English family, but I found myself needing to leave the room very often to compose myself. I began doubting everything I had believed. My life was falling apart. I wanted to be back at the farm before this mess started. I wanted to be with my friends at school, my biggest supporters right now. The word "run" was passed around like that was the answer to all our problems.

To this day I have trouble remembering the next sequence of events. I remember going to school, my dad getting out, and Doctor English's funeral. The rumors began all over again. Half the town wanted my mother gone. Some said we were going to be forced out of the English house. Others were still talking about where my mom had been that week she had been missing.

The town split in two, based on whose side they were taking— my mom's or my dad's. Some said the shooting happened because my mom and Doctor English were having an affair and my dad had had enough of it. They began talking about how dangerous my dad was, how at any moment in time he could snap, and go on a killing spree.

At Doctor English's funeral, some of the men from the church pulled me aside. They explained to me that I was now the man of the house. They said that my mom would need my support, no matter where we went or what we decided to do. But I didn't want to hear this. I didn't want to leave Glen Rose and I didn't want to be the man of the house.

I wanted to go back to being a normal fifteen-year-old, enjoying my youth. Back to football, the farm life, the band, my friends. I wanted to go back to those mornings when I fed the cows. Most of all, I wanted to go back to the farm. Hearing the phrase "wherever we went" shook me. I didn't want to go anywhere. I felt like nobody was listening to me. Surrounded by darkness, I felt that even God had turned His back on me. I just wanted Him to reveal to us what we had done to deserve this.

Shortly after the funeral, my mom sat us down and told us we were leaving Glen Rose and going to Pensacola, Florida. This was where her parents and family lived, and we would be safe there. None of us liked that at all. We had been down to Pensacola for Christmas on several occasions; my parents had packed us all in the car and driven straight through, a twelve-hour drive. The only stops had been for gas and the occasional bathroom break, and a bathroom break for us boys meant going on the side of the road or at a gas station.

My parents had bought a Chevy station wagon at a government auction. It was a utility car without a backseat, used for hauling. My dad bought it because when we bought a baby calf, we could put the calf in the back with me and my two oldest brothers and we could hold onto it as we drove. It was a sight to see—the three of us in the back with a baby cow. It must have been a Texas thing. Not once were we stopped for it.

On our earlier trips to Pensacola, we put blankets down in the back and lay on the floor. If you slid off the blanket onto the wooden floor, there was a good chance you would get splinters. We were allowed to bring any toys we wanted, not too many, but enough to stay busy. We would lay in the back, play with our toys, trying to be as quiet as possible. If you asked dad where we were, you'd get hit. If you wanted to know, you would whisper to Mom and she would tell you that we were five minutes closer than we were five minutes ago. Most of the time we just laid in the back and stayed quiet.

Even though a majority of the people loved Doctor English, there were always rumors. People spoke about the circumstances when he moved to the area and how he was a player with women, so there was speculation about Mom and Doctor English. In light of this, moving to Pensacola seemed to be the best solution, so Mom packed up and away we went. We stopped one night in Fort Worth to say goodbye to Joy and continued our journey to Florida.

Even though we wanted to stay in Glen Rose, it was not an option. Mom had a good support system in Pensacola and felt they would help us out and keep us safe.

During this period, I found out who our friends really were. Some of those I considered friends of the "family" were really just friends of my dad. They made it clear that my mom was not welcome in Glen Rose anymore. Very few people supported my mom. The majority of the town was happy to see her go.

Later in my life, I found out that my dad was just as popular as Doctor English. My dad was "one of them": a hard-working, blue-collar man, working during the day for a military contractor with General Dynamics, and busy being a rancher and a farmer in his afterhours and on the weekends. Plenty of people loved Doctor English as well, but unbeknownst to me at the time, there had been lots of rumors about him and women for a long time.

We left the English house for a motel in a nearby town. No one wanted to take us in because they were scared that my dad would come after them. The next day there was a packed trailer outside, and my mom told me I had eight hours to say goodbye to everyone in town.

She dropped me off at school and I went around telling everyone that although we had to go, I would be back. I didn't know how, but I knew that I would, even if it meant running away from Pensacola. I dreamt that my dad would get sentenced to life for killing Doctor English or maybe even get the death penalty.

When that day came, we could move back to Glen Rose. I could resume my life without my dad, without living in fear of him. A new dream formed in my head—we would leave only to return to the best homecoming ever. As I said goodbye, I was busy planning my inevitable return. Little did I know that happy homecoming would never come.

The drive down to Florida was uneventful. We had a couple of scares when the trailer started to sway on us, like when the hubcap rubbed against the railing on the Mississippi bridge, startling us all awake. In less than forty-eight hours though, we were in Pensacola.

We arrived around the first of October. It was hard to believe that it had only been three weeks since all this had started. The uncertainty of our future was putting a lot of strain on the relationship between my mother and me. We were barely talking at this point.

Three days after we arrived, I realized that my mom and her mom did not get along. I would hear them fighting, each one firing shots back at the other. It got so bad that my mom would go to her room to be alone, cry, and then come back out to fight with her more. I think it really bothered my mom that her family was her only support. We had little to no money, and she was completely dependent upon them—something she hated.

My grandparents lived in the suburbs of Pensacola in a town called Cantonment. Those living in Cantonment that didn't drive to Pensacola for work or weren't in the navy, were probably working for the two plants nearby: Monsanto and St. Regis.

One of the first things we noticed about living in Pensacola was the smell. On a still night in Cantonment, the air was filled with the pungent odor of the St. Regis paper mill. The smell was the ongoing joke when you told people you lived in Cantonment.

My grandfather, Pat, was a truck driver. I remember him going through Fort Worth one time when I was little with parts of an amusement park, heading out to California. He told us he was taking those parts to Disneyland. We thought he was the coolest guy in the world. We thought that we were going to grow up to be just like Grandpa Pat, or Papa as we called him.

At times, I felt like he was the one person I could talk to. He would smoke a pipe and listen. He wouldn't take any grief. He had also grown up in a time of swift punishment, so we never crossed him, but he tried to listen to us and helped us when we had problems.

My grandmother, Nanny, and my Aunt Jan told my mom that they would help her get a job at the trucking company where they worked. My grandparents let us stay in a two-bedroom trailer they had on their property while mom saved up money to move. They had stayed in the trailer themselves while they were building their house. I thought things were finally looking up for our family, but Mom hated living there and being in debt to them. I tried to cheer her up, but she wouldn't listen to me.

The relationship between my mom and my grandmother continued to worsen. I didn't realize how deep the resentment between the two of them was until my relationship with my mom got worse too. My mom was still dealing with what happened with Dad, just like the rest of us. I sometimes tried to talk about it, but she pushed me away and remained distant, reminding me of the way my father acted.

During our first few weeks in Florida, we lived with my grandparents in their home. I'm not sure how we were able to do that. It was a three-bedroom home with seven people in it—my grandparents, my Uncle Charlie, my mom, and us.

My Uncle Charlie was only three years older than me. He made us laugh, acting like a clown. He was the comic relief we needed at the time. Charlie may have been older than me, but we were the same size. I used to catch him stealing my clothes all the time. His justification was that since we were living in his mom's house, he could go through all of our stuff if he wanted. I went to Mom about it and she just reminded me that this living situation was temporary and that I was just going to have to deal with it.

Charlie joined the Air Force, and six months later he was sent to Vietnam. After six months, we received a call that he had been injured and was on his way home. The first time I saw him again, he was on crutches. He told us he had been blown out of a tower and broken his back.

Later, I was told by relatives that what actually happened was that he slipped on spilt milk in the mess hall and tweaked his back. Either way, the family was happy to have him back. I liked to listen to all his "war stories" from his time served. He introduced me to what was happening in Vietnam and marijuana too. He was constantly smoking it. Anytime I was around him, he was smoking pot. He said it helped him with the pain in his back, but I just think he liked the feeling of being high. During high school if any of my friends wanted weed, I pointed them to my Uncle Charlie.

In the weeks while we were getting the trailer cleaned up, we lived out of boxes. Within a week of us moving there, Mom got a job at the trucking company where my grandma and aunt worked. As soon as possible my mom made me go back to school.

As soon as we pulled into the parking lot of J.M. Tate High School I knew it was going to be nothing like Glen Rose. It was huge. Instantly I didn't want to go. There were over four hundred students in my class, a total of two thousand on campus. I went from a big man on campus who knew everyone to a tiny fish in a big pond, not knowing anyone.

It was a complete culture shock. I knew that if I wanted to get out of the house, I would have to start making friends, but I had no idea how to do that. I felt out of place here. I just wanted to go back to Texas. On my first day at Tate, I was encouraged to join the band and the football team. I was thinking that maybe things weren't as bad as I thought they were, and maybe I would get so distracted that I would forget about Glen Rose and give Pensacola a try.

I was lost on my first day. I had to go to homeroom which was something I never did before. The purpose of homeroom was to take attendance and hear the announcements. Looking around the class, I realized that this was only a fragment of the sophomore class.

I also discovered that the school was not segregated. I could see several African American students—this would have never been allowed at Glen Rose. My mom always taught me not to see color, but to judge people by how they acted. This anti-racist stance would cost me a job in later years, but I thought it was the right way to treat people.

I was led from class to class by another student. I was glad for that, because otherwise, I never would have found my way. On the first day everyone thought my name was Howard James. That was frustrating. I hated Howard as a first name. As a last name it was fine, but never as a first name. The joke soon became that I had two first names. It wasn't a good way to start my tenure at J.M. Tate.

Eventually I was able to find the band room. That made me feel even more out of place. Instead of a forty-person band like I had known, I was standing in a hall of one hundred. Ms. Sidorfsky, the music director, asked me what instrument I played. I told her I played French horn, and when she asked how good I was, I just said I didn't know. In my small school I was great, but I wasn't sure how I would stand up against a band this large. She had me do a tryout and placed me in second chair. After a few private lessons she told me that if I continued to practice, I could make first chair in a year. In my mind, I wasn't going to be there another year. As soon as my dad was thrown in jail, I was moving back to Texas.

At the end of the day, I finally made it over to the gym to try out for the football team. The season had already started, and the coaches told me that I could only practice with the team until my transcripts from Glen Rose came. I was okay with that. All I wanted to do was play.

Playing with the Tate team was an eye-opener. In Glen Rose, if you were breathing, you played football. Here, you had to try out to be on the team. These guys were the best I had ever seen. I got creamed in the first practice I played with them. I was put on defense, trying to get to the quarterback. The two offensive linemen in front of me seemed to know exactly what I was going to do and when I was going to do it. In my defense, not only did they weigh at least twenty pounds more than me, but they also knew their stuff. I got pancaked, chop blocked, and all sorts of other blocks I had never seen before.

Even though I kept getting knocked down, I didn't give up. Every time I got hit, I got up ready for the next play. When practice was over, one of the linemen came up to me and told me he was impressed with me. He wasn't impressed with my football skills; he was impressed that I didn't give up. To be honest, I was loving being back on the field.

October ninth was my sixteenth birthday. We were still living with my grandparents, and my mom gave me a turtleneck. Back then, turtlenecks were not only in style, but also way over our budget. My mom told me she wanted me to have something nice because of everything that we had been through. She said that she knew this was as hard on me as it was on her, and that got me thinking.

I thought about how my mom was always there to support and protect us. She had come back for us. As I was thinking though, my mom told me I needed to forget about Glen Rose. Of course, I got angry all over again. I didn't want to forget Glen Rose. In my mind I was still going back. I remembered everything—the fights, her leaving, the shooting, and having to say goodbye to all my friends and family. I couldn't understand how my mom could simply forget it all. She just wanted to move on, but I couldn't do that. I was already mad at God for letting this happen, and now I was mad at my mom for the part she had played too. Perhaps if she had just listened to Dad or given him a second chance, things would have turned out better.

On that day, I felt more alone than ever. I realized that if I wanted to go anywhere in life, the only person I could count on was myself. Not God. Not my parents. Not my family. Just me. Nobody else was going to make me happy but me, and I wasn't willing to let anyone stand in my way.

When we finally got into the trailer, it certainly was a sight to see. We had two bedrooms for five people. Fortunately, the bunkbeds we had from the farm just fit in the back bedroom. We had a small place for a dresser and a closet, but we didn't have room to turn around. Mom didn't have bedroom furniture so all she had was a mattress and box spring on the floor and a dresser that was built into the trailer.

But even though the space was cramped, it was safe. We didn't think Dad would come and find us. Looking back, I'm sure he knew we were in Florida. Our friends didn't know because mom advised us to only tell a few people we trusted about our move. Despite my sense of safety, dreams came at night. Dreams of Dad finding and hurting us.

Since I could not sleep, I began sneaking out at night, just for an hour or two. I sat and thought about plans to get back to Glen Rose—and I had a couple. I figured I could get to the state line and then hitchhike the rest of the way. Best-case scenario was that my grandpa would have to make a trip out of state, and I would hide in the back until he got close to Texas. I decided that I was not staying in Florida, even if it meant leaving my family behind. I was going to find a way to get home.

I started to get more and more into music. My dream had changed. Instead of being a minister of music, I just wanted to be a musician. Ms. Sidorfsky continued giving me private horn lessons and encouraged me to perform in a quartet. I started making friends in the band, but I made sure not to tell any of them about my family history. It was a secret and I wanted it to stay that way.

During our stay in Florida, I attempted to go to church a couple times. I was still angry with God, but there was this something that kept bringing me back to church anyway. My mom, on the other hand, stopped going altogether. She said there were too many hypocrites there.

I heard pastors talk about how God is a loving Father, but the only father I had known had ruined my life. I began to think like my mom: All Christians were just hypocrites. I became judgmental. I really liked one Sunday school until I walked outside after the service and saw the teachers smoking cigarettes. They taught that the body is a temple, but here they were outside ruining that temple by smoking. I heard about other Christians that went to bars at night. They said one thing and did another. All of this just cemented my mother's belief. Soon I started to agree with her. I decided that if this is what Christianity was all about, then I didn't want any part of it. Instead I started to learn how to use Christianity to meet girls, bringing a whole new meaning to reading the Bible.

In November, we got word that the trial was starting for my dad. Mom, my brother Joel, and my grandmother were all subpoenaed to testify at the trial. I didn't understand why my grandmother was asked to testify. As far as I knew, she had nothing to do with my dad's case. I asked my mom why, but she wouldn't tell me. Later, that answer, and many other secrets, would spill out and the truth about how bad things really were in Texas would cause me more pain.

To me, my dad's trial meant a trip back to Texas. My mom told me not to get my hopes up, assuring me that things had changed for the worse in the short time we had been gone. I didn't care; all I wanted to do was see my friends again.

We drove to Texas and stayed in a hotel in Cleburne, about thirty miles away from Glen Rose. Mom would head over to the courthouse and drop us off in town, giving us a time to meet her when she was done. I contacted a couple of my friends from school. They picked me up and we hung out, and just like that it was like I never left. We caught up on things that were going on in town and I told them how big my new school was. I told them I planned to be back one way or another the following year. I figured my dad would get life in jail and I would find someone to live with in town. It didn't matter if my mom didn't want me to go. I was sixteen and my mom couldn't stop me.

As the trial progressed, I could see that things were not going the way we had hoped they would. The state was going for the charge of murder with malice, which meant my dad would get life in prison, but when my mom returned from the trial, she was upset. She told us that the twelve-member jury was comprised of all men from Glen Rose, most of whom knew my dad. We were concerned that they would let my dad off the hook, feeling sympathetic for him.

It was then that the bombshell hit that I knew could get my dad sentenced for life. It turned out that my father called my grandmother and told her that he was going to kill the whole family and Doctor English. This shocked me. Suddenly all of the things my mother had said about my father made sense to me. I realized for the first time that this man I had respected may never have cared about me at all. Perhaps my father really was mentally ill. It was the only way I could justify a man wanting to kill his entire family. I couldn't imagine a sane man ever saying something like that.

The only information I was getting from the trial was through my mom. Rumors around town were spreading like they had before we left, and the friends who picked me up started filling me in. One day they told me they heard that my mom had stayed in a hotel room rented by Doctor English in Fort Worth when she had left.

The word "affair" was again being tossed around in relation to my mom and Doctor English. People were coming forward and saying that they saw my mom and Doctor English in compromising positions. The ongoing story was that my mom and Doctor English were going to run off with each other, but they came back to get us.

The overwhelming speculation was that Doctor English was going to run off with my mom and leave his wife and children behind. This brought up the question of whether my mom was planning on leaving me and my brothers behind too. If Doctor English was going to leave his family, it made sense that my mom would also leave hers.

When we got back to the hotel that night, I thought my mom was going to fall apart. Once again, the whole town had turned against her and made her out to be the bad guy. The entire town of Glen Rose blamed her for this tragedy. I defended her honor, mostly because I knew how bad my dad's temper was, and I couldn't believe that Doctor English would ever do anything like they were claiming he had. Besides, Carlie English would have never let us stay at her house if she thought my mom and Doctor English were having an affair. I chose to believe that all these rumors were just lies.

The next day, Carlie English took the stand. She told the jury that her husband, Doctor English, had been counseling my mom. Carlie said that it was her idea for us to move in with the family, and that she knew of the hotel situation. She had paid the bill and there was nothing going on.

Another friend of the family went on the stand, someone who had been a part of the church. She said she had been on many trips with Mom and Doctor English and never felt that there was anything but friendship between the two of them. She said that Doctor English had counseled her too, and there was nothing unusual about it.

Their testimonies made me feel better about my mom and Doctor English. I believed the rumors had been planted by the defense to get my dad off. I figured there was no way my dad was getting off for the murder after the testimony of Carlie English and our friend. I was wrong.

On the final day of the trial, the state said that my dad planned to kill the whole family and Doctor English. The proof of this was all in the phone call he had made to my grandmother that day. The state said that he had been planning this since the first of September. The defense said that my dad was the victim, that my mom gave divorce papers to my dad a week after she had spent thirteen days with Doctor English in a Fort Worth hotel. My dad had testified that he followed Doctor English out to his car just to talk with him about what was going on, but when the doctor got in his car and locked the doors, he got mad and shot and killed him instead.

My dad kept saying that he only planned to talk to Doctor English. A psychiatrist testified that my dad was under a lot of stress due to the divorce and the loss of his family. He said the stress caused him to kill Doctor English. His opinion was that my dad was not schizophrenic, which was one of the rumors that had been circulating around town.

The jury took over nine hours to come back with the verdict that my dad was not guilty of murder with malice but was guilty of murder by reason of temporary insanity. They felt that the pressure of everything going on in my dad's life drove him over the edge. The evidence said that my mom and Doctor English had spent over a week together in a hotel followed by my mom not talking to my dad and her filing for divorce. They said that in church that night, my dad had tried to sit with my brother Joel, but Joel had taken a seat with Doctor English and Howie instead; and after the service, my dad was just trying to have a conversation with Doctor English, who ignored him, got in his car, and locked the doors. My dad admitted to shooting Doctor English, but he claimed that he was so angry that he didn't even remember doing it.

After the verdict, we knew the sentencing for my dad was going to be light. We figured that there was no sense in staying and waiting around for the verdict. My dad was sentenced five years in Huntsville Prison, but could get out in less than three years for good behavior. Just like before, we left Glen Rose in a rush with no thought of returning.

As soon as we got back to Florida, I turned my attention to school and the band. I started finding any way I could to get away from the house and my mom. Since the trial, the pressure on my mom was rising. Life between the two of us became unbearable at times. My mom was stressed with raising all of us and also dealing with my increasing anger issues. We went from my dad being quick with a belt on us to her becoming quick with her hands to our faces. If I said one thing out of line, she hit me, sometimes to the point of seeing stars.

She went from one job to two and eventually a third, to save enough to move us out of our grandmother's trailer. I asked her if I could get my license, and her response was that as long as I could pay for my own insurance, I could. We both knew that wasn't going to happen, seeing that I didn't have a job at the time and insurance for a sixteen-year-old boy was expensive. The more I dug in about getting it, the more resistance she gave me. Once I found out that I needed a parent's signature to get my license I knew it was going to be a long time before I ever got mine.

It was during this time, that we noticed a big change in Mom. She didn't drink alcohol, yet we would catch her acting like she was drunk. Her speech was slurred, and she stumbled into things. One day, a friend and I had missed the bus, so we went back to the house to ask Mom if she could drive us. She told us to give her a few seconds to get herself together and then fell to the floor. I ran into her room and saw her trying to stand but she could not.

Knowing she didn't drink, I thought there was something medically wrong with her. She explained that she was just looking for her shoe and fell over again. Then she told me to get out of her room. I went back into the living room and my friend asked me if she was alright. Honestly, I didn't know. I had never seen her like this before. She came out of her room bouncing off the walls, telling us to get to the car. We walked down the steps out of the trailer, and I turned and saw her fall off of them.

My friend and I ran to go help her, but she just yelled at us that she was fine. I was really worried about her, but I just got into the car as she directed. I climbed in front and my friend sat in the back. While she was driving, she was talking to us about missing the bus and I noticed that her words were slurred. I asked her if she wanted me to drive, but she just snapped and said that she was okay.

It was then that I heard the strangest sound and I turned to see my friend tug on his seatbelt. We didn't have to use seatbelts in the 70s, and rarely bothered with them, but my mom was scaring him so bad that he dug out the seatbelt from between the seats and put it on. On the way, she pulled out in front of cars, ran into a ditch, and by some miracle got us to school without hitting anyone.

As soon as we got there, my friend jumped out of the car and ran to class. My mom called me back and said that if I hadn't mentioned anything then my friend wouldn't have noticed anything was wrong. Her speech was slurred so badly at this point that I could barely understand her. I prayed that my mom would make it home safely. That afternoon she was still mad at me, but otherwise seemed normal.

Later in life, I found out that she had started taking Valium for her anxiety. She was either too proud or in denial about how they made her feel to tell us anything. She didn't like to depend on anybody or anything.

Meanwhile, I tried my best to focus on school. I was still practicing with the football team, but I wasn't able to play a game in uniform until the last game of the season. It was one of the best days I had had in a while. It was a Saturday playoff game; and even though I didn't get to play on the field, just standing there with my football uniform on was enough. I hoped I would be able to be back on the team next year but knowing the size and caliber of the guys on the team at Tate, I knew my chances were slim. I doubted I would ever put on a football jersey for real except maybe a Cowboys jersey to watch the game on TV, so I decided to put all my focus into music.

I was convinced that the only way I was going to get out of the house was through music. Every time I had the opportunity to play, I took it. Playing in the band become one of my escapes, but it also introduced me to a whole new group of friends. Since the band program was so strict, most of the people in it were friends I could count on. A lot of them went to church on Sunday. I was invited to the First Baptist Church of Pensacola by some of the members and I joined the youth choir. It gave me an opportunity to get out of the house—one my mom approved.

I didn't really want to go to church. I only went because there was a girl there that I was interested in. Plus, every time I went, the church bought us a McDonald's hamburger with fries. It was a great time. Oddly enough, my mom still thought I was going to be a music minister.

Eventually I got a job. One of the neighbors worked for a guy that made air conditioning ducts. His business was operated out of his house and was located directly behind my grandparents' home, so I could walk to work. I hoped I could make enough to get car insurance, but it was a job I wouldn't wish on anybody.

The business was in the guy's garage. He had turned it into an AC duct factory. His job was to cut the sheets of tin into the sizes of AC ducts and our job was to glue down the insulation to the tins. We put glue on the duct and then took the fiberglass insulation, cut it, and laid it down on the tin sheet. It didn't take long to get enough of the glue and fiberglass insulation on your person for the itching to begin.

Ironically, he didn't have AC in his AC-duct making factory. Once it got hot, you would unconsciously wipe the sweat away, and end up getting fiberglass all over yourself. It was miserable, but the pay was good. However, once I began working, my mom made me pay my own way if I wanted to do anything and then I didn't have enough to pay for insurance. I realized I was fighting a losing battle, and after three weeks working in the heat, I quit.

Towards the end of my sophomore year, my mom sat me down and told me that she had had enough of Florida and wanted to move back to Texas. She didn't know if we would return to Glen Rose, but she decided that she wanted to move back. The next day, I was like a kid who finally got a break from a living nightmare. I told all my new friends that as soon as school was over I was moving back to Texas. She told us to start packing and only keep out necessities.

My grandfather was driving to Fort Worth and he was going to bring us a shipping container. We were told to pack it with everything we could fit in it. We would be leaving as soon as school was over.

Several days later, we were down to our beds and enough clothes to last us through a week. We even shipped our TV. We were so excited about the move. We packed all of our extra belongings. Now all we had to do was wait till the end of the school year.

I got up every day knowing we were one day closer to being home. I just wanted to leave. I knew that even if we didn't go to Glen Rose, I would be close enough to still see my friends. I was excited about the potential of moving to a small town and getting to play on a football team again. Ms. Sidorfsky had helped me improve in my music and I knew I could get into whatever band I wanted.

Life was going great, except for a few hiccups along the way. Now that football season was over, it was basketball season. I was never good at basketball and I figured that since we were leaving at the end of the year, there was no point in trying out. That meant that I got thrown in with the misfits of gym class. We were at the mercy of the extra gym teacher of the day. We did whatever he felt like doing.

One Friday, he decided that we were going to play touch football and it turned into an all-out war. We had about six guys on both teams. Two of my buddies that had been on the football team and the band with me were on my side with three other kids. It was a fight to the finish, and we were ahead by one score. The last play of the game the other side had the ball and threw a "Hail Mary" pass. For those of you that don't watch football, this is a last-ditch effort to win the game in its last few seconds. You just step back and throw the ball as far as you can, hoping that one of your players will catch it. I was with the kid that was meant to catch it, but at the last second, I jumped up and hit the ball so he couldn't get it, winning the game for my side.

As I came down from my jump, I felt him underneath me and tried to avoid him but landed on my leg the wrong way. I heard a loud pop and was instantly in pain. My two buddies came and picked me up, supporting me and pounding me on the back in celebration. But when I tried to stand, I fell instantly. As they were standing over me, I told them that I heard something pop when I fell and a guy from across the field said he had heard it as well.

I knew something was wrong, but I was hoping that it was just a sprain; otherwise my mom was going to be mad. My friends helped me off the field and took me home, and by this point, my leg was so swollen I couldn't even walk on it. When my mom got home, I had no choice but to tell her what happened. She threw me in the back of the car and took me to the emergency room.

After the ER doctors reviewed the X-rays, they told my mom it was just a bad sprain. They said to soak it and in a couple of days I should be good as new. They wouldn't give me any crutches so I had to hop back to the car because I still couldn't put any weight on it. The next day, she called our family doctor to have them look at the X-rays. They called her back, saying that my leg was definitely broken, and they needed to see me so they could set it.

For my last few months at school, I was hobbling around with crutches and a broken leg. The break meant the final end of my football dreams. I talked to my mom about the injury, upset about the fact that I had been playing tackle football for four years without injury but during touch football I broke my leg. I expressed to her how I hoped that this wouldn't ruin my chances to try out next year and she told me that there wouldn't be a next year.

She wanted me to put all my effort into music, meaning no football, even if my leg healed in time. A parent's signature was required to play, and she wouldn't sign it. The resentment I harbored towards my mother continued to grow. I was determined that Texas or no Texas, I couldn't wait to get away from her.

One of the many jobs my mom had was working for the bookstore at Pensacola Junior College. One day, she told me she was going out. She had met a guy at the college, and they had been talking for a while. She told him she had four boys at home, but he was still interested in her. She felt that it wouldn't go anywhere. We were leaving soon, and he was stationed here in the navy.

I didn't know how to handle the news. I told her to have a good time, but in the back of my mind I was hoping it would go badly. She came home that night and said that he was nice, but that she didn't see it going any further. I was relieved; I had my bags packed ready to go to Texas and I didn't want anything jeopardizing that.

The end of the school year couldn't get here soon enough. Even though I had had a really good year at Tate, it wasn't Texas. I said goodbye to my new friends, wished them the best of luck, and told them that if they ever were in Texas to look me up. I didn't care that I was still hobbling around with my foot in a cast; I was ready to go home.

I didn't know where we were moving, but anywhere in Texas sounded good to me. I was hoping for a small town where everyone knew my name, where I would finally be able to play sports again. Even if I had to forge my mom's name for the permission slip, I was going to get back into football.

But after school ended, we didn't move. A week after we had planned on leaving, my mom brought the guy she was dating home to meet us. His name was Bob and he was nothing like we had pictured. Don't get me wrong. Bob was a very nice guy, but almost immediately we saw why mom had wanted to date him. It was because she wanted to control him. Right off the bat you could see she was grooming him to do her bidding.

Two weeks after school ended turned into four weeks. The topic of Texas was being avoided like the plague. Every time Bob came to the trailer (which was a lot) I resented him more. He was doing his best to get us to like him, but he was the only thing standing between me and Texas. He didn't have a chance. I didn't need any more distractions; our belongings had already been shipped and all we needed to do was drive. I'm sure they both felt my frustration. I didn't hide it. I had told everyone I was leaving, and I was ready, but once again what I wanted wasn't going to happen.

Mom finally sat us down and told us that we were staying in Pensacola. She and Bob were talking about getting married and he would help take care of us. He was in the navy and we would have medical insurance and a house.

It all went in one ear and out the other. I felt that she was betraying us all over again—choosing her way instead of listening to what we wanted. Football was over, getting my driver's license was shot, and I wasn't going to see my friends or my old girlfriend. I was mad at the world. Why did God do this to me? I was so angry that I just wanted to get away from this catastrophe we called a family. I decided that as soon as I found a way out, I would take it. I just needed a plan.

It was the summer of rebellion. If my mom went right, I would go left. I didn't care. Bob became the mediator between my mom and me. He always took her side, but he tried to help us talk about what was going on. Somewhere in the middle of the summer, she told us she had found a new place for us to live. It was still in the J.M. Tate School district, so at least we would still be with our new friends.

The new place had three bedrooms, meaning we would only have two boys per room. It was a move up for us. Mom was able to get away from Grandma, taking some pressure off her. She told me that we were going to fly to Texas and get all the stuff we had shipped there.

Now it felt final. The only way I was going to Glen Rose was on my own. I accepted the trip for two reasons. One, I had never flown before. Two, I was hoping I would be able to see my old friends. I did have fun on the plane, but I didn't get to see anyone. We never even made it close to Glen Rose.

One positive was that I saw Joy and some of Mom's relatives. We got to spend a day at the Fort Worth Zoo too. At the gift shop, I found this floppy leather cowboy hat. It was unique to say the least. I tried it on just to see how it would look. Mom told me to take it off because she wasn't going to let me buy such a goofy hat. As soon as I heard that, I walked right up to the counter and used all my money to buy that hat.

That upset her, but Bob stepped in, saying that since it was my money, I could spend it the way I wanted. She didn't respond, but if looks could have killed, she would have had one less child to worry about.

We got the trailer loaded with all our possessions, and on the way home I wore that hat all the time just to irritate my mom. It worked. The trip back was a constant battle between us. I'd ask to drive since I had my learner's permit, but my mom always said no. Bob asked what the harm was, and against my mom's wishes, I got to drive anyway.

I was beginning to like Bob more and more. If I could get him trained to look at my side of things, maybe he'd help me get my driver's license. Even though I started to admire Bob, my mom did not let up on him. Despite that, he stayed around. Mom was a lady with four boys and a dark past, but Bob kept coming back. After the trip to Texas, I decided that having to stay in Pensacola was not all Bob's fault. If he helped us get some relief from Mom, it would be nice to have him around.

I decided if I was going to be stuck in this new house, I might as well make the best of it. I reached out to a couple of the guys in the band and found out they lived nearby and started to get closer with them. The rest of the summer was spent unpacking boxes and staying out of my mother's way. It was easy to get out of the house with my friends nearby, I just told my mom I was going to someone's house and walked out the door.

She gave me a curfew, but sometimes I came home before the curfew, only to sneak out again later. I never did anything that would get me in trouble, I just walked the streets after dark. It gave me peace and quiet. It also gave me solitude. I liked being alone and knowing that I was the only one I could trust. I was tired of getting hurt.

Since sports was out, I focused everything on music in my junior year. Ms. Sidorfsky retired, and a new and younger band teacher arrived full of grand ideas. One of the first things Mr. Slayton did was decide that our band uniforms were out-of-date. We were happy as our old uniforms were wool and incredibly hot. The school granted some funds for the new uniforms, but we had to raise the rest ourselves. This gave me another chance to get out of the house. We went door-to-door selling all sorts of items: J.M. Tate seat cushions for the bleachers, screwdriver sets, and of course, the inevitable raffle tickets. After a while, people in our neighborhood stopped answering their doors.

Slayton was very progressive; he wanted to move the band into a different marching style and music. This meant we had to try out for new positions, and I got first chair for the French horn. This upped my status, and I became "somebody" at J.M. Tate. Not that many people knew me as a sophomore which had suited me fine when I thought we'd be leaving for Texas, but now I was first chair and it had perks.

Slayton would call all the first chairs together and talk about our plans. For the first time since we moved, I felt like I was regaining some of the prestige I had enjoyed in Glen Rose. I wasn't a jock, but a leader in the band instead. Best of all, the more I was asked to do for the band, the more time I had out of the house.

Mr. Slayton was always up for new ideas. I had started listening to movie soundtracks. One of my favorites was Jerry Goldsmith's soundtrack for *Patton*. One day I was in Slayton's office and played him the title song. I suggested that we could recreate it on the field; it would be really cool. We could have clarinets playing the organ part, soft trumpets echoing in the background, the French horns bringing up the volume, and then have everyone else join in. He listened to me intently, and we talked for a few minutes about how we could pull it off. He finally said it would be too difficult to do while marching, thanked me for the suggestion, and then practically pushed me out of his office. What I didn't know is that he really liked it, so much so that one day he would not only make the band play it but take credit for it too.

I was finding it easier to make friends. I decided that Glen Rose was a fading dream. The more I gained popularity, the more I was able to forget about Glen Rose. I didn't tell anyone at Tate about my past. I told them that my parents had a nasty divorce and that was it. I was still angry at the world. On bad days I would go into my room, turn my music up loud, and dream of a day when I could leave this world behind.

The further I got from Glen Rose in my head, the further I got from church too. My taste in music also changed. Simon and Garfunkel and James Taylor turned into the James Gang, Steppenwolf, the Doors, and Led Zeppelin. I still loved the band sounds of Chicago and Blood, Sweat, and Tears, but hard rock introduced me to a whole new group of people that my mom didn't like.

Our lack of funds and long hair made it seem cool to resist authority. I started to meet more people around the neighborhood that my mom definitely did not approve. The boys that lived next to my grandmother loved to race cars, steal car parts, and were always out drinking. At first, I didn't participate. I tried smoking a cigarette once or twice, but always got sick. If someone had marijuana though, I never refused.

I just liked riding around with the guys and hanging out with girls that were as fast as the cars. My mom was always warning me about girls and having sex before marriage, but I often saw Bob come over and spend the night. Even though she never said anything, I knew what was going on. I didn't date much, mostly because I didn't have money and a car.

If it weren't for the band, I would have probably gotten arrested. Even though I liked hanging out with the wild crowd, deep down I still didn't want to disappoint my mom, even though we were always fighting, and I couldn't wait to get away from her.

After a couple of the guys I hung around with got arrested for doing stupid things, I decided it was time to start hanging with the nerds. That crowd just went to movies and hung out at someone's house, smoking weed and listening to records. Most drove their parent's cars, so they were scared of going too fast and losing their privileges.

Church was becoming more and more of an afterthought. When people asked me if I was Christian, my answer depended on who was asking. If it were someone from band or a girl I was trying to impress, I said yes. Sometimes I just avoided answering the question altogether because I wasn't really sure. I was still mad at God, and everywhere I looked at home reminded me of what happened.

I just couldn't shake the thought that if there was a loving God, then He would not have allowed what happened to my family. The only example I had of a father was one who was a brutal killer, so hearing that God was supposed to be my heavenly Father only turned me further away from Him and church. Additionally, none of my prayers of moving back to Glen Rose had been answered so far. I figured no one was listening.

Besides a few band trips and double dates, my junior year was uneventful. I avoided my mom the best I could with Bob running interference for me. They didn't get married, but he kept hanging around. Since he was in the navy, I was dreading the day he would leave on a six-month cruise and leave me to face my mother alone.

When my mom got food stamps, I realized we were officially kids from "on the other side of the tracks" now. We were poor. I hated going with her to the grocery store because I was always scared someone I knew would see my mom using food stamps. This was another source of friction between us. She didn't care about the food stamps. She saw them as a way to put food on the table.

In school I started to notice the separation of the classes. In Glen Rose, everyone worked—either on a farm or a factory, but there was hardly any separation between classes, at least not that I had seen. But at Tate there was a real separation between the "haves" and "have nots" and I belonged to the latter group.

This was also my first year of noticing racial separation. My dad never allowed us to have friends of a different race over and we couldn't attend their parties when invited. There was not one African American family in Glen Rose and the ongoing joke was that there better not be one there after dark.

Although my new school was not strictly segregated, there were some areas that you could only go into if you were a certain race. I never treated anyone differently, but there were areas of the school that "whites" didn't go to. Once there was going to be a fight and I heard later that it had been between the "blacks and the whites." I tried to stay out of that as much as I could and treated everyone the same.

Toward the end of the year, we moved again. This time, we moved to a larger house with a bigger yard. An added bonus was that it was closer to the school. It also had a large utility shed that was made like a playhouse. It was big enough for four or five of us to hang out in, so this became our little clubhouse. I also discovered that even though I was only seventeen, I looked eighteen which was the legal drinking age. I used to go to a convenience store in the area and buy wine for the guys. The clerk never asked for ID and soon I became popular.

I would buy a bottle of Boone's Farm Strawberry Hill or Apple Blossom, one of the guys would bring his cassette tape player, and we would sit around the clubhouse and talk about the future. I quickly learned I was not the only one that didn't have a good relationship with their parents. Most nights, we passed the bottle around and talked about what we were going to do after our senior year.

I decided with one of my friends that we were going to buy a van, paint it like the American flag, and travel the country. We didn't know how we planned on financing this, but that was always our grand plan: to see the country and leave Florida behind, never looking back.

Summer came and my mother had plans for me. She was working for a builder and he had property that needed to be tended to once a week. On Saturdays I mowed the grass at one of his properties with multiple rentals on it. It wasn't a hard job; it was just boring. I finally got a little transistor radio with a single earbud so I could listen to Casey Kasem's American Top Forty. I would time it so I could always listen to the number one song of the week.

Mom also had a few friends that had children, and she sometimes rented me out as a babysitter. I was genuinely surprised by how many people trusted me with their kids. As soon as I showed up at their home, they'd tell me what time they'd be back and leave. I wouldn't know anything else, and I figured if I ever had an issue, I would just call Mom. I think the reason Mom was working me so hard was so she could keep me off the streets.

Despite all that, I still found time to hang out with my friends. I still didn't have a car, so most of my times out on a "date" were with another couple. I constantly brought this up to my mom, asking her to let me get my license, but she always said I had to be able to pay for my own insurance first. It was a constant battle that pushed us further and further away from one another.

During one of our arguments, she told me I was just like my dad. She said I only thought about myself, that I was going to end up in jail like him because of my temper, and that I was going to kill someone too. I didn't know where this was coming from because as far as I was concerned, I was the exact opposite of my father. But in her eyes, we were the same.

This led to more yelling, more hitting from her, and after one particularly hard slap, I was tempted to hit her back. After that I planned to run away. I had a friend whose family really liked me; and after I told them what was going on at my house, they said I could live with them for a while. Since I was turning eighteen in three months, I decided it was time to leave. I packed up all my stuff, waited until she left for work, and moved in with my friend and his family.

It didn't even last twenty-four hours. As soon as she got home, my brothers told her what happened, and she lost her mind. She called around until she found where I was and got me on the phone. She told me that if I weren't back at the house in an hour, she would have the family I was staying with arrested for harboring a runaway. I didn't know if she could really do it, but I didn't want anything to happen to them, so I went home.

When I got there, she was locked in her room and we never talked about it. I think she was afraid that if she pushed the subject, I wouldn't run to one of my friend's, but back to Texas. She also realized that I was turning eighteen soon. I would be an adult and there was nothing she could do to get me to stay then.

I don't know how she did it, but she found me another job with the company she was working for. I was a brick layer's assistant's assistant. It was a tough job, but the two guys I worked with were great people. I mixed the mud and carried bricks to the brick layer. The guys treated me well, but at the end of the day, I was worn out with the constant manual labor. I'm pretty sure it was part of my mom's plan to wear me out so I wouldn't have enough energy to fight with her. It worked. We hardly spoke to each other.

This job lasted for about a month. After the bricklayers finished their project, they moved to a different location, and since I had no transportation, I couldn't follow them. I went back to doing maintenance on the properties and babysitting.

Right before my senior year, three things happened. I went to band camp, we moved again, and we found out that my dad had gotten out of prison. Mom was able to buy a house from the developer she worked for. We didn't share our new address. We just changed the address at the post office to forward our mail and cut all our ties with Texas.

I'm not sure what Bob's role was in this move, but he was back from one of his tours overseas and always at the house. There was talk of them getting married but of course no set date. Once again, I decided to bury myself in music. This year, I wasn't only in band, but also in chorus. Chorus traveled like the band, so I was even more excited to join. The new house became available, so we said goodbye to the clubhouse, packed our stuff, and moved for the last time as a family in Pensacola.

JIM HOWARD

My senior year officially started at band camp. I don't remember where it was, but it was a regular camp with all the amenities: girls' and guys' barracks, a lake, a large field, mess hall, and even a large baseball diamond. I felt like I had finally achieved the same status I had at Glen Rose. I was a big duck in a small pond and I took advantage of it.

Because I was first chair in French horn and familiar with a completely different marching style, I was brought into the band's inner circle to make sure we could do what Mr. Slayton wanted that season. We had used the basic military style previously, but now Slayton wanted to use the new corps style. New corps had short, measured, rolling steps, with our feet barely leaving the ground. I liked this style better because it was easier to play while marching across the field. We spent our mornings marching and getting used to the new style and our afternoons playing new music.

Slayton decided that we were going to use this new style of marching and a new routine for our first performance. We would be starting off with a low melody with an echoing trumpet piece in the background. Then the flutes would play, followed by the French horns and trombones, and finally the whole band playing the same tune at the same time. He called it "Patton's March."

He had stolen my idea and was running with it. It would become one of our signature performances. I didn't really care, but it did get me thinking about how my life was being pushed more and more toward music. As long as I was playing music, it didn't bother me that Slayton was taking credit for my idea. I was happy. I loved playing and it felt good to be in the position of first chair.

Plus, being in the chorus was the first time I had been in an organized singing group since Glen Rose. Ms. Beck, the music teacher, saw talent in me and made me lead tenor. She believed that if you worked hard, you could go places, but I was still angry inside. This difference in view caused us to constantly butt heads.

However, something happened in chorus that caused me to play along with Ms. Beck's game plan. I became popular with the girls. I could have my pick of any one of them. I also noticed that talking about God and Christ made me more popular, so I used my past training in the Baptist church to become the most popular guy in the chorus.

Right off the bat, I started seeing girls in the group. Some of the girls had their driver's licenses, so they could take me out. I was always the gentlemen, and never went too far with any of them; but it was nice knowing that if it didn't work out with this girl, there was always another one in the wings. It drove Ms. Beck crazy; she wasn't used to having a boy like me in her group. She demanded I did not date anyone from the chorus many times, but I never listened.

October was a big month for me. I turned eighteen and could now legally buy alcohol, making my popularity soar. Most of my classmates were only seventeen in their senior year, so I made all sorts of new friends because I could buy booze. I was never a big drinker, but I was always up for some Boone's Farm; and later, after my first bar, a rum and Coke.

I ran with two different groups. One was Ms. Beck and the chorus comprised of all the kids who didn't drink or smoke and wanted to talk about Jesus more than anything else. I was always sure to be on my best behavior around them, so all the parents trusted me. I was always a gentleman around the girls.

And then there was the second group—the band group. (I never really ran with the *really* bad kids.) When I was with the band group, we drank wine and drove around, listening to music and talking about how we couldn't wait to get out of school. We did stupid things like taking a baseball bat to mailboxes, but we never broke into a house or stole a car. There was a lot of built-up anger in us, but we knew that if we did something really bad, we would not only have our parents to deal with, which was scary by itself, but we would be kicked out of band. For a lot of us, band was our only ticket out of Florida, so we did nothing that would jeopardize the band.

When I turned eighteen, I finally got my license. A friend took me to the DMV. I took the written test, and then I used his dad's three-speed Chevy Corvair for the driving portion. I didn't tell my mom, but I did show my brothers. It took her less than twenty-four hours to find out.

At first, she told me that I lived under her roof and didn't have her permission to get a license. I told her that I was eighteen and didn't need her permission. For the first time in our fights, I could see some hesitation on her part. I think she knew that if she pushed me too hard, I would leave again; and if I did that, she had no way of getting me back.

Because of my sporadic church attendance, she still hoped I would become a music minister. She thought she would be redeemed because of what she had accomplished if I did. On the other hand, if she pushed me out the door, she didn't think I would finish high school and I'd end up with a job at a gas station, never amounting to anything. Then I could blame her for all that went wrong.

I still didn't have insurance and couldn't drive the family car, but I had a newfound freedom and it felt good. There was no stopping me now.

Senior year in the band and chorus was the best. We got to go to all the football games. We went on lots of trips where we would march or play in different events and went to places like Underground Atlanta and Stone Mountain. There were band competitions all over the state and parties afterwards. Then there were also chorus trios. Competitions took us all over Florida from Tallahassee to Panama City.

The traveling caused fights at home, of course. I mowed yards, worked for the property owners, and reached out to my old babysitting clients to get money for the trips. I was working any Friday and Saturday and babysitting whenever I wanted. It was good money and to be honest, I really didn't have to do a lot to get it. I had my own babysitting method: If they were old enough to run, I played hide-and-seek until they were so tired that after a couple minutes in front of the television, they'd fall asleep. Then I called whichever girl I was dating at the time and talked while watching TV. They were great gigs. The parents and the kids loved me, so I had an instant supply of cash whenever I wanted it.

Using Christ to meet girls was a powerful tool. All girls were looking for that perfect gentleman. A good Christian guy they could introduce to their parents. Someone they could marry in time. In the back of my mind, I didn't have an issue with that, but it didn't mean that I ever tried to push the limit with them. Every time I had a disagreement with a girlfriend, I started looking for another one. I knew that once we started having problems, the girl would leave me. That's what my mother had done. At the time, I couldn't see the whole picture of what had happened with my parents. I only saw the breakup, and that was clearly her fault.

I was often angry with my mom and screamed at her, telling her that if she had only stayed with my dad, we would not be in this situation. Later in life, I realized that the reason for my revolving girlfriends was my fear of abandonment. I pushed them away before they could break it off. Every once in a while, I would meet someone that I thought might be "the one" but with all the baggage I was carrying, it was only a matter of time before they dumped me. This made it harder for me to keep my feelings in check. I felt that I could trust no one. I only had myself, so at the first sign of trouble in a relationship, I initiated my exit strategy.

Mom didn't think every girl I brought home was a "good girl" either. She was always voicing her opinion about whoever I was dating. When she said that she didn't like a girl, I wanted to date them even more.

Once I dated a girl that claimed she was psychic. She said that she had a ghost living inside her house. There were a couple of times I picked her up, only to find her outside because she had been "chased out" by the ghost. She was also good at predicting things. She predicted who would win the high school football games. Tate's football team during my senior year was the best in the school's history, so it wasn't that difficult to know they would probably win, but at an away game once, she told me not to get my hopes up because Tate was going to lose. I just laughed it off because all the statistics supported a win. We lost.

In the final game of the season, I asked her if Tate was going to win. She said she couldn't figure it out. She didn't see us winning, but she didn't see us losing either. The game ended in a tie. (She didn't know football games could end that way.) My mom pulled me aside and told me this girl was from the Devil, and that I needed to break up with her. That only pushed me toward her even more. My pushing made her break up with me, and for a long time I blamed my mom and went on the hunt to find another girl to fill the void the other one had left.

The incident with the girl with the "psychic powers" ushered in a whole new set of issues. My mom always wanted me to bring the girls I was dating to the house. Every time I brought a girl home, she critiqued them, and she didn't like most of them. She had lots to say: She didn't like the way they dressed or the way they wouldn't stop talking or how they were acting too friendly toward me. It was a nonstop battle between us. After a harsh review of one of my dates, my mom often said that there would never be anyone good enough for her boys. This just drove a deeper wedge between the two of us.

We had a scare the winter of my senior year. We heard someone outside. It sounded like they had tripped over something in our yard. John, Joel, and I were watching television when it happened, and I walked over to the front door to see who it was, thinking it was one of my friends being stupid. They shouted the name "Jimmy" but everyone we knew in Florida called me James. It sounded like my father, so we quickly locked the door and turned off all the lights. We were afraid to look outside for fear of seeing my dad in our front yard.

We told my mother what happened, and she quickly started calling relatives who might know where he was. No one could give us a straight answer, so for the next month or so, we were on high alert. Just thinking that my dad might be in the area caused my mom to practically have a nervous breakdown. We weren't sure if it had been him, but our fear of him had been awakened.

We knew he was out of jail, and although we had not heard from him for several years, we were nervous. My mom never actually said anything, but I had a feeling she thought I had tried to contact my dad so I could get away from her. She started comparing me to him more and more often, constantly telling me I would end up in jail like him. She didn't know that I had finally accepted being in Florida and wanted to stay now. I was having fun at school.

Near the end of the last semester, I met the first girl I ever loved. We had a lot in common: chorus and the "Christ thing." She introduced me to her family, and they took me in immediately. I was in love, and we even talked about marriage a couple of times. She was the first person with whom I was intimate. For many years, I had just been testing the waters, but now I was finally hooked. I became obsessed with her. She didn't refuse me, but she did keep me in check because of her relationship with her parents and Ms. Beck. She was Ms. Beck's favorite; and Ms. Beck did not want her to have a relationship with me.

When we talked of the future, mine was a little cloudy because I didn't really know what I wanted. She, on the other hand, had hers all lined up. She was taking a vocational course and knew exactly where she would end up after high school. All I wanted to do was get out of the house. I still had that dream of buying a van and traveling the country. My friend and I still did not have the money for that trip, and my girl was not very fond of our plan. Every time I talked about running away, she brought me back with a touch. I was falling more and more in love with her, and soon my dream of traveling the country faded away.

Her parents had a rural paper route. Once another rural route opened up, they put in a good word for me and I got it. The nice thing about rural paper routes is that the people were usually a different class, meaning you'd get a bigger tip. The only issue was that I needed a car to do the route. Before going to mom about using the car, I went to Bob. He and mom were planning to get married sometime around my graduation, so he was around the house a lot more now.

Using him to help me talk to my mom made her more willing to let me borrow the car. At first, she said I could only use it for work, but soon she was letting me use it to go on dates and pick up my brothers.

This newfound freedom was intoxicating. The paper route was a pain, but it got me out of the house with a car; it also gave me a chance to be alone with my girlfriend. Getting up so early in the morning and putting the papers together to do the delivery was difficult, but collecting the payment was a whole other thing.

The paper company would sell the papers to me for a discounted price. Then I had to go around and collect from the subscribers. Some were good about being there and paying, but there were others that avoided me like the plague. I learned pretty quickly who they were and stopped delivering to them. That always led us to a nasty call from the district representative who would tell me that "the customer was always right" and then I had to deliver to them anyway.

I remember one time that I was so mad about a subscriber not paying that I decided to collect their payment in a different way. Each week they got their groceries delivered to their house, so I decided to help myself to some cases of soda since they hadn't paid. They never caught me, but they did call the front office and offered a truce. They would pay me back everything they owed, if I left their groceries alone.

The only really good thing about the paper route was the fact that my girlfriend went with me. It wasn't an official date, but once we went to the houses and collected enough money, we could do something together.

My girlfriend's dad really took a liking to me and started talking to me about my next step in life. I don't remember ever saying anything to him about wanting to marry his daughter, but I think he automatically saw it in our future. Close to the end of my senior year, we found out that Bob had been transferred to Norfolk, Virginia and that he and my mom finally had a wedding date. My graduation date was nearing, so I had to decide what I was going to do. I either had to go with mom and Bob or find a place to stay in Pensacola.

My girlfriend had the perfect plan: I could move in with one of her aunts. Her aunt travelled a lot, so we often used her house to be alone together. It was a small, two-bedroom house and perfect. It was cheap too. Her family could keep an eye on me, and I could finally get away from my mom. My path decided, my future seemed clear.

However, it started a war between me and my mom. I thought she would be happy that I was out of the house, but I was wrong. Moving out meant she didn't have control over me anymore, which she feared would end my chances of being a music minister.

Mom hated the fact that my girlfriend and I had a physical relationship, but she really didn't have anything else to say. My girlfriend was a good kid. She went to church and was well-liked around town and school. If I stayed with her, my mom thought I would also stay on the path to be a music minister, but music and school were the last things on my mind.

I was close to graduating and getting on with my life and just wanted to get away from my mom, marry my girlfriend, get a job, and enjoy living life as I pleased without having to worry about my mom. Freedom was right in front of me and I wasn't about to give it up. I graduated from J.M. Tate in June of 1973, and in July I said goodbye to Mom, Bob, and my three brothers and hello to total freedom.

It didn't take long before I realized that I had just moved from one controlling family to another. Additionally, I was a wreck inside and without strong influences outside. I knew I was going to end up being that person I never wanted to be. I didn't party a lot or smoke; and with my girlfriend, my life was pretty stable, but I still didn't know who I was or where I was going. That had caused my rebellion in the last part of my senior year.

My girlfriend and I were both in chorus, and sometimes she had to stand up for me because of my actions in school. Even though it got me away from Mom, I was done with school. I was eighteen, an adult, and I just wanted to get away from it all.

My girlfriend saw this. She knew that in order for me to accomplish anything, she had to be in control. She gained that control through physical contact. Without her, she and I both knew I would be a wreck. At first this was a good thing, but later it would end our relationship.

With my family gone, her family stepped in to fill the void. They helped me get my first car, a 1968 Volkswagen Squareback. Her family owned it and sold it to me to help me out. It was a zippy little Volkswagen with a stick shift, but it was great on gas and more importantly, great for zooming around the paper route and with a big back end in which to pile the papers. I remember going to the gas station when gas was twenty-five cents a gallon; it only cost me five dollars to fill up the tank for an entire week.

The other thing that was great for me is that when my girlfriend went to her grandmother's house (which was also nearby), I could sneak over and see her. Her grandmother lived on a hill so I could get enough speed to shut off the engine near the top of the hill and coast the rest of the way up. When I left, I just let it roll down the hill and waited until I was far enough away to pop the clutch in second gear and speed off. Life was good, but it eventually dawned on me that it was time for me to get a serious job.

During this time, I met a guy who was working at Monsanto, well, not really Monsanto. There was a staffing agency that sent workers to Monsanto to do menial jobs like janitorial work and all the manual labor. He explained that it was decent work with decent pay and if you did well, there was a chance you could actually move up to get a position with Monsanto. That was the real dream.

Working with Monsanto got you medical insurance, vacation days, holidays off, and great pay with retirement benefits attached.

I don't think I actually heard a word he said; I was sold on getting a job there. I wanted to get away from the paper route business. The next thing I knew I had an interview with the staffing company working at Monsanto (not *for* yet); I was placed in the textiles chemical treatment area of the company.

During the Korean War, Monsanto created a synthetic grass called "Chemgrass" which was later named Astroturf. Astroturf was put in the Astrodome because it looked and felt like real grass. I worked in an area that treated the textiles that became part of Astroturf or any other type of carpet. On my first day, I understood why they hired guys like us to work in this area.

First, it was hot, and with that came a smell. They took a large roll of textile and placed it on a spindle, which fed it through what looked like a large room where you could paint a car. They treated the fabric with chemicals, so it was ready to be glued to the bottom of the Astroturf or carpet.

We had to watch for spills and clean them if they occurred. We also helped get the large rolls of fabric off the spindles. You had to be careful around the chemicals because too much exposure to the smell alone was overwhelming. If it got on your skin, it burned, so we were always scared of accidentally encountering the rolls. On top of all that, we were tasked with taking out the garbage and making sure the floor was clear of all debris.

The other part of the job that was bad was that the *real* Monsanto employees didn't really talk to you. You had to perform above and beyond average because most of the hires were family and friends of those in the company. If you didn't know anyone, it was nearly impossible to get hired. I was an outsider, and I didn't talk unless spoken to first.

They didn't do much to make me feel like less of an outsider either. They looked for any reason to fire me, constantly watching to see if I was goofing off or doing the job properly. There was usually only one other non-Monsanto employee, and if you didn't get along, it was going to be a long day.

Despite that, there was one benefit of working there: I learned to drive a forklift. They would send us out to the warehouse to get rolls of fabric. The rolls were over ten feet long and weighed over five hundred pounds, and some were even larger. I had to pick them up with the forklift truck and bring them back to the machines. When the fabric was finished, we took the roll back to the warehouse, ready for the next step.

When I started, I was on the night shift. I worked hard. I didn't talk to anyone and kept my mind on my work. If they told me to do something, I answered with "yes, ma'am" or "yes, sir," and nothing else. Soon, I had the reputation of a being hard worker, but I was still not *one of them*. It didn't matter. I planned to be one within a year.

Finally, one guy started talking to me. I shared my plan to work for Monsanto. He told me I'd never get hired full-time working in this area. This area made you or broke you, and most quit before they were able to advance at all. If I wanted to get a full-time position, I had to start working at the warehouse. The work there was hard, but if they noticed you, it was easy to get full-time. From that moment on, I began working toward getting into the warehouse.

In less than a month, I was offered a position there. I was finally moving up. The warehouse was a completely different environment than the treatment area had been. It was wide open and well lit. It didn't smell like chemicals and it was busy.

On my first day, I worked with a guy named Ernie Stallworth. Ernie had a big contagious smile and the perfect disposition behind the smile. We had to take textile rolls that had been cut to a specific size and wrap and pack them in boxes. When we filled a box, another person took it to shipping. The process was impressive.

The rolls were cut at one station and sent to us for wrapping. We wrapped them with two end pieces and brown paper and then put them in boxes for shipping. The rolls weighed between thirty-five and fifty pounds and sometimes we got fifty to one hundred rolls a day.

Ernie would get an order and we'd have a race to see who could wrap the rolls the fastest. There's a trick to wrapping. You had this big stand with a pole on it that was the size of the cardboard tube in the middle of the roll. If there were fifty rolls to be wrapped, we would take twenty-five of the cardboard donuts and place them on the end of the pole. Doing it this way allowed us to take the roll and slide it down the cardboard donut, cut a piece of the brown wrapping paper, and start wrapping the roll.

The trick was that you didn't keep track of how many you wrapped, only how fast you ran out of the cardboard donuts. I knew there was no way I could beat Ernie though. He was a pro, so whenever he went to get more brown paper, I used to throw one of my donuts on his pole. He would come back to wrap another one while I was still on my first, but I would still finish before him because of my technique. You know what they say: If you ain't cheating, you ain't trying. It didn't take him long to figure out what I was doing, but he just laughed and kept wrapping rolls. He never got mad.

When I got to work in the morning, orders were already waiting for me. I started at eight, busted my butt until ten, got a thirty-minute break, went back to wrapping until noon, took an hour for lunch, and went back at it. Then there was another break at three and I went home at five. Those were the official union work hours, but you really worked until everything was finished. There was a lot of overtime which was fine with me. I liked the money.

I also liked working with Ernie, but once again I ran into class separation, only worse. Not only did the full-time Monsanto employees treat the hired hands worse than they did in the chemical treatment area, but there was also a big division between races, and Ernie was African American. I was oblivious about how much this would affect me, but I was caught in the middle of a racial war at work.

At some point in all this, my girlfriend and I went for a drive and found a 1970 Plymouth Barracuda for sale. We instantly fell in love with it and somehow convinced her father to cosign the loan. I had a fairly good-sized car payment for that Barracuda, plus the car insurance went up, so I was always working overtime at Monsanto.

I found that most of the white guys didn't want the Saturday part-time hours, so most of the African American workers took them instead. Most of them were just like me: they needed the money. Ernie was married with children and most of the others were in the same position. They wanted to work hard and get hired full-time at Monsanto, so they jumped at the opportunity to showcase their work.

There were several weekends that I showed up and found that I was the only white guy in the group, but I didn't care. It bothered others, but not me. On my first weekend, I had a nice lunch with the guys and talked about cars, women, and sports. They found out that I had just bought a Barracuda and we talked about the engine, transmission, and how that car was a total chick magnet. They also made fun of it because it was the smaller V8 engine. We just sat around joking and having a good time.

The more I worked, the more I noticed the division between the classes and races though. It was my first exposure to true racism. I had worked weekends with these guys and had fun with them. One Monday morning, I was asked by one of the white guys if I wanted to join them for lunch. Over lunch, one of them asked me how it was working with all the "niggers" on Saturday.

I wasn't sure what the expression on my face was, but one of them jumped in and said they needed to be careful because they didn't know if I was a "N" lover or not. I was so taken back by the conversation that I wasn't sure how to respond. I think I mumbled that I had a good time on Saturday, but all I really wanted was to get away from that table and fast.

Back at work, Ernie asked me how lunch went. I told him it was okay, but the tone of my voice and my face said it all. He just looked at me with his big smile and told me not to worry about it. He and the others knew that theirs was an uphill battle at Monsanto, but he was willing to take the challenge. My respect for those guys grew every single day I worked in the warehouse.

After my lunch with the racist redneck crew, I decided to make a stand. Instead of sitting with them, I asked to join the all-black table instead. It was there I met Sherman Dorsey. Everyone called him Haystack, a nickname he earned because he was over six feet tall and as broad as a haystack. Sherman was trying to get a tryout with the Kansas City Chiefs. He was from the Kansas City area but had somehow ended up in Florida. Now he wanted to go home and chase his dream.

I never understood why he worked at Monsanto, but I was glad he did. His voice filled the room and his wit kept everyone in stiches. When I asked if I could join them, he belted out, "Once you go black you never go back," and after that, we became good friends.

We had the perfect combination at the fabric packing stations. Haystack and another guy by the name of David did the cutting and Ernie and I wrapped. We rocked the place. Haystack was afraid of no one and everyone was afraid of Haystack. With Haystack next to me, I was living the classic "buddy movie."

It got to the point that if anyone said anything racist, sexist, or demeaning, I would take them on and Haystack would let out one of his bellowing laughs that scared everyone. It was the perfect attack. I took crap from no one and no one messed with me. However, I learned later that you had to be careful because you never knew when it might backfire on you.

It soon became apparent to management that I was a problem. There were some in management who felt that if I were moved away from the "troublemakers," I could be saved from myself. One day I came in and Ernie told me that they wanted to see me in the main office. I genuinely thought I was about to get fired for pushing issues too far; instead I got somewhat of a promotion.

One of the forklift drivers had backed off a loading dock and was now forbidden to drive, so they asked me if I would be interested in driving it. I jumped at the chance, thinking this would make me look more valuable. When I told Ernie the good news, he cautioned me to take care. I would be away from Sherman and he wouldn't be there to protect me anymore. If they caught me screwing up, they could easily fire me. I just winked at Ernie and told him that I knew how to play the game.

The next day I came in and got certified on the forklift. I was ready to go. I would show up for work and get a sheet with all the rolls that needed to be pulled for the cutting station, take the rolls to Sherman and David and drop them at the station and go for the next pull. In the past when other guys worked the truck, they would give Sherman and David a hard time and call them lazy and slow. Sherman would take so much and then go to a supervisor and snap at them. Either way, things normally went south.

We all knew they were trying to get Sherman to do something stupid enough to get him fired. In turn, Sherman knew just how far he could push them before he laughed and got back to work. They really didn't know what to do with him and I saw a way to keep this from happening.

I went and pulled a roll that needed to be cut and then went back for my next roll to see whether Sherman and David were ready. If they were finished, I would drop that roll and head to the next one. If not, I would jump off the truck and help them finish the cut. With both of them cutting and me carrying the rolls over to Ernie, it sped up the process. No more complaining, just more efficient working. If Ernie got behind in the wrapping and packing, I jumped in and helped him.

These guys became my brothers. We started doing things together outside of work and life was good. Or so I thought.

When I was off work, I started to drift. Music had been my dream for a long time, but I didn't know where I wanted to go next. I enjoyed working at Monsanto with the guys. Things with my girlfriend were also going well, besides the fact that we had not set a date for our wedding yet. This concerned me just a little. I wanted to move in with her, but back in those days, moving in before marriage was unheard of. When she was at work, I hung out with the guys from work. This wasn't bad, but I saw myself becoming like all the rest: going to work, going home, and drinking or smoking marijuana.

That was their lifestyle. I still hung out with my friends from high school, but most of them had college plans whereas I was working at a factory. They remembered my musical talent and kept asking me if I was okay with just letting that fade away. Right then I just didn't know.

My high school friends were pushing me to try out for a band at one of the junior colleges to get a scholarship. My buddies at work were telling me I was a bound to get hired full-time at Monsanto because of my work. I was unsure what to do, but because of my relationship with Sherman and a drastic change in my life, I was soon to move in a direction I never imagined before.

In October of 1973, I was constantly uncertain about what I wanted to do with my life. My girlfriend was pushing me to go back to school, but I was enjoying work at Monsanto and the friends I had there. One of the guys I had worked with in the textile treatment area made his way to the warehouse too, so we added another member to our group. He lived near me so when my girlfriend was working, I often went to his house. We would sit around, smoke pot, listen to music, and talk about how great our lives were.

I think my plan at the time was to get a full-time job at Monsanto. I figured that after that my life would be perfect. I was with a group of friends from high school with the same mindset as mine: no college, potentially travel some, find a job that paid well, get married, and be satisfied with wherever we ended up. We had no real ambition to do anything else.

All my friends were the same. Others said we could do better, but we were simply happy with what we had. We hadn't really experienced life yet. However, all that was about to change.

One Saturday, my girlfriend and I planned a picnic. I stopped at a convenience store near my house to get last minute provisions. I had just gotten back to my car when an African American male tapped on the hood of my car. When I turned to look at him, I noticed he held his fingers out motioning for a cigarette.

I shook my head. I didn't smoke. I put the car in reverse but before I could back up, the guy yanked open the passenger door and got in my car. I was shocked at his boldness and told him to get out of my car. He told me to drive. When I told him to get out again, he told me he had a gun and if I didn't do what he wanted, he'd kill me.

I sat there for what seemed like minutes trying to comprehend what was happening, and I didn't move until he told me to drive again. I drove the car out of the parking lot and asked him where he wanted to go. He gave me directions toward Monsanto. At first, I thought it was strange that he was taking me near where I worked, but nothing made sense to me at that time.

He was constantly looking around nervously around and giving me commands. He would tell me to slow down, not to drive where we could see police cars, and if I did what he said, he wouldn't shoot me. The next thing I knew I was on a rural road. There were a ton of unpaved roads, and he told me to turn down one and keep driving. We got to another unpaved road and he told me to turn onto it. Suddenly, we were in the middle of the woods.

I thought that he had brought me there to kill me so I started thinking of different ways I could get away from him. I had never been in a situation like this before and I had no idea how to handle it. I was lost. I was scared to death that I wouldn't live to see my girlfriend, my friends, or my family, and I just kept trying to think of ways I could get away. I was hoping that if I ran out of the car and down the road, I would be a difficult target to hit. When shooting as a boy, moving targets were the hardest to hit, so I hoped if I became one, I might survive.

Before I could try any of my ideas, he told me to stop the car and get out. He said he wanted to know what was in my trunk. My escape plan was that as soon as he opened the trunk and looked inside, I would break away and run.

As we walked toward the trunk, all I could think of was the phrase "feet don't fail me now." I looked around and noted a couple of trees. I thought if I could hide behind them (or in them) maybe I could get away from him.

I was getting ready for the run. I had a feeling that this was the end, and he was going to have me get into the trunk and then kill me. I don't remember putting the key into the trunk, but as soon as I did and the trunk lid started to pop up, I turned. In that split second I remember seeing that there was nothing in the trunk. I took my first step to run only to see his hand fly to the top of the trunk and slam the door down.

The slam of the door made me think for a second that I had just been shot. I stood frozen and could only think about how fast my plan had fallen apart. I thought he had seen through my plan and shot me right there on the spot.

He said something that caused me to look back at him with a totally blank face. He saw it and this time barked at me to get back in the car and drive him somewhere else. It was only then I realized I hadn't been shot. Still confused, I got back into the car and drove where he wanted to go—toward civilization and possible help.

The guy asked for my wallet, watch, and class ring. My class ring was my most prized possession. When I ordered it I wasn't sure how it would turn out, but as soon as I saw it I loved it. It had a blue stone and a white, cursive T for Tate that made it look like a "J." The coolest part was that when you put it under a black light, the "T" glowed. It was the talk of the seniors when I got it, but I was in survival mode now, and I handed it over to him. I only had twenty-one dollars, a watch worth $12.95, and my class ring. I gave it all to him.

After coming out of the woods, he had me turn into a vacant strip mall. We went around the back in the car and he told me that if he ever saw me again he would kill me. I watched him walk away, turned the car around, and drove off. It had been a little over two hours since he got in my car.

I drove about two miles away from where I had dropped him off and found a phone inside of a clothing store. I told them what happened and they let me use their phone. I called my girlfriend and let her know I was okay, and then called the police.

The police dispatcher told me to sit in my car and wait for a deputy. I sat there shaking. It was then that it all really hit me. Sick, I almost threw up a couple times just thinking about it. Why had this happened to me? Why did this guy choose me?

I got angry. I was angry at God for letting a crime of this type happen to me now too. I was angry at my parents for putting me in this situation in Florida in the first place. This would never have happened to me if we were still in little Glen Rose.

By the time the deputy got to me, my emotions were off the charts. The more I talked to him, the more I felt like he wasn't listening and the angrier I got. He kept asking me if there was anything else, I needed to tell him about what happened. I kept repeating that I had told him everything and was upset because I had just been robbed.

I wondered why he was still talking to me in the first place. Shouldn't he be assembling the troops to go out looking for this guy? I gave him a great description. They needed to find this guy. The deputy eventually asked me if he could look in my car. I thought that he was looking for fingerprints or other evidence, so of course I said yes.

I asked him if he was going to have the car processed (I had seen way too many police shows by this point). He told me he had everything he needed and asked me one more time if there was anything else that I needed to tell him.

I got frustrated and told him I was done talking. Thirty minutes ago, I was expecting to be murdered in a vacant field, and now I was being interrogated by a deputy as if *I* was the bad guy? The deputy told me that a detective would contact me later, told me to "have a nice day," and left.

I sat in my car. One thought, and one thought only, ran through my head: *What the hell just happened?* I was really angry. A guy robbed me, convinced me he was going to kill me, and then this deputy treated *me* like the criminal! Later, when I was talking to one of my friends, and shared my frustration, they laughed. That made me madder, but they explained, "Jim, look at you. You're a young guy with long hair driving a Barracuda. This had 'drug deal gone bad' written all over it."

I couldn't believe what I was hearing. (That shows how naïve I was.) Then it began to make sense to me, and I figured I would never see my class ring again. The police didn't believe me. They thought I was just another drug dealer who got what he deserved.

I had had enough. Something snapped. Life was too unfair. I slipped into a depression. Once again, I was the victim, and no one was listening to me. My girlfriend and friends kept telling me that I should just be thankful to be alive, but I was mad. I was mad because this guy had taken away something I loved and made me scared of my own shadow as I walked down the streets on top of that. I lived in constant fear of running into him, thinking he would kill me like he said he would. I didn't think that the police were even looking for him. What I didn't realize is how far from the truth all of that was and how drastic a turn my life was about to take.

About two weeks later, I picked up a friend and was driving us both to work. We were driving down a street in my neighborhood when I noticed a guy standing on the corner. As we drove by, I realized it was the same guy who had robbed me. I couldn't believe that my robber was just standing on a street corner in broad daylight. I told my friend that we should go get him and hold him until deputies got there. I threw the car in reverse but almost immediately heard a loud bang.

In my haste to go after the guy, I had forgotten to look behind me. When I shot back in reverse, I had plowed into another car. My friend and I tried to explain to the driver behind us what was happening and asked if we could leave for a second and come right back. The guy wouldn't let us leave, thinking we were probably just trying to get away from the accident.

Once again, it was a case of "long-haired men driving a sports car up to no good." We waited until the Florida Highway Patrol showed up and took the report. The trooper didn't seem to care about the reason for the accident. He just took the report, issued me a summons for improper backing, told me to be more careful and "have a nice day." At that point I didn't think my month could get any worse. Once again, I was wrong.

Through all this, I was not in a good place. It seemed like everywhere I turned I was getting bad news or dealing with bad situations. At this same time, my girlfriend began working the late shift, which added extra hours to her job at the hospital. She didn't know when she would be able to see me for a while. I found out from a mutual friend that she was really seeing other people while she was supposedly at work.

I couldn't understand why she would do that. We had planned to get married and I was living with her family. She was part of the reason I had stayed in Pensacola, and now we were in danger of falling apart. When we finally discussed it, she told me she wanted to see other people. I had to find a new place to live.

This was almost too much for me to handle. I didn't think I was a bad person, so I couldn't understand why all of this was happening to me. All this turmoil was too much for a lonely eighteen-year-old to bear. My friends were trying to help, but once again I fixated on the question: *Why me?* Everything just reaffirmed my belief that I could not truly trust anyone but myself. Not my friends, not my girlfriend. Not my family and definitely not God. Just me. I built my wall higher still and looked for a place where I could get away from all my problems.

Once again while driving the same route to work with my friend I saw the guy who robbed me at the same street corner. My friend, wishing to avoid any conflict, asked me to drop him off near his house. I did and then headed for the phone at the same convenience store where the guy had initially grabbed me.

Again, the dispatcher told me to wait in my car for the deputy to arrive. I hoped it would not be the same deputy. If it was, I was sure it would be another bad day for me. To my surprise, in just a couple of minutes an Escambia County deputy came sliding into the parking lot.

He stepped out of his vehicle and yelled to me to get in his car. It felt like I wasn't even fully in it before he shut the door and was off, tires squealing and speeding off in the direction of the corner where I last saw the guy. The deputy told me that this guy had robbed several people in the neighborhood and that out of all of them, I was the only one who could identify him. He told me that one of the victims had been his girlfriend, which made him intent on being the one to catch him.

We were driving with the lights and sirens on, swerving in and out of traffic. I was hanging on to the bar above the seat. All I could think about was how great this was. Someone actually believed me. Now I could not only get justice, and my class ring back, but I also finally got a deputy I liked.

As we turned the corner to where the guy had been, my heart sank. He wasn't there anymore. I thought that we had missed him again. As I thought hard about that, it suddenly hit me that it was a bus stop.

I told the deputy that. He picked up the radio and ordered all other vehicles in the area to stop every bus that had come from this direction. He explained that he had someone who could identify a robbery suspect that could be on one of the buses. He turned back and winked at me, and said, "Don't worry. We're going to get this guy."

Finally, there was someone who believed in me. Not only that, but I was starting to enjoy myself. We drove back and forth for some time in case he wasn't on a bus and then another deputy radioed that he was getting ready to stop a bus from our area.

The afterburners on the deputy's vehicle kicked in and we went off to the location of that last radio transmission. For the first time in my life, I actually looked for the seatbelt. Ironically, I couldn't find it, so I just hung on tighter. As we were weaving in and out of traffic, I did my best to calm myself down by remembering that the deputy was a trained professional. I just tried to enjoy the excitement.

This was like nothing I had ever experienced before. While one part of me was concerned about how fast we were driving, another part was screaming about how cool this was. The other deputy told us he had stopped the bus and was ready for me to identify the guy.

Coming out onto the main road, I swear we went up to eighty miles per hour. I could see up another county car with its lights flashing ahead, and we sped up to catch up with him. I looked for the seatbelt one more time, but at that point, I was so excited that I couldn't bring myself to care.

The other deputy had pulled the bus over next to a big parking lot. We flew into the lot and hit the brakes, putting the car into a slide, and coming to a halt next to what appeared to be an unmarked police car. Before the dust had even settled, the deputy was out of the car and calling to me to follow him. As I jumped out, I suddenly remembered the last words the guy had said to me. He had threatened that if he ever saw me again, he would kill me. My excitement was immediately replaced with terror.

I would have to point the guy out, and now I wasn't sure I was brave enough to do it. The deputy looked at me and asked me what was wrong. I told him that I didn't want to leave the car. Could he get everyone off the bus and I could point him out from the car? I told him what they guy had said, and the deputy gave me the biggest grin I had ever seen in my life.

The look on his face was totally confident—like he had done this a thousand times and never lost a witness. He told me to trust him; he had me covered. I just needed to do my part and point the guy out; the deputies could do the rest. He gave me that confident look one more time and told me to come on and help him catch this guy.

In times of this type of stress, the world seems to go in slow motion, making a few minutes feel like hours. I really don't remember how I was able to get on that bus. The first step seemed like it was five feet high. I remember just thinking: *Don't fall, be cool,* but I was anything but. My knees were shaking, and my mouth was dry, but I just put one foot in front of the other and walked through the bus, staying as close as I could to the deputy the entire time.

When we got further down the bus, I saw my robber. He had his head down like he knew what was about to happen. I had one moment of doubt, wondering if this could really be the same guy, but I knew it was. The whole time I had been with him, I had done my best to memorize his face. I was sure it was him. He suddenly looked up, and for a moment I was so shocked that I took a step back. He wouldn't look directly at me, but I was sure that it was him. I must have mumbled the first time I did speak because the deputy asked me to repeat myself. I said it louder: It was him. The next thing I remember was being pushed into a seat while the two deputies manhandled the guy off the bus.

I sat there on the bus for what seemed like a long time, thinking maybe I should just ride the bus. I didn't care where I was now. All I cared about was that we had finally caught the guy. The deputies held him against one of the cars, handcuffed him, and put him in the back of the other deputy's vehicle. I got off the bus and went back to my deputy. He was all smiles, giving me this big hand-shake, pumping my arms and telling me what a great job I had done. He said he was proud of me.

He walked me back to his patrol car and told me to have a seat. He needed to get some information from the suspect, but that after that he would take me back to my car. I sat there shaking like I had never shaken before. It was the strangest feeling. I wasn't afraid, I was just euphoric. I felt that I could accomplish anything. I felt unstoppable.

I had faced danger head-on, and it was the most alive I had ever felt. I had heard about this feeling, when people faced danger and all they could talk about was how alive they felt afterward, and the exhilaration they felt. I was still shaking when the deputy got back to the car. He looked at me with that grin and asked how I was feeling. I told him how I felt, but that I was confused because I couldn't stop shaking.

He said that he and other deputies got that feeling all the time when they went on "hot calls" like this. It was the adrenaline in my system. Right now, it was flowing through my body. He told me he was an adrenaline junkie. That was why he had this job.

He told me I had done great, and that I should be proud of myself for standing up to that guy. He said I had saved a lot of other potential victims by helping him put this guy away. Then he told me to buckle up. He would take me back to my car, and later a detective would get in touch with me.

As we were driving back, the shaking stopped but the adrena-line feeling did not. As we pulled up to the parking lot, I told him

I wanted his job. I wanted to be a deputy. This was the most alive I had felt in my entire life, and that I had to keep feeling this way.

Smiling, he asked me how old I was. I told him I was eighteen. He said that even though I was old enough to drink in Escambia County, I needed to be twenty-one to be a deputy. As my face immediately deflated, he went on to say that I should join the military, do some policing there, and then they would hire me as soon as I got out.

He continued to praise me for how well I had done and told me I would make a great deputy one day. I thanked him for all that he had done for me that day. I told him how I felt like nobody believed me and that he had restored my faith in the police. When we reached the parking lot, we said our goodbyes and I got into my car and finally headed to work.

When I got there, most of the guys were waiting for me, all high fives and congratulations for finally catching the guy. Most of them hadn't thought it would happen, but they were happy it had. In my mind, I couldn't get over the feeling I had experienced. I knew I needed to go talk to someone in the military. I didn't want to tell anyone what I was considering for fear that they would try and talk me out of it, but that night lying in bed, all I could think about was the chase and how I couldn't wait to do that again.

I spent the next couple of days looking at the branches of the armed services. I knew that my stepdad Bob had been in the navy, but the shore patrol didn't interest me. I started talking to an U.S. Air Force Reserve recruiter. I told him what I wanted to do, and he told me that the AFR was the place to go. He told me that security police was what I was looking for and that if I liked my time in Reserves, I could go into the regular air force. After my training and the one hundred and eighty days of active duty, I could leave, and they would help pay for college to get me where I wanted to go. The U. S. Air Force sounded like the place for me, so I signed up. My enlistment date was January, so all I had to do was keep working at Monsanto until then, and I would be good.

Excited about the news, I couldn't wait to tell my soon to be ex-girlfriend. I hoped that this news might rekindle our relationship and change her mind. I still hoped that we could get back to normal. She patiently listened to my story about my experience with the deputy, and then the Air Force recruiter, and how I planned to go to the Escambia County Sheriff's Office after my enlistment. To me, this meant we could get back together, and keep all those plans we had made together.

After I finished, she said she was happy for me. It seemed as though I had finally found a plan for my life. Even so, she was not ready to get back together with me. I needed to move out of her family's house because we weren't together anymore. Marriage was nowhere near in her future and she wanted to move on to other people. She told me that I should feel the same way. She wished me the best of luck, said she hoped we could still be friends, and left.

That conversation solidified my plan of joining the Air Force. I just had one problem. I didn't have anywhere to stay. I had recently been invited to a church where a high school friend of mine attended. I don't know why I went there the next weekend, but while I was there I ran into a girl I had known in chorus. We had always had this friendly flirtatious relationship, so she invited me over to her house to meet her mom.

While I was there, we started talking about my dilemma. I must have seemed desperate because her mother invited me to live with them until I went into the air force. I don't know why I took the invitation, but the next thing I knew I was moving out of my ex-girlfriend's aunt's house and staying with another mother and her two daughters whom I barely knew. What I did know is that it seemed like the right thing to do at the time. I was still working at Monsanto, so I offered to help with the monthly bills. She graciously accepted. I thought I could finally settle down until I got into the Air Force in January. Once again though, it seemed that as soon as I had a plan, God threw another roadblock in my path and everything went south.

The one constant in my life was that I was having a great time at work. Another constant was that I always felt as though I was being watched. I kept myself busy, but I still didn't take any crap from anyone.

Sherman still had my back, but now the racist white guys regarded me with malice. It was almost like they were biding their time, waiting for something to happen. I was doing the same thing, but I was just biding my time until January, waiting until I could leave.

I didn't tell many people about my plans. I wanted to work until I had to leave, and I didn't want anything to jeopardize that. Sherman was talking about how he was planning to go home for a tryout with the Kansas City Chiefs. It seemed like everything was coming together in preparation for my departure. I planned to lay low when Sherman left in December. In two weeks, I would be on my way.

Soon after, I got a call from a detective. He asked me to come down to the station. When I got there, he told me that I had done a great job with catching the guy. He had confessed to all the robberies that had been happening in the area. They had suggested to the guy that if he were to give back all that he stole, he would get a lighter sentence.

I said that sounded great to me. I still wanted my class ring back. The conversation was short and direct. He told me that if he needed anything else, he would get back to me. When I walked out of the station, I felt even more confident in my decision. I knew that law enforcement was my ticket out of here.

Then the wheels came off the wagon. I started having car trouble with the Barracuda. At first, we thought it was the battery, so we purchased a new one and that fixed the problem for a while. Sherman's exit date was in a couple of weeks, so I started to back off my attacks and started mending fences with my supervisors. It seemed like everything was finally coming together. It was mid-November and all I had to do was hold on until the end of December. Piece of cake, right?

The day came for Sherman to leave and we had a small goodbye party for him. We loved Sherman, but he didn't help matters. He spoke to some of the staff about how poorly the hired hands were treated. He just told the truth. He wasn't angry at them, but he told them that they needed to stop treating people the way they did. He must have thought that confronting them about their racism was going to help, but it didn't. Sherman urged them to unite with us.

There were all smiles and nods, and it really looked as though this talk might bring us together. However, as he said goodbye and walked out the door, I noticed that one of the supervisors was watching him intently. I remember thinking that was odd. What I didn't realize was that he was waiting until Sherman passed the gate, so he couldn't come back in. As soon as he did, he called me into his office and fired me.

I was confused as to why I was fired. My supervisors said I had been fired for falsifying my timecard by leaving early and having someone else clock out for me. As far as I was concerned, I had always done good work. Sure, I stood up to the supervisors that said things in bad taste, but besides that I was a model employee. Then it dawned on me then. I remembered my feelings of being watched, remembered just passing it off as paranoia. Instead, it turned out I was justified.

I realized they had been watching me, and for the past month my coworkers and supervisors had been setting me up. I had worked one weekend with a guy that was known for being the office snitch. We had teased him a couple of times, but nothing too serious. We had worked together on a Saturday and he told me that I could go, and he would punch out for me. He told me it would only be about fifteen minutes but when I saw the card later, it was a full hour.

There were other reasons why I was fired, but despite the injustice of it all, I knew I couldn't win. There was nothing I could do about it. I just kept pondering what the real reason behind it all might have been. Eventually I realized that it was because I had befriended several African American men. They were great guys, as solid as could be, but they were called out relentlessly. I was fired because I always stuck up for them. As soon as Sherman walked out of that gate, they made an example of me. It was racism, plain and simple.

I went to a human resources employee and tried to plead my case. I told him about the inequities in the warehouse. At first, he didn't listen to me, but then I told him I was leaving for the service soon and just wanted to stay till that time. I still don't know if he felt sorry for me or wanted to send me away to a worse job, but he told me that the only job open was repairing the roofs.

I told him I would take it. Heck, it was the middle of November; I figured a few more weeks wouldn't kill me. I thought I could do it. Man, was I wrong.

It was brutal. I wouldn't wish that job on anyone. I'm pretty sure they sent anyone that had gotten in trouble and really wanted a job there just to punish them. The roofs were flat tar and gravel. You had to peel the old roof off and then add the new one. Some guys cut up the old roof. My job was to pick up the pieces and throw them into a big trash container. The hot tar of the roof raised the already sweltering temperature to a much steamier level, and after two weeks broiling in the blazing heat, I was done.

I visited human resources again and told them that if they didn't have anything else for me, I would go back to textile treatment. They told me it was either working on the roof or nothing. I told him it was nothing and left.

I had less than a month before I was due to leave, but I was without a job or money. I could no longer financially assist the family that had just taken me in. Out of sheer kindness they told me not to worry about it. It was only a month.

The car had also started giving me more problems. Sometimes it wouldn't start unless it got a jump. On one of the days I had to go to Eglin Air Force Base, there was an accident on the interstate. A truck had jackknifed, flipped over and was blocking all the lanes. I got off and stopped at a gas station to get a breakfast sandwich and kill time until the road was clear. There was only one other car in the parking lot and I made sure to park as far away from it as I could.

I wasn't there ten minutes when the owner of the other car came into the store, asking who had the other white car in the parking lot. He said that he had just hit it. He bent in the fender. It was noticeable but not so bad that I couldn't drive it. He said that he had a lot on his mind as he owned the truck that had just flipped on the highway. He asked me to call him about the damage later and he'd write a check to take care of it. A week later I called him, and said the damage was $200. He sent me a check. I figured I could use that money to live on for now and get the car fixed later.

The closer I got to leaving for the service, the more issues kept popping up. The church of the family I was staying with was giving them a hard time for letting me stay with them. Christians, really? I tried not to get involved, but sometimes when I walked past the mother's room, I could hear her crying. We sometimes spoke about how badly her ex-husband had treated her and her girls. I told her a little of what I had gone through. I really could relate to her. I don't know how much my words helped but seeing her go through what she did helped me realize that my family was not the only one with issues.

Once again, it all made me mad at the church. I didn't understand why they wouldn't try and help her. Instead they complained that she had let me stay in her home. I was sure that it was her ex-husband that was leading the church against her.

Eventually my car quit on me. It didn't matter how many new batteries I put into it, there was something wrong that I couldn't see. My friend's mother paid to get it to a garage, and after a while, they determined that it was the alternator. It was only a couple of hundred dollars to fix, but for me right then, it might as well have been a million. I didn't have the money to cover it.

A few days later, I got a call from my ex-girlfriend's dad. He wanted to remove his name from the loan on the car since he had cosigned it. He asked me if he could just have it since I was leaving soon. I felt like I had been kicked when I was down. Not only had my girlfriend whom I planned to spend the rest of my life with broken up with me, but now her whole family had turned against me too. I told him I would do what I could and prepared to get rid of the car. There was nothing else I could do.

When you had built up walls like mine, you had to let someone in every once and in a while or you'd do something really stupid. The family that had taken me in turned out to be one of the best things that could have ever happened to me. My friend from school and her siblings became the sisters I never had. Their mom was one of the most supportive people I had ever known. She was constantly praying for me and my future, even when her own life wasn't going so great. They were there for me when I didn't understand where my life was going, but they always saw hope.

Other school friends also appeared and helped me through those uncertain times. In my last two weeks in Pensacola, I realized I would never be alone with friends like these. I couldn't think of what to do with the car besides giving it to my ex-girlfriend's dad. I couldn't afford to keep it in storage, so I left it at her house and let them do whatever they wanted with it. Besides all that, I had bought it with my girlfriend. Now she could decide whether she wanted to keep it or not. The day after I dropped off the car, I got on a jet and flew to San Antonio, Texas to begin basic training.

JIM HOWARD

January in San Antonio turned out to be very cold and very wet. As soon as we got there, we learned the term "hurry up and wait." I was instructed to go to a pickup location, but first I had to wait until all the other recruits arrived. While waiting, I thought about the fact that I was only a little over four hours away from Glen Rose.

I wondered about renting a car over some future long weekend and driving up there. I could meet with some of my old high school friends and see how everything was going. I dismissed the idea quickly. I figured everyone would have forgotten about me by then, and on top of that, I didn't know if I really would ever have the time. Before I knew it, everyone had arrived, and we were on our way to Lackland Air Force Base.

When we got there, an instructor started yelling at us almost immediately. He commanded us to get off the bus, line up, and once they found out where we were going, run to our new home for the next six weeks.

I got there on a Saturday, and for a while it almost felt like I was at summer camp. All the recruits that were supposed to be in my unit had not arrived yet, so when they took us to our barracks we stayed in our civilian clothes. We were assigned temporary bunks until everyone else got there, then led out to get food and sit around and talk. An instructor asked us where we were from and why we had chosen to join.

I learned a few interesting things. One was that this was only a Reserves and Guards group. There were no normal Air Force cadets with us. The other thing was that these guys were from all over the United States. Several were married and older. That took me by surprise.

I didn't think that anyone over twenty joined the Air Force. I thought that it was a young man's game. If you were in your thirties and had a job already, why join the Air Force? Those first few nights, we sat around, getting to know each other. Over the next few days, more and more recruits arrived, but it stayed the same. We talked, ate, and hung out in the barracks. I kept thinking that this really wasn't so bad. This was going to be a piece of cake for me. I had no clue that this was the calm before the storm.

One night the sergeant that had been showing us around told us to go to bed early. He informed us that our training began in the morning. Lying in bed that night, I wasn't nervous. How bad could it be?

At five o'clock the next morning, all hell broke loose. Our Training Instructor (TI) burst through the door in a fury, yelling at us. We flew out of bed, some running into each other and others into their lockers. He welcomed us into the U. S. Air Force by telling us that from now on we were *his* property until we graduated to another training. Barely awake, I wondered if the earlier nice treatment was nothing but a trick so we would get our guard down and relax. All my thoughts about how easy the Air Force was going to be disappeared in a matter of seconds. Now I was just hoping to make it through the day.

We quickly got changed into our civilian clothes and went down to the tarmac attached to the barracks. We learned how to get into formation and get in it quickly. Other personnel jeered at us. They called us "rainbows" because of the different colors of our clothes. They told us to enjoy the little time we had left because hell was right around the corner.

It was still cold and raining. Half of us didn't have any kind of jackets or winter gear. The whole time we were there, the TI yelled at us. He told us how bad we looked and how we wouldn't survive this training. He promised that in the six weeks we were his, he'd get us in shape.

We marched in formation to the mess hall where the etiquette of eating was explained. Everything was done as a team. You could eat anything you wanted, but you were not allowed to leave anything on the plate. They did not tolerate waste.

During the next few days, we became real recruits. We got uniforms, underwear, boots, and haircuts. Nobody was spared from the closely shorn head; they made sure that everyone looked the same. We were clean-shaven with clean uniforms and were now being taught the basics of the U. S. Air Force.

I hated the immunization shots they gave us for every disease known to man most of all. They lined us up and as we moved in the line, a corpsman was ready with a pneumatic injector. The pneumatic injector was a medical device that used a high-pressured shot of medication to pierce through the skin and deliver the shot.

When I first saw one, I thought the Air Force must be super advanced. I had seen what looked to be the same thing on Star Trek. On Star Trek, they looked painless. There were no needles, just a spray of fluid into the skin. I figured it wouldn't hurt at all.

But after watching the guy in front of me flinch and gasp in pain, I quickly realized that this was going to hurt a lot more than

I expected. How bad the shot hurt depended on a couple of things. One of them was simply the injection that you were getting. Different shots required different densities of the liquid. The other thing that went into the shot was whether you moved or tensed your arm beforehand. If you did, there was a good chance the pressure was going to cut you. I remember seeing some guys walk away with blood running down their arms. Some actually fainted. No one was immune to its discomfort.

I quickly learned that if you paid attention to your TI's instructions and did exactly what they told you to do, you would excel in basic training. Doing something wrong was inevitable, but after a good chewing out from the TI, you never did it again. Marching in formation, physical fitness, and making sure your area was sharp were top priorities. After our first inspection, the TI came in and unloaded on us. He told us that the officer doing the inspection told him that we were the worst recruits he had seen in twenty years. He went through and listed all our infractions. As a result, everyone was going to have to do extra duty to make up for all our mistakes. He flipped over some beds, screamed at us, and walked out. We looked at each other in silence for a moment and then began working to make our barracks better.

What helped me the most, was that one of the guys next to my bunk was a novice pilot. Our TI was also a novice pilot, and he started to ask the recruit questions about flying. He asked how he would handle going into a turn with the wind at his back or what he would suggest doing in a stall. The recruit got the questions right and the TI made him the "house mouse" (the recruit that cleaned the instructor's offices). That recruit and I later became close friends. He told me that while he cleaned, he often snooped around. He found out that we had actually done okay for our first inspection. The yelling was just to scare us to do better.

After that I realized that if I just played the game right, I might get through basic training easily. When they said to get out of bed, I was the first one to hit the floor. When they asked for volunteers, I was the first one to step forward. The more I got involved, the easier the jobs they gave me became. I listened intently to every command and obliged without question or complaint. My primary motivation was getting into the Air Force Security Police and later, do actual police work.

Eventually my life was amazing in basic training. I was having such a good time that I considered joining the actual Air Force. Unfortunately, those dreams, along with those of the other recruits, were ruined. A man from the legal department came in to talk with us. After we started asking him questions, we realized that most of us had been lied to in order to get us to sign up. We found out that if we wanted to join the actual Air Force, we had to start training all over again. He also shattered my college plan. Apparently the promised one hundred and eighty days of training that would lead to college assistance didn't apply to the training we were in.

One recruit asked if we could quit now that we had discovered we had been tricked. The guy said that since we didn't have any documentation in writing, we were still legally bound to be there. He apologized and told us that they were trying to fix this recurrent problem, but that there was nothing we could do. I, like many others, just tried to make the best out of a bad situation.

Despite all that, the Air Force was good to me. They gave me three square meals a day, and all I had to do was do what I was told.

Life was good. I couldn't wait to get out of basic training and go to Air Force Security Police School so I could get on with my life.

Additionally, I was finally fully out of my mom's reach. She no longer had any say in the decisions I made, and it felt freeing. The government was giving me clothes to wear and food to eat as well as something else: they were making a man out of me. For a long time, I had been worried about my life's direction, but now I had a plan. I was going to get out of training and go into police work. If this was going to take me to where I wanted to go, then I was going to keep going. I had been lied to before and I knew it wouldn't be the last time. I just had to keep moving forward. All things considered, life was good for me in the Air Force.

Another thing that helped me through the Air Force was the support from my new family that I had made with my friend, her sisters, and her mom. I must have left a good impression on them because I don't think a day went by without receiving a card or letter from one of them. I also kept getting stuff from all the friends I had made in Pensacola. Most of them were from school, and I never expected the overwhelming support I got from them. Every day I got something in the mail from someone, and that helped keep my hopes up.

Those letters kept me going, but there were some recruits that didn't have that support. There were some that hated being there so much that they would do anything to get out. One of the recruits said he was having LSD flashbacks during an exercise. When that didn't get him kicked out, he told the TI he was gay, and when that also didn't work, he was removed from the class and we never saw him again.

Some couldn't wait to get out and leave, but I was happy to be there. I was far away from home and getting trained to be successfully independent. I learned how to work on my own, and also how to rely on my teammates when I needed help.

Toward the end of our basic training, our instructors started treating us differently. They could see all the work that we were putting into finishing the training and started to talk to us about our future. They would explain what we did well now instead of yelling at us about what we did wrong. I started to feel that I was capable of doing anything that I put my mind to doing. Instead of listening to my mom telling me I would end up in jail just like my dad, or my father treating me like I would go nowhere, I had people encouraging me and constantly telling me I could do anything I focused on. I finally began gaining some freedom from my past baggage.

I never did get the chance to go to Glen Rose. When I was able to get off base, I normally headed to downtown San Antonio. During basic training, we still had to wear our uniforms when we left the barracks. We would take the bus into town, and as soon as we got off the bus, the offers began:

"Hey airman! You wanna meet my virgin sister?" or "Hey airman, you wanna buy some weed?" At every stop, we were bombarded with offers of sex and drugs. It amazed me how many recruits fell for it. We had been instructed not to carry all our money off base in case we got robbed, but on one of our first trips, one of the guys didn't listen and took it anyway. He wasn't in town for two hours when he was robbed blind after being promised marijuana by two strangers. I found him back at the base, crying because he had lost every dollar he had.

At first, I felt bad for him because I had also been robbed back in Pensacola, but then a friend of mine put the situation in perspective. When I was robbed, I had done nothing wrong. When this guy was robbed, he was doing something illegal. He was traveling far from the rest of us to buy drugs. He was lucky that all they took was his money. I had been a victim; the recruit was just stupid.

Seeing the Alamo was a highlight for me. At first, I was like everyone else: I thought it was bigger. But then I remembered that the majority of the battle was fought in the courtyard, and not in the front of the mission like in all the movies. Despite its small size, it was something to see.

Every young Texan knows the names of Jim Bowie, David Crockett, and William B. Travis: the heroes who died during the famous Battle of the Alamo. The mission was sacred ground for all Texans, and I was finally there. I also got the chance to see the River Walk where the 1968 World Fair (or the HemisFair '68) was held. I also went to a few of the many restaurants on the River Walk.

It was a peaceful escape from the base, but more than that, it reminded me of Glen Rose. The business owners were also nice to the military personnel in the area. Many nights found me and a handful of other recruits on the River Walk.

My time in basic training came and went. I had the opportunity to go back to Pensacola before the Air Force Police Training School started and had a warm homecoming. There was a lot of talk about where I would end up after school. Although I was happy to be back, there were some changes that made me think my welcome would be short-lived.

The oldest daughter in the family I had lived with had just gotten a new boyfriend, and he was less than thrilled that I was staying at the house. On top of that, the church was still giving the family trouble for letting a young man stay with them. Some things would never change. I did my best to ignore all that and had a great forty-eight hours with them. After that, I was back to San Antonio for the Security Police Training.

Security Police Training was not what I expected. The first thing I noticed was that I was now mixed in with every branch of the Air Force. There were Guards, Reserves, and Regulars in the school. Nobody really cared where we were going, only that we got the school done so each could move on to their next duty station. Some of the recruits were going places like Malmstrom Air Force Base in Montana. Malmstrom was a Minuteman III intercontinental ballistic missile base. Most were either going there or heading overseas to the Kunsan K-8 Air Base in South Korea.

This was the first time I was glad I had decided to be in the Reserves. When my training would end, I would get to go back home. My future base, Eglin Airforce Base, was a little over an hour from Pensacola. This meant I could go home to my friends once my shift was over. That was the main benefit of being in the Reserve. Some of the guys were going places they had never heard of before and they weren't too happy about it. Most of them did it because they understood the cause and wanted to serve. After boot camp, I never heard one person complain about what they were doing. I was really the only one that felt I had been lied to about my job.

We learned about setting up physical security on bases—how to properly set up perimeters and protect expensive aircraft, missiles, or radar installations and personnel from enemy attacks. It was all about the base itself rather than the law enforcement aspect. Even though I wasn't interested in the training, the group of guys I was with and the fellowship we had made it more interesting.

There really is no playing around when you are out on these flight lines guarding expensive jets. That was how the training was done. No horseplay, no goofing around. Everything we did was serious.

One of my classmates put it rather bluntly. We were the ground infantry for the Air Force. When the shit hit the fan, we were supposed to be the first line of defense against the enemy. This brought a whole new meaning to the class, and I started to look at my job as important, not minimal.

Of course, playing with the M-16s and other weapons was a lot of fun. The more we studied, the more we realized that there was a lot of mental preparedness behind this type of training. We had to look at our strengths and weaknesses and work on each one to make sure that we were able to completely lock down the base we were protecting.

I made friends with several of the airmen, and any chance we got, we headed to downtown San Antonio. We would hit one of the many restaurants on River Walk, eat food and drink cheap wine, and then stumble our way back to the base. Since we traveled in a group, we never had any altercations with the locals. By the time we got back, we had sobered up just enough that we wouldn't get into any trouble.

I enjoyed military life and genuinely had a good time. That didn't change the fact that being lied to in the first place had left a bad taste in my mouth. Being stopped from becoming full-time military just cemented my dream of becoming a police officer. I wanted to do my best in training and then move on with my life.

Time went by and soon I found myself graduating from SP school and going to my duty base. My base was Eglin Air Force Base near Fort Walton Beach, Florida, about forty miles from Pensacola. On a good day with light traffic you could make the drive in under an hour.

I was finally going back home, or what I now considered home. In all my time in San Antonio, I never once went back to Glen Rose. I blamed it on not having enough time, but I think a part of me feared what I would find there if I went back. I knew my dad was out of jail, but I didn't know where he was. I didn't want to walk off the bus in Glen Rose and just run into him somewhere, and then have to face him. I was still hurt over everything that had happened, and as far as I was concerned, the day we left Glen Rose was the day everyone in that town had forgotten about us. It was best for me to forget the past and turn my sights on what was in front of me: my goal of becoming a police officer.

I arrived at Eglin Air Force Base in March of 1974. I was shown to my barracks, which I shared with another airman. The living conditions were great. We had our rooms, the showers, and a common room where the guys got together and watched television. My roommate seemed okay, but I quickly noticed he was a slob.

He left food and his dirty clothes everywhere. Even though I was going to be there for a little over three months, I tried my best just to grin and bear it. Luck came my way when after a little over two weeks, a separate room opened up, and for some strange reason, they let me have it. I now had my own room. I think they knew about the guy's living habits and felt sorry for me for having to bunk with him.

During my first week at Eglin, the family I was staying with in Pensacola came over and took me home for the weekend. I knew that they wouldn't be able to do that every week, so the first thing I did was look for a car. Eventually I found an older couple selling their 1965 Ford Falcon. It was in pristine shape, not a scratch on it, and abnormally low mileage for a '65.

I paid five hundred dollars cash for the car, and just like that I had my own car again. My only complaint about my Falcon was that it didn't have air conditioning. If I wasn't doing 55 mph on the roads with the windows all down, that car got *hot*.

But it was completely mine. I didn't owe a cent on it. I could stay on the base for my work week and drive down to Pensacola for the weekends and stay with anyone who would have me. The family that had taken me in was more than gracious, but it became clear that they wanted me to find my own place. I started staying on the base, where I had a free room and free food. When I had joined, I was five foot eleven inches and weighed 135 pounds. Coming into Eglin, that was upped to 145 and when I left, I added another ten pounds. Base cooking was the best.

My first night there, the tech sergeant that ran our unit took me on a tour. He was a tall guy that reminded me of Fess Parker, the actor who played Davy Crockett and later Daniel Boone.

Eglin Air Force Base is massive. It covers 463,128 acres or 640 square miles. I was lost within the first ten minutes of the tour. The sergeant explained that it was a military testing facility, meaning new jets tested their weapons here. Every once in a while, we might get a call to check out an unexploded bomb. We had to watch over it until someone came out and made it safe.

The TS told me that when I was there, my primary responsibility was to guard the jets housed at Eglin. We had to make sure no one breached the perimeter or did anything to the aircraft. Some days I worked the guard shack at one of the entrances to make sure no unauthorized personnel entered. If I was lucky, I would get a shift at the radar station. Before I left Eglin, I got to do all three positions. It wasn't exactly what I would call "police work." It was more like the infantry, but I took my job seriously. We were the guardians of the Florida coast, the first line of defense against the enemy. That sounded good to me.

My first night on the flight line, I found out that most of the security policemen on base were big partiers. All of them drank and most of them smoked marijuana. There were a few that didn't smoke, but almost all of the men in my barracks drank heavily every night. It was their way to pass the time.

I had other things I wanted to do and was rarely at one of their parties, but hardly a night went by on the ramp that someone didn't pass a joint around. Many nights found us lying around once everyone had left, looking up at the stars and talking about what we would do once we left there. Most of the men I hung out with were what we called "short-timers"—only four to six years in and then they were out. It had either not turned out as they had planned, or they wanted to join something different afterward like I did.

Walking around a Phantom F-4 jet on cold and rainy nights made me wonder if this was really what I still wanted to do. I didn't like the fact that most of the others that were supposed to be protecting our government were alcoholics and dopers. Ironically, the commander of the Air Force Police (the law enforcement side of the Air Force) didn't like the regular Security Police so it was a constant battle between them with him trying to get us in trouble.

Surprise inspections with drug dogs were a continual threat to us. Somehow, word always got out just beforehand, so all the guys were able to hide their contraband. I felt like I was in a bad movie.

I had increasing doubts about going into law enforcement. If this was what it was going to be like, I didn't want any part of it. I had to admit though that incompetence excepted, there were still some good guys. I tried to hang out with them and not the majority, but I was still considered an untrustworthy outsider. I just did my best at work and then drove back to Pensacola.

The Security Police also had our own groupies. If you went out to one of their parties, you did not return to your barracks alone. Once one of the groupies found out that you had a room to yourself, you were sure to get someone for the night. Most of the time it was a one-night stand—no commitments and no promises. Most were interested in how many SPs they could sleep with in a certain period of time.

To me, these relationships were nothing but shallow. I was still looking for that one person to spend the rest of my life with, and I knew I wasn't going to find it there. I wanted someone I could settle down with more than I wanted a quick relationship with someone I didn't know.

But the more I experienced the secular side of the world, the more I started to figure out that it was all about taking care of one's self. It was about what you could get for yourself using what you had—whether that was your money, your body, or your assets. For example, if you had a car, most of the women would trade favors for a ride off base, even if it was in an old Falcon '65 with no air conditioning. They didn't care.

The more that I learned about this side of the squad, the more I wanted out of Eglin. I wanted to actually get out and do something with my life. Police work didn't look like what I wanted to do anymore. I felt completely and totally alone. I was also still mad at God.

On base one week, they played a movie called *Shamus*, a tough private detective played by Burt Reynolds, who scored with all the women, and got the job done, no matter what. I walked out of that movie theater, thinking that maybe I had another option. If I got out of the Air Force and worked for a department for a while, then I could work for myself.

I started thinking about my future. There was an old saying that if you sold your soul to the Devil, he'd give you everything you wanted. I was sure I could have everything I wanted and more. God hadn't helped me so far, and I did not see Him doing anything any time soon. It was then I remembered my old philosophy: I could only trust myself. I wasn't exactly sure how I was going to reach my dreams, but boy, was I glad that I hadn't signed up for the regular Air Force. The Security Police at Eglin was depressing enough.

I hadn't talked to my mom since I had signed up. Eventually I found her number and I called. I shared what I had been doing and what my next step was going to be, telling her that I didn't have any future plan after my recent disappointment with the Air Force. I was still too young to join a department, but I only knew that I wanted to get out of the service as fast as possible.

I had to look for a full-time job when I got out while continuing my monthly Reserve duty, but once again my future was uncertain. To my surprise, despite all of our fights, she sounded different. Almost supportive, like she wanted to help me sort all this stuff out.

She basically told me that now that I had the "police officer" phase out of my system, it was time to go back to what I did best: music. She suggested a school with a great music program in Norfolk, Virginia, where she was living. She offered to help me pay for college if I agreed to live with her, Bob, and the boys. I could work part-time and get back on track to be the minister of music she had always wanted me to be.

Even though I knew she wanted me to be the music minister of her dreams, she mostly sounded like she wanted to help. She seemed sincere, and honestly, I was running out of options. In a few days my active duty would be over. In a week, I'd be homeless.

I figured there wasn't much to lose, so I planned to leave Florida and go to Virginia. She, Bob, and the boys were coming to Florida for vacation soon, so we planned that I would follow them back. I figured the change of scenery would do me good. Of course, there was one little discrepancy in the plan that I didn't tell my mom about. Even though she wanted me to become a music minister, I was going to be a rock star.

By August of 1974, I was back living with my mom, Bob, and my brothers. They had rented a nice place in Virginia Beach, a three-bedroom house in a nice neighborhood. It was good to see the guys and catch up. It appeared that things with them had changed for the better.

My brothers had nice bikes, nice clothes, and not a care in the world. It seemed like Mom marrying Bob had changed things.

Even my mom had changed. It reminded me of Glen Rose before things got bad. She seemed different; and for the first time in a long time, I felt there was some hope that we could repair our relationship.

Since it was too late to sign up for a semester at the college, she planned to get me a job at the K-Mart where she worked. She said it was a way for me to get some down time before I started my studies.

I was stunned. Here was a version of the mother I had always wanted. I didn't know what had caused this change. Perhaps she realized how much she had missed me and understood that I wasn't anything like my father. Maybe she believed in me now, and knew that with a little assistance, I could do anything I set my mind to do. I didn't know what started the change or why it had happened, but I planned on riding it out and enjoying it while it lasted.

Reality snapped into place only two days later. She called, telling me that she had made us an appointment with the college counselor. They told her that it wasn't too late for me to get in this semester if I tried. At first, I wondered: *What about getting some down time?* But Mom said that the sooner I got in, the sooner I'd graduate.

She reminded me that it had been quite some time since I had played French horn. And the longer I put off playing, the longer it would take for me to regain my earlier expertise. I thought I was going to have more time to relax, so I was disappointed, but I knew I couldn't refuse her since she was helping to foot the bill. The next day, we sat down with the college counselor and talked about my next step.

Every single time the advisor asked me a question, my mom answered for me. Before I could even blink, she had signed me up as a full-time student with classes every day. I was shocked, not realizing that she would start me off with a full load right off the bat, but I figured that if she was paying, I could handle it.

As we left there, I thought to myself that my schedule wouldn't be hard if I didn't have to worry about work. That's when she told me she had also gotten me the job at K-Mart. I questioned being able to do both, but she said that if she could handle three part-time jobs at once, I could handle working part-time and "a couple little college classes."

As soon as she told me to stop complaining, I realized that she was trying to control my life once again. Just as before, her plan was to keep me busy, so she wouldn't have to worry about me getting in trouble. The new "part-time" position she was telling me about was five days a week from five in the afternoon until closing. This was on top of the classes she had just signed me up for. My only days off were Sunday and one other day of my choosing. A part of me knew that she had set me up again, but another part of me thought that I could do it and still have fun, and that somehow, someway, I would prove her wrong.

I started off with a bang. I got my schedule and eked out free time between classes and work. There wasn't a lot. The part-time job at K-Mart was basically a janitor's job. I came in at five and cleaned the bathrooms, mopped the floors, emptied the trash cans, and did any other cleaning that came along the way. It didn't give me any time to study, so that's what I did as soon as I got home.

I went to school, then work, studied, slept, and repeated it all again the next day. Instead of going home and doing homework,

I looked for other places to go, so I could get out of the house. I found the Baptist Student Union. Before I say anything else, they did do a lot of great work for the students there, but that was not why I was there. I was looking for girls, using my tried and true I-am-a-Christian method. Sure enough, there were plenty that loved a guy who was not only a gentleman but could also quote the Bible.

I didn't have any trouble finding dates. It got to the point where I didn't even need to look for girls, they came to me. I don't know how to explain it. It was as if they wanted someone to help them experiment with sex in a safe way. I was always happy to help. Once again, hypocritical Christians were everywhere.

So was homosexuality. This was my first exposure to the gay lifestyle, and I wasn't sure how to handle it. It disgusted me, but every time I thought I had found a friend, it turned out he actually preferred men. Don't get me wrong, they were great guys. They had amazing musical talent and were fun to hang out with, but when it came down to chasing women or chasing men, they chose the latter.

They didn't bother me about the fact that I was straight, but they sometimes pushed the envelope to see if they could sway me. My private French horn teacher went either way, despite the fact that he was married. Once during one of my sessions, he was yelling at me to use my diaphragm and pushed on my stomach to make sure I was. When he finished, he asked me if his touch had bothered me; he said this like a pickup line. I told him that as long as it was professional and not personal, I didn't mind, but he just repeated the sentence back to me. I think he could tell that I was uncomfortable, so after that our sessions were strictly professional.

During the first part of the semester, the college started looking for pledges to the music fraternity. I was asked to join, and the first get-together they had was at what I thought was an Irish pub because they had green beer. I was sitting with one of my straight friends watching a couple of girls on stage practicing a dance routine. The redhead kept looking over at me, so I told my friend that after another beer I was going to ask her out.

His face was priceless. He slammed his beer down on the counter and started screaming at me. He said he didn't think I was "one of them—a queer." I reaffirmed that I was straight and only liked women. Then he asked me where I thought we were. I told him I didn't really know. It turned out the establish we were in was called the Cue Club, and then I started piecing the puzzle together. It wasn't referring to a cue stick. We were at a gay bar and that redhead that had been flirting with me was a drag queen. I explained what happened, and we both laughed. We paid our bill and left, deciding that club just wasn't for us.

One of the students that lived with my private French horn teacher worked at a small-time department store. Because my instructor recommended me, the student got me a job at the store. The place hired off-duty police officers as security, and pretty soon I was getting to know some of Norfolk's finest.

They would come to my department and talk to me about working as an officer. The more I heard, the more I felt my old dream beckoning. I started having doubts about music and wondering if law enforcement was really the right path for me. The officers asked my age, and I told them I wasn't twenty-one yet. They said I should wait until then, but once I was ready, they'd put in references for me. Working a full-time academic schedule plus twenty hours a week at work started to weigh on me, but there was no way I was prepared for what happened next.

Mom, in all her wisdom, didn't like my '65 Ford Falcon. She felt that it wasn't a dependable car, so she took me down to the car dealership and "bought" me a new car. It was a 1975 Opel Manta. I never had a new car before so at first, I was ecstatic. Then she handed me the bill and told me I had to pay for it. I shook my head and told her I would just stick with my Falcon. However, she had already used it as a trade-in. There was no way I could get it back now.

I didn't understand how she could do that. I owned the Falcon, so I should have made that decision. She just said the deal was done, and that I had nothing to worry about. If I got in trouble with the car payment, she would help me out. I didn't understand her logic. Even though the Manta was a cute car and had a lot of new features, it still didn't have air conditioning. In my mind I had traded a dependable car for a *newer* dependable car. She didn't agree with me.

It didn't matter what I thought though; the deal was done and there was nothing I could do. I was naïve, so I just took the Manta and began thinking of ways I could prove her wrong with the car.

My first semester was rough. I had to balance my new job and school and wasn't into my classes as much as I thought I would be. I squeaked by on the academics, always doing well, but never putting my heart into it. I met several "good girls" at the Baptist Student Union that kept up my interest in school. I could talk like a good Christian, and even became a lead vocalist for their Christian band for a season.

I loved the music, but I didn't like the classes. I did have my first experience with backpacking though. We went to either Blue Ridge or the Appalachian Trail and spent a couple of days out there. If there was ever a time when I thought there was actually a God, this was it.

It was on one of those trips that I realized that my love for music was a hobby, not a job. If I could play in my spare time I would, but I didn't want to sit through classes and learn about it. It was that and many other things I didn't like in the music department that made me seriously consider dropping out, but I had yet to hit the last roadblock that drew the final curtain on my potential music career.

At the end of the first semester, I asked Mom about financing for my second semester. She told me it was my turn to take it over now. She had helped me for the first semester out of obligation. I thought this was another way for her to control my life. If I had to take care of both a car payment and school, I would be too busy to focus on anything else.

She also instituted a curfew for me. Every night I had to be home by midnight and there would be consequences if I was late. She kept repeating the phrase "my roof my rules." Since I couldn't even afford my car and college payment, there was no way for me to afford my own place right now. She told me I'd have plenty of time to have fun after college, but right now I needed to focus. Once again, she had mastered total control over my life.

Several things happened right after the second semester started. One of the "good girls" I had been dating broke up with me. Right before that, we had been going to church together and I was seriously thinking about giving God another chance. Things were going great between us, but then her boyfriend was a week away from getting off his military cruise.

She decided that the best way to handle that was to ask me to marry her. I told her that I wasn't ready for marriage. She said that her other boyfriend was, and then she broke up with me. *Another hypocritical Christian.* We had been seeing each other and going to church together for six months. I met new Christian friends and even volunteered with the Royal Ambassadors a couple of times.

However, once we broke up, she told me to stay away from "her" church. Once again, I confronted God with why He had let this happen to me. My education was going south, I disliked my job, and I was getting deeper in debt as time passed. I wanted to get away from my mom, and once again I didn't like where my future seemed to be going. My only relief during all this was talking to the off-duty police officers at the store. The stories they told got me excited about law enforcement, but I felt trapped because I couldn't do anything about that until I was older.

One night I was at school for one of my later classes, walking across the campus to talk to a teacher. I felt miserable, was doing poorly and needed help with this class, and it was cold and raining. I finally got to the administration office and saw a college police sergeant. He stopped me when he noticed I had a patch on my jacket from my job as Security Police at Eglin.

He told me that he had also been at Eglin, so for a while we just talked about our experiences. I told him that school wasn't going in the direction I planned, and he asked me if I was still interested in law enforcement. He said that if I was twenty, I could apply for the Norfolk Police Department now because they had just started accepting applications from twenty-year-olds.

That was all I needed to hear. Later that week I told my brothers of my plan and within twenty-four hours my mom came and told me that she would not stand for me joining the department. She told me that I wasn't allowed to drop out of college.

The next day I dropped out of school and applied at the Norfolk Police Department.

CHAPTER 7

It took about six months for me to be hired by the Norfolk Police Department. All the paperwork, interviews, and polygraphs took time.

For my interview, I was in the room with several deputy chiefs and a captain. One of the deputy chiefs, an older gruff man, noticed that I had written that I was a Christian on my application. He asked if I would pray to my God if I were ever in a shootout. I said yes, I would. After he looked up from the folder, I told him I would pray for God to steady my aim, so I could take out the bad guy. I guess he liked my answer. After that, he just closed the folder and wished me good luck.

I had passed everything up to that point. The last thing I needed was a physical, but they wouldn't do that until I had an employment date. The next academy started in October, but I was told I wasn't going to be able to make that one and would have to wait for January.

I had already dropped out of college, so at this point I was working at a department store almost full-time. My home life was tense, to say the least. My mom had completely stopped talking to me. At the time, I considered that a blessing. Whenever she did speak, all she said was that mothers should not have to worry about their sons being shot and killed by criminals. I responded by telling her that as far as I was concerned, I could get hit by a bus walking across the street. It didn't matter what I was doing; if it was my time to go, it was my time to go.

I played "hurry up and wait." Since I couldn't get into the October academy, I just needed to be patient until January. I needed to stay out of trouble, and soon I would have the life I wanted.

Almost three weeks after my twenty-first birthday, I got a call that there was an opening in the October academy. If I could get down to the public health department on Friday and pass the physical exam, I could start the academy the following Monday.

I told my work about my situation and they wished me the best of luck. On October 27, 1975, I joined the other cadets in the Norfolk Police Department's Ninth Academy and never looked back.

Academy life was totally different than military life. For one, we didn't live on the base. We all drove to the academy in the morning and home in the afternoon. This left me a lot of time to get in trouble.

Other cadets went to the bar after academy. I remembered how it was at Eglin with all the alcohol and drugs, and decided I wasn't going to do anything to potentially jeopardize my career.

I used Christianity as my excuse as to why I wouldn't go out with the guys. Instead I went home and studied. There was another Christian in the academy. He was a nice guy but reminded me too much of a "holy roller." I stayed away from him as much as I could.

Sometimes we got ridiculed by the other cadets in the academy, but I didn't care. I was focused on my dream of becoming a police officer. Too many of the other guys reminded me of the screw-ups in the Air Force Academy. I wanted to be as far away from them as possible.

I continued hanging out at the Baptist Student Union. Mostly because there were still a few girls there that I liked, but also because I felt safe there. Between studying and the BSU, I kept myself busy and out of trouble.

After three months of classes on constitutional law, search and seizure, laws of arrest, defense tactics and firearms training, I was in. I got my uniform, weapon, flashlight, and handcuffs. I got orders to report to the Second Precinct in the Ocean View part of Norfolk, working the midnight shift.

I certainly was a sight to see on my first night. My uniform was new and freshly pressed. It was our winter uniforms, so it had long sleeves with a tie. I had my new gun belt, nightstick, and gun with speed loaders. I had my hat folded just right with the brim shining as brightly as my shoes. I looked sharp.

I remember going into the precinct, getting the tour and my new locker and then heading out to roll call. I was led into a room with veterans and had my first taste of being a real police officer.

The officers who were younger, cleaner, and more in shape had a uniform that looked sharp and neat. The older the officer looked, the more it looked like they had slept in theirs. They were wrinkled with food stains on their tie. Some of the officers looked like they couldn't run a half-mile, much less get out of their cars without being out of breath.

There were just as many tall and skinny officers as there were short and fat ones. It was nothing like you see on TV or in the movies. Insults filled the air. I was called a rookie and other words that weren't so nice. They told me to go sit in the corner.

At first, I thought I was in the wrong room. Finally, an officer around my age told me to sit next to him. He said not to worry

NPD 9th Academy 1975, 1st row on steps, second from right

about the guys. Most of them were good men, he said, just a little rough around the collar. That was an understatement.

I was assigned to a Field Training Officer (FTO) and while waiting for final instructions from the sergeant, I was told to go downstairs and wait.

While waiting, I leaned against the wall in the entrance hallway. I was excited about my first night as a Norfolk police officer. Not really knowing what to expect, I let my mind drift back to my experience with the Pensacola deputy.

Before I was able to get too deep in my thoughts, the front door to the precinct burst open. The door hit the wall I was leaning on with a bang so loud I thought it was a gunshot. It quickly brought me back to reality.

A man ran through the door, his shirt ripped and bloody, a shiner under one eye. He was a mess, and I realized I knew him.

While in the academy, we had watched a detective who was a professional boxer. He had some of the fastest hands I had ever seen. I got to watch him pummel the guy at the fight, but right now he was running for his life and had just taken a beating.

He yelled that he needed help. My first thought was that if he just got his butt beat, there wasn't much anyone could do. The only true fight I had ever been in was with my brothers. Even though we were family, there had been some big ones. The last one we had ended with some shiners and bruised egos, but besides that, I had never been in a fight.

Here stood a professional boxer asking me for help. For a split second I thought I had made a mistake. I should forget about police work and just go back to music.

However, it was that night that I saw what police officers do when one of their own was in trouble: they respond to the call. They not only band together to protect their own but unleash the entire fury of the department. Suddenly, every officer in that precinct was there. The battered detective explained that he had been working a narcotics buy when it went bad on him. Two guys had tried to jump him and rob him.

Narcotics detectives and supervisors came in and took over the entire precinct. They grabbed my FTO and another seasoned officer and told us we were going with them to look for the suspects. The next thing I knew we were in the patrol car, trying to keep up with the unmarked narcotics cars, as we drove to our first location

The detective had gone to a specific bar and met with the dealers to make the buy. Our first stop was the bar. As we got out of our vehicles, I was impressed at the show of force. There were eight of us going from bar to bar, looking for the guys who attacked the detective.

I watched the narcotics sergeant. He was a short guy but walked in and declared martial law in every bar. He would walk up to the biggest guy in the place and berate him. It was almost like he was daring him to do something stupid, while trying to find the names of the ones who had jumped the detective. Once the sergeant threatened to shut down all the bars on the strip, it wasn't long before we got the names of the two suspects.

Within an hour, we had them in custody. Of course, it wasn't without a physical interrogation. It was the first time I saw first-hand what some would call police brutality.

We found the first suspect hiding in another bar. Before they put him in handcuffs and threw him in the back of the police car, everyone took a shot at him. Being a rookie, I was shocked. The other detectives said it was what he deserved for going after one of us.

The second guy we found at his home. There was no official process at all. One of the guys knocked on his door and whoever opened it was pushed away, while everyone else stormed inside. Once they found the suspect, the beating began.

That moment of doubt disappeared as soon as I felt the same adrenaline I had experienced in Pensacola. I felt like I was in the right place. A place where we protected our own. I found the family unit I had been searching for, and I was going to do anything to be a part of it.

That was how my career in law enforcement started. I ate, slept, and drank police work. When I wasn't on the job, I was reading about it or working out with the guys in the platoon. I wanted to learn from them so I could be the best. I'm not going to say that I wasn't afraid, but I always knew that all I had to do was get on the radio and call for help. I knew that they had my back.

I learned quickly that the police department was a family. A dysfunctional one with its own dirty little secrets. The difference was this: If these secrets got out, they ruined an officer's career.

I was quickly accepted by the younger guys. Some of the older officers were a little standoffish because they felt as though I hadn't proven myself yet. When I joined the department, I was 5'11" and weighed 155 pounds. Most felt that I couldn't stand straight against a strong Nor'easter, much less fight. After a period of time, my FTO, who was considered one of the old timers, let the others know that I wasn't afraid to jump into anything. It wasn't long before they listened to him and I was accepted by them as well.

The district I was assigned to with my FTO was a mostly residential/small business area. Our boundary was East Little Creek Road and Tidewater Drive down to Camellia Road. The area covered the north side of Little Creek Road.

There were small businesses on Little Creek Road with some residential areas behind them. The K-Mart I used to work at was now in my patrol district. I occasionally stopped by to see everyone. They were proud of me for getting out of K-Mart.

Even though our district kept us busy with routine police calls, the action I longed for was in the sector to the north called Ocean View. The bars we went to the first night of the job were there.

East Ocean View Avenue and Shore Drive was called The Strip. The Strip started on the 7900 block of Shore Drive and went to the 8100 block. In that short distance of three blocks, there were about fifteen different bars in which a sailor or marine could get himself in trouble. Bikers, long-haired rednecks, sailors, and marines were just some of the characters that frequented the bars on The Strip.

On the first and fifteenth of every month, it was like the Wild West on The Strip. If you heard a call over the radio for places like The Purple Onion, Jolly Roger, Pirates Cove, JR's, or the Wing Ding, you knew a fight had broken out or had just broken up and they needed an ambulance. Sometimes we heard a call go out that other units were needed, and we would speed toward the bars only to be told that we were too late, and the excitement was over.

We worked on rotating shifts. We worked seven days, two days off, seven nights, another two days off, seven evenings, and then a three-day weekend. On the last shift of the evenings, most of the guys got together and had what we called "Choir Practice."

It got this nickname from Joseph Wambaugh's book, *The Choirboys*. Wambaugh was required reading for all police officers at this time. *The Choirboys* was about a platoon of Los Angeles cops who worked hard and partied harder. They would tell their spouses that they were going to choir practice when they went out to party. We picked up the term, but the spouses of the guys at Norfolk knew there was no singing going on.

No singing but lots of booze and loose women. It was always an interesting time.

At choir practice, you learned a lot about your fellow officers. When the alcohol started flowing, they shared war stories. As I listened, I learned that some of these guys were living life like it was their last day on earth. They were fearless. They told stories of how someone would look at them the wrong way and they would start fights with them. They talked about how they beat the guy up and laughed about it together.

Then they'd have another drink and move on to the next story. After a while, I realized that most of these guys weren't fearless; they were just bullies. They probably felt like the only thing they could do in life was be a police officer—a police officer complete with a gun and a badge that made them feel like they could do whatever they wanted. Hell, they were entitled. After all, who would choose to work all these crazy hours and get poor pay, but also have aid whenever disaster struck? It was all part of the job.

At choir practices, I remembered what they told us at the academy: There were three things that could cause a police officer to lose his job: money, alcohol, and women. They didn't mention drugs because a lot of the young officers smoked pot. The supervisors knew about it, but never really said anything. If it came up in conversation, the supervisor voiced his opinion and had another drink. I think they liked to pretend that it didn't exist.

After three months of working with my FTO and attending lots of choir practices, I began to pick and choose the officers I wanted to be around. I avoided the others like the plague. I had the feeling that most of them would be gone in a few years. They would either retire or get fired. In the coming years, a lot of them were fired.

For a while, I tried to fit in by going to the choir practices, but soon I saw that most of the guys that liked to get totally wasted all the time weren't the norm. A lot of the guys had a beer or two and went home. Most of them were good family men.

The supervisors wanted to be "one of the guys" but after two beers it was time to leave. They didn't want to witness the rest.

Once you got promoted, you moved away from the partying crowd and into more subdued company.

I wanted to find a happy medium, a little crazy and fun, but not *that* crazy. I walked a thin line. I would have a beer or two and then head out. I usually told them I was leaving early to meet a girl. Eventually they started harassing me and telling me to bring her in, but I just laughed and left.

The next week I often heard that someone had drunk too much, fired his weapon, wrecked his motorcycle, or stole someone else's girl, causing a fight. I soon decided choir practice was down a singer.

Every day, I just felt more naïve. I wasn't on the street three months before I started seeing the seedy side of life—not only in the police department, but in the world.

The other thing we were told would get us in trouble was women, so it surprised me that so many married men had women on the side. Sometimes I just didn't want to believe it. I had been raised that once you were married, you got that promiscuity out of your system.

The general routine for work with my FTO was that we would get our police car, load up, and head out to a Fotomat located close to our district. A Fotomat was a drive-through kiosk that developed film back in the 70s and 80s. Their claim to fame was that they could develop film in twenty-four hours.

There was a very young, petite blonde that worked there. My FTO went there first thing after his shift began, and sometimes we sat there for long periods of time, as long as he felt we were safe and couldn't get in trouble. Every day he asked her if there was anything she needed, and if there was, we went and got it for her.

My FTO was about twice the girl's age, so at first, I thought she was the daughter of a friend of his. I didn't think much about it. I had met my FTO's wife before. She was pretty, and I thought she was the better half of the marriage. Don't get me wrong, my FTO was a great guy and a good instructor, but he was also overweight and sometimes a bit of a slob. I always joked that he married up and he agreed.

They had a couple of kids and on paper, their marriage looked perfect. At least that's what I thought. Then one night he came into work really shook up. He had been in a fight with another officer because they found out that they were *both* having an affair with the Fotomat girl.

Both were twice her age, and I was shocked that both of them were seeing her on the side. This was my first experience with "police groupies."

Most of the women I encountered while out on the street either loved the uniform or hated it. There was no in-between. I also found that if you could get those that hated it alone, it didn't take much to convince them to meet you after work. Sometimes that brought a whole new problem.

Most groupies I met had a place of their own, so I could meet them at their place when I got off work. I still had to be home before a certain time though. I still had a curfew because I was living at my mom's house with Bob and the boys. I couldn't come home with alcohol on my breath or I got into trouble the next day.

Here I was: twenty-one years old, carrying a gun and able to arrest people, but I still had a curfew! I only stayed there because I didn't think I could afford living anywhere else. At first, I accepted it, but soon it interfered with not only my personal life, but my career as well. I had my new family. My police brothers and sisters supported me. They accepted me and understood what I was going through. It was time to move on.

I remember the day I told my mom I was moving out. At first, she fought it. She didn't understand why I would waste money on an apartment when I could live with her rent free. I told her that I would stay if she lifted her restrictions, but she stuck to it.

I explained that the curfew was just one of the reasons I was leaving and then she just stopped speaking to me. I decided I would always love her because she was my mother, but this was my life, and I needed to rely on the support I got from the department and get as far away from her as I possibly could.

I became a nomad, moving from place to place. I planned to have a place of my own but realized that I wasn't making enough money for all the things I wanted. I sometimes returned home for a few months, saved enough to buy something, look for a new place, and then leave.

Most of the time I left because of Mom's rules. I had too many new girlfriends that wanted me to stay the night. This caused several rounds of fighting with my mom. Eventually, I just got tired of it. I would convince one of my police friends to be my roommate and I would move out. Although I was bouncing around from place to place, I was happy. I had my freedom, my work, and I felt like I was unstoppable.

As soon as I was released from my FTO and the sector I was working, my career took off. I got transferred to the sector that worked the Ocean View area. It was great. Most every sergeant I worked for just turned me loose.

I started making a name for myself. If an unpopular job came up, I somehow always got it. I'd moan and groan a bit, but eventually someone would pull me aside and tell me that they chose me because I was the only one they trusted to do the job. That was all I needed to hear.

I realized that none of these jobs were punishment; they were just jobs that needed to be done right. I was the guy that they would turn to for that. Walking details, stakeouts, selective patrol, I was into it.

I would get into friendly competitions with guys in the platoon on who could make the most arrests or write the most traffic tickets. I always won.

Before long, sergeants would come up to me and talk to me about joining their units. I ended up joining the Fifth Platoon which was at the beck and call of the captain of the precinct. We got to wear plainclothes, drive unmarked cars, and cruise the streets looking for things to get into. I got detailed twice to Vice and Narcotics. I decided that was where I wanted to go.

Fifth Platoon also thrived on its internal politics. In time, I got tired of that and went back to my uniform. Now I was one of the senior officers on the platoon and had more responsibilities.

While in patrol, I was nominated for Exemplary Police Office of the Year. It was a great honor and I knew I was in the right place as far as my job went. Relationships? Well, that was another story.

It took about two years after I moved out for my mom to start talking to me again. We had short phone conversations every once in a while. It was all cordial until we got into an argument or said something we regretted. Then we quickly said our goodbyes and hung up.

She would invite me to family functions, dinners or birthday parties and I would show up. Whenever I attended, even at Thanksgiving and Christmas, it was tense.

My younger brother, Jeff, was following in my footsteps as far as music went, and it looked like Mom was going to get her music minister after all. He was playing French horn and learning the piano. Mom was right by his side helping him achieve all his goals.

My brothers John and Joel were moving on in their lives, but none of us were really close. At one of our get-togethers, John and Joel announced they were both joining the Norfolk Police Department and preparing to attend the academy.

Mom was mad. She blamed me. In reality, I had nothing to do with it. I guess they saw how happy I was and wanted to do something that made them happy too. That was great for them, but thanks to them, I was back in the doghouse again after finally making amends.

I was getting tired of the dating scene too. I could be with anyone I wanted, but most of the time, I would find a flaw in the girl I was dating or act like a jerk and we would break up. I went from relationship to relationship, almost always being the one that broke it off.

Every once in a while, I would meet someone that I thought was going to be "the one" only to have my heart broken all over again. I was caught in a cycle, and I got the reputation of being both a loner and a womanizer. How ironic. The two were complete opposites.

Once I found that women liked the uniform, I started moving more and more away from Christianity. I no longer needed to impress women with my knowledge of the Word, and being a good

Christian constantly got in the way of my new lifestyle. I was still mad at God, and just started dating a large variety of girls. It was almost too easy.

I could be driving in my patrol car, minding my own business, and a girl would flag me down at a light and invite me over to her place after work. When I did go to church and talk about my job, the Christians looked at me as though I were a monster.

I got in a bar fight one Saturday that didn't end well. When I tried to talk to a church group about it, I could feel them begin to move away from me. It got to the point that I felt they were pointing and whispering about me. They gave me fake smiles, and I began to understand that there were two worlds out there.

There was the normal one in which people went to work, came home, cooked dinner, watched television, and went to bed. They locked their doors at night and rested, reassured that God was going to protect them. I lived and dealt with the other world—the subculture that we talked about at work and only whispered about in public groups. I felt like I couldn't live in both, so I decided to walk away from the church and God entirely.

I met my first wife, Donna, while I was still working at the department store. She did modeling for the store's catalog. She was very attractive and always an item at a party. She ran with management and we talked briefly. After I left the store, I didn't think much about her.

After I joined the police department, I ran into her at a 7-Eleven. She was going in and I was leaving. She smiled and said hello. I called out her name and told her that I had met her before, but she didn't recognize me.

Being polite, she asked me about the job, and I watched her whole attitude change. Later on, I realized she was a closet police groupie, so we started hanging out. She was into the police stories, but not the police officers themselves.

We started dating, and in my mind, I felt that she was the one. There was just something different about her. She had a good job and a great family. I quickly became friends with her brother, sister-in-law, and mother. I felt like this was the natural progression of life: grow up, get a job, meet a girl, get married. We dated for about six months and then we decided to get married. But something about her changed as soon as she said "I do," and six weeks into the marriage, I started looking for an exit strategy.

Life was not all bad with Donna. When we went on vacation together, we discussed the issues I was having. We talked about the jealousy she showed about almost everything I did. At one time she had loved police stories, but now she hated the department. To her, all police officers were now jerks because they were all like me—uncaring and on my side.

She started hating the relationship I had with her brother. She complained that I liked him more than her. I talked to her about it and she listened. She told me she was so jealous because she had lost her father at eighteen and was worried that she was going to lose me too.

I told her she wasn't going to lose me, and that I would work with her on her fears. For a while, it looked like things might work out. I didn't realize that everything was just going to get stranger instead.

We didn't even have time to unpack our bags from our honeymoon when I got a call from Joy in Fort Worth, telling me that my dad and his new wife, Winnie, were on their way to Virginia and possibly already there. We hadn't seen him or heard from him since the trial, so it was somewhat of a shock to have him just appear out of the blue. Joy told me that he was going to call me as soon as he got into town, only it didn't happen that way.

The relationship between my mom and me was tense, but it was about to get worse. Instead of my dad calling me when he got to Norfolk, he found a Norfolk police officer and asked him if he knew any of the Howard Boys. At this time, we were known all over the police department and this specific officer was a good friend of John's. He knew that we had a father and that he was from Texas but that was about it. The officer asked for ID and when my father verified who he was, the officer gave him John's home number without a second thought. The problem was John and Joel were still living with my mom.

When Dad called John at my mom's number, all hell broke loose. John asked Dad where he was, and Dad gave him the address of his hotel. John told him to stay there and that he would come to him.

Both John and Joel went to the hotel and told Dad that if he attempted to contact Mom in any way—either by showing up on her property or calling the house again—they would put him in jail. They advised him to pack up his bags and go back to Texas.

While John and Joel were threatening Dad, Mom was able to get in touch with me. She asked if I knew that Dad was in town and I told her that Joy had called me. Before I could say anything else, she started screaming at me, telling me that I should have told her. I could see that nothing was going to calm her down. Even when I did have a chance to defend myself, she just started scream-ing again.

She was sure that I was going to be happy when Dad showed up at the house and someone got killed. The call wasn't going well. On top of that, I still didn't know where Dad was. I had not heard from him yet.

Shortly after my mom finished raking me over the coals, my dad called. I, like John, asked him where he was, and I told him I would be there soon. He asked me if I was planning to threaten him too. I just asked him to stay where he was.

I took Donna with me and we went to the hotel room where Dad and Winnie were staying. When we got there, I was unpre-pared. Standing in front of me for the first time since 1970 was the man I had hated for years. I hated him for what he had done to our family, and how he had ruined our lives.

He looked old, and although I was still mad at him, something told me to listen. I felt sorry for him.

Before I had the chance to say anything, Donna stepped in. She told my dad that it was great to meet him. She walked right over to Winnie and next thing I knew, my dad and I were having a beer to-gether. I didn't even know my dad drank beer! Donna took charge and before it was all over, we were planning a trip to Fort Worth to visit my dad, Winnie, and Joy.

On my way home, I was trying to figure out what had just hap-pened. Donna's response was that he was my father and I should have some sort of relationship with him. Then it hit me. This was her way of getting back at my mom. Donna couldn't stand my mom. I didn't argue with her though. If this type of thing helped our relationship, then I would go along with it. One thing I did know was that there was going to be a lot of soul searching in the next couple of days. I needed to decide whether I was going to let my dad back into my life or not.

Several months after my dad made his surprise visit, my mom calmed down enough to call me. I tried to explain to her what happened: that Joy had called and told me Dad would call me first. I had planned to call John and Joel and tell them what was going on after that and handle all the communications between them.

If nobody wanted to see him then I would have told him that. I had no idea someone would give Dad John's number. I told her I was sorry. She cut me off halfway through my apology and told me to never let it happen again. If Dad ever decided to come back to Virginia, she wanted to be the first to know.

I didn't think it would happen again, but I told her that I would reach out to her first if it did. Even so, it would indeed happen again.

My stepfather, Bob, and I bowled in a league together for years. Bob had always been the rational side of Mom. I could talk to him, and he always tried to listen to my side of the story, even though he took mom's side in the end. I understood why, and I respected him for all he had done for my mom. I genuinely enjoyed our time together.

The first night we bowled after the incident with my dad, I expected Bob would be mad at me. Instead, he just looked at me and said, "Jimmy, I understand why your dad came to Virginia. I have a daughter and I would do anything to see her." Bob helped me understand what I was feeling. I wanted to see my dad again.

In 1979, the Houston Police Department began recruiting experienced officers. My brothers and I had always talked about going back to Texas. Joining the Houston P.D. seemed like a real possibility. I had just had my fifth anniversary with Norfolk and thought this would be the perfect time for a change.

Even though I loved working in Norfolk, Donna was pushing for the move. I figured if it helped our relationship, it would be worth it. I called Dad, told him our plans, and Donna and I flew into Dallas. It was like the "Glen Rose Incident" had never happened. Donna and Winnie got along great. I also got the chance to see Joy. We even took a trip down to Glen Rose.

We drove out to where the farm had been. The house was gone. Despite that, there were several trees there, and one still had our swing on it. We walked around downtown. I hoped I would see someone I knew, but I never did. I felt as though Glen Rose had forgotten about me, and I could finally move on.

The four of us drove to the Houston Police Department and I talked to one of their recruiters. He was excited that I came down and gave me a handful of applications. He told me to take them back to Norfolk and see if I could recruit other officers too.

The whole idea of moving back to Texas kept sounding better and better. Donna and I would move down and get a fresh start. Maybe this would help us work out our issues. We made our way back to Dad's, visited a few more days, and got ready to head out.

Right before he took us to the airport, he pulled me aside. He told me that if he had his way, he would not have allowed any of us to join the police department. I didn't know what to say, but suddenly, he was that guy again. The guy that ruined my life.

Instead of being mad though, I just felt bad for him. I couldn't wait to get away from him and back to Virginia.

Dad's remark made me hesitant to leave Norfolk. I had recently put in a transfer request for Vice and Narcotics and my chances were looking good. I changed my mind and decided that if I got in, I would stay in Norfolk. A lot of the guys I knew from my early days on the force had been transferred there, and the stories they shared sounded exactly like what I wanted to do. I had read an article about how the Houston Police Department was going through a tough time, so I felt like staying put.

Donna and I went back and forth trying to work on our marriage for over two years. No matter what we did, things just got worse. On multiple occasions, she baited me to hit her by screaming and pushing me. She would threaten to call the police and tell them I hit her. She lost her job and told me she got sick every time she thought of work. We were down to one salary and it took a toll on our relationship.

I went to her brother and asked him if he knew what was going on, and his response shocked me. Apparently, the whole family knew about her fits, but they had all thought I could help her. Instead, the relationship continued to deteriorate. The more problems we had, the more time I spent away from home. Some of that was because of my job, but I also started seeing other women. I had given up and was looking for somebody new. Then I wouldn't be so hurt when she left me.

After one particularly bad episode, I decided we needed professional help if we were going to stay together. I didn't like to fail at anything, and I felt like I was failing at marriage. I wasn't proud of my choices, but I justified them anyway. I didn't want to be alone. I got Donna to go with me to counseling. However, after several weeks getting nowhere, Donna told me she was who she was and she was not going to change. If I didn't like it, I could leave.

I moved out the next week. I got my transfer to Vice and Narcotics and threw myself into my work. I told myself I didn't need anyone. I had my brothers- and sisters- in-arms watching out for me. Donna's actions had really frightened me. I always did better on my own, so I eventually reverted to my old ways: juggling relationships but fully dedicated only to the job.

Right before Donna and I broke up, I started having health issues. I got an ulcer from all the stress. My doctor chastised me about my high blood pressure and my weight. I had gone from one hundred and fifty-five pounds to two hundred. He told me I needed to make some lifestyle changes.

I needed to get in shape and lose weight or I would have worse health issues later. His words reminded me of a friend of mine who ran, and often invited me to join him. Before this, I had never considered it. I used to tell him that the only time I ran was during television commercials to go to the bathroom or get a drink before the show came back on.

I didn't think I would ever enjoy running, but because of the doctor's warning, I decided to give it a shot. How hard could it be? I didn't expect it to be a life changer. But for right now, once I got transferred to Vice and Narcotics, everything else in my life (including my health and running) went on the back burner.

was soon transferred to the narcotics side of Vice and Narcotics. Now that I was away from Donna, I was able to give everything to my job. In a downward spiral due to the breakup, I started hanging out with the partying crowd.

I drank almost every night. I didn't drink on duty, just afterward. Originally, I had thought that the groupies were only into the regular uniformed police, but pretty soon I found out that there were just as many into the plainclothes Vice and Narcotics crew as well.

We were called investigators instead of detectives. We started our own investigations, whereas detectives investigated a crime after it happened. As Investigator Howard, I easily shifted into my new role.

My first night on the job, we had gotten word that there was a guy selling marijuana outside a bar in West Ocean View. Because I was the new guy, they wanted to see if I could score on my first night. I was ready for the challenge.

I was certainly dressed for the part. With my short hair and leather flight jacket, I looked just like a sailor, and sailors were the lion's share of the bar clientele in the West Ocean View area. The informant gave us the name and physical description of the dealer. He had been standing outside Greenies and selling out of his car. We decided that the best way to get him was a buy/bust operation, meaning that as soon as I got him to sell me the marijuana, the other officers would arrest him.

We set up in the parking lot and I walked in, only for the suspect to walk out with another client. Then I saw a girl I knew from my patrol days, and was scared that she might recognize me, but I soon learned that as soon as you're out of uniform, most of the girls didn't recognize you anymore.

I noticed her smiling at me, so I took a chance and asked her if she knew the dealer. She did. I sparked conversation with her, telling her I heard he had really good stuff. She told me he had just left, but he would be right back.

I stood outside making small talk with her, and I kept expecting her to suddenly realize I was the cop she used to know, but she never recognized me. Pretty soon, the suspect came back. At first, he gave me a hard look and I thought he was going to tell me to leave, so I just told him I was interested in buying pot. The girl vouched for me, and the suspect smiled and led me to the parking lot.

It was dark as we walked to his car. I knew my backup was nearby, but I was still a little hesitant. Many sailors had been robbed in this area. I reached up and felt for the two-and-a-half inch .357 I had in my coat pocket.

He told me to get in his car, and when I did, he threw it in reverse and out of the parking lot before I could say anything. I knew the guys watching me were wondering just what the heck I thought I was doing.

I looked at the suspect, and he said he didn't like the parking lot. Too many eyes. He told me to reach under the seat and pick out how much marijuana I wanted. When I got the bag, I saw that it was a gallon Ziplock filled with a half-pound of marijuana separated in ounce bags. He told me he liked to drive around while his clients looked at his supply, so he waited for me to make my choice.

I picked out an ounce, gave him my money, and we drove back to the parking lot. As soon as he parked, he looked at me and asked me if I was a cop. I informed him that asking me that *after* he sold me the dope was the absolute worst thing he could do.

As I got out of the car, the troops showed up and arrested him. While being handcuffed, he told me he knew I was a cop. Apparently, I had written him a misdemeanor summons for having beer on the beach.

Later, I went to my desk, pulled out my latest summons, and there he was. Less than three weeks before I had written him and the girl a summons for having alcohol on the beach. He didn't recognize me until after he had sold me the dope, but even then, he thought that I was cool and smoked. That would not be the last time I bought drugs from people I knew. Dope and money made you do stupid things.

If this was all narcotics was, I was in a pretty good place, but instead of staying in that unit, I was sent downtown to deal with the heroin dealers. I didn't even know my way around.

I didn't know the area and I didn't know the players, so my first month there was frustrating. Their idea of an investigation was to do surveillance until they found the big dealers. They sat around waiting and not making arrests. After six months, I was ready to move back to the street where I could do *real* police work.

My supervisor noticed my frustration and moved me to a different side. My new partner, Lou, was more my style of investigator.

We hit it off quickly. We started doing some small time buy/bust and were working our way up the chain in the Ocean View Area.

Lou was also single, so we often found ourselves chasing bad guys and women. Fridays on day shift were called Therapy Day. We would get off work at four. Most of the guys told their wives or girlfriends they were working, but we really went out and hit the bars for happy hour. We spent the rest of the night trying to hook up with someone.

A major problem with Lou was that as soon as he had alcohol in his system, he couldn't keep his mouth shut. Alcohol in him was like a truth serum. He always told people *exactly* how he was feeling. His friends knew how to handle him, but it was still dangerous. He often got into fights because of his mouth. Sometimes it got so bad that he would take out his gun and just start shooting things. One time, he shot one of the other investigator's paychecks. He just put his .45 to the check and pulled the trigger. I loved Lou to death, but I knew that eventually he could be the cause of the demise of my career in the narcotics division.

Our partying days came to a screeching halt after Lou ended up at a party with some of our supervisors. He got drunk, couldn't contain himself, and began to squeal on everyone about things going on within the group. I got an apology call from him the day after the party. He put in for a transfer to traffic. He said he covered for me when he realized his mistake and went back and told everyone that I was a great investigator. He said that since I was the new guy, I was just following the old guys around in their ways.

I think Lou saved me because that following Monday, there was an all-hands meeting and the hammer came down on everyone that Lou had ratted out. The wrath of the sergeant came down hard, and he threatened that there would be major changes if any-one was caught doing what they had done in the past.

We had been warned. If we got caught screwing up again, we would be transferred. Some listened, but others did not: it went in one ear and out the other. I was one of those that listened. I had been given a second chance. My new partner, on the other hand, wasn't afraid of the brass and thought he could do whatever he wanted.

Because of him, my next three months nearly blew my career in narcotics. One of the things the sergeant warned us about was going to a specific bar. It was known for its drug deals, and yet our guys were in there drinking and partying. I had never been to the bar before, but my new partner was a frequent visitor.

On one of our first nights together, he said he was meeting some new friends there and invited me to come along. I reminded him that our supervisor said he didn't want us going there. He shared a few choice words about our supervisors and told me I could either stay at work or come with him. I had him drop me off at my girlfriend's house. He informed me he would be back later to pick me up.

He never came back. Instead I had to have my girlfriend take me to the station. Minutes after I got there, he came in drunk. I exploded and we got into a big fight right in the middle of the squad room. After he passed out at his desk, I decided it was time for a move.

I went to my supervisor and told him that I was worried about my partner's activities. Even though I had been in the squad for a year, I was still considered a new guy. Because of this, they gave me a new partner but told me that this was my last chance. I asked them what they were going to do with my current partner, and they said they would talk to him. They never did. At the time, he was more valuable than I was. This was not what I thought narcotics was going to be like. Once again, I decided to do things my own way. I would show them.

The new partner they gave me was another do-nothing kind of guy. He would drive around downtown and sit down in the street of known heroin dealers. He would point them out to me and tell me about their past.

I would ask him if we could go down to Ocean View and work on some leads I had been building with Lou, but he just told me not to get into "trouble" because this was my last chance.

I knew that if I wanted to last in narcotics, I needed to take matters into my own hands, so I started building leads behind his back. Even though I knew it was a huge risk, I felt like I needed to do it anyway. I had no way of knowing that the case I was working on would change my entire career path.

Before I continue, you need to understand how the Norfolk Police Department worked. All commands were run by a captain. There was a captain over the First Precinct, the Second Precinct, the Traffic Division, Central Records, the Detective Division, Internal Affairs, and of course, over Vice and Narcotics. The captains were moved around every two years because in the old days, supervisors felt that if captains were in charge for too long in the same area, they would be susceptible to graft.

It was an outdated policy. All the captains knew that they would only be in the position they were in for two years. Instead of trying to change it for the better, they focused on getting a better position next.

I had been in Vice and Narcotics for a little over a year when a new captain came in. When captains went to their next command, troops they liked and trusted were usually right behind them. Because of this, transfers normally followed every command shift.

We had an all-hands meeting with the new captain, and he told us that as of right now, we were all starting off fresh. We didn't know him, and he didn't know us, but as we got more familiar with each other, he warned us there would be changes.

I knew this was my chance. Either I was going to prove myself to the new captain, or I was going to be looking for a new precinct.

While working with Lou, I had obtained an informant. One day this informant contacted me, saying that a woman was about to move a lot of weight in marijuana. I asked exactly how much weight was "a lot" and he responded with as much as sixty pounds.

He had my attention. He gave me a name: Cathy. He told me she was leaving in the morning, traveling all day, and would be returning with the drugs. He said that she ran a top-notch operation. He explained that she had the drugs packed in cardboard boxes designed to look like deliveries from UPS. She only sold in pounds and the pounds were bundled in shrink-wrap and looked like logs. They would be in one-to-two-pound deliveries and shipped out to the buyers. All of this would happen in the course of a day; by the next day, she began taking orders for the next batch. She normally left on a Tuesday morning.

I was able to find where Cathy lived through our computer system. She lived in a modest home back in my old stomping grounds in Ocean View. She had no real criminal history: just a traffic ticket or two.

I worked to find her public records and other information. She was a grandmother and her granddaughter lived with her. I really didn't want my current partner to know about this. He didn't know my informant, and my evidence on Cathy was weak. I was afraid he would lecture me about losing my narcotics career if I tried to convince him that this little old granny was moving over fifty pounds of weed with her granddaughter at home. I was already concerned about my career if the information was wrong. I knew I needed help, but I didn't know how to get it. I ended up getting it, but in a very surprising way.

When I first transferred to narcotics, another guy transferred the same day. His name was Larry Hill. Larry was a unique character. He was born and raised in Norfolk and grew up in Ocean View on the Chesapeake Bay. He was an avid fisherman, hunter, trapper, and your average "good old boy." Larry and his partner had been on the same squad as Lou and I, so we had experienced a lot of "therapy nights" together.

I got to know Larry, and really liked his preferred method of getting drugs off the street. He hated long term investigations, especially when you knew the drugs were being delivered. He didn't like letting guys go just to get the "bigger fish." Letting drugs get onto the street was Larry's biggest pet peeve, and it was mine too. We had an opportunity to run around together for a while, but after the Lou incident, I was moved to the other squad and didn't see Larry as much.

Larry knew most of the big players in Ocean View, so I decided to call him one day while he was working. I asked him if he knew about Cathy and told him I was working a case on her. There was a long silence on his end of the phone and then he told me he knew her.

He said that he had been out watching her house because he heard a tip that she was moving pounds of marijuana. With Larry's information and mine, I felt like we had a good case. I finally felt confident enough to work it. I thought that since Larry and I were on opposite shifts, we might get approval to run a twenty-four-hour surveillance on her.

I told Larry about my plan and could hear the excitement in his voice. He thought it was a great idea; all we needed was permission. I met him at his office within an hour to pitch our proposal to the captain.

Larry and I went to the captain without our partners. Larry's partner was on his way out of narcotics. He was one of the oldest members on the squad and thought it was his time to get out. He told Larry it was okay to meet with me.

I, on the other hand, never told my partner. I was tired of letting drugs stay on the street and I knew that if my partner heard about what we were trying to do, he would want to start a long investigation on Cathy and find her source first. This would let all of her drugs continue to flow for as long as the investigation went on. Larry and I both agreed on a tactic: Get the drugs off the street, pull in the little fish and use them as informants, then get the bigger fish.

The captain agreed with our plan and Larry took the first shift. I had court in the morning but after that, I would join him on the stakeout. My partner and I both had the day off that day. I spent it working the case with Larry. The captain called my partner, saying that until further notice, I was on a special detail. He reassured him that as soon as I was done, I'd be back with him doing surveillance.

While I was coming out of court that morning, one of the investigators pulled me aside and told me that Larry and Cathy were on the move. This was way before cell phones, and our walkie-talkies were short distance at best. Repeaters stationed around the city tried to help with the signal, but sometimes car-to-car transmissions were spotty.

I ran to the squad room and grabbed the keys to a 1975 Camaro we had just recently confiscated. It was the fastest car we had, so if Larry was far ahead of me, it gave me a chance to catch up. I also grabbed another investigator. At first, he didn't want to because he was hung over, but he agreed once I told him I would let him sleep in the car.

We sped out of the station toward Ocean View. Dispatch was relaying transmissions between Larry and me. I told him I was on my way. Larry said something, but I only heard something about the Portsmouth Tunnel. Ocean View and the Portsmouth Tunnel were in two different directions, so I turned the car around and drove toward the tunnel. When I got close, I told dispatch I was entering and after that, it was like being on the dark side of the moon. Suddenly, it was dark and silent because all transmissions had to be put on hold until we got out of the tunnel.

We were going so fast that we were shot out of the tunnel. Once we got through, I knew that radio transmissions would begin to fade between walkie-talkies and dispatch. Before that happened, I needed to get my bearing on the locations of both Larry and Cathy. Dispatch called me and told me that Larry's vehicle ran out of gas, and I needed to come pick him up.

I called back to dispatch and asked about Larry's location. We were going about ninety miles per hour when dispatch finally answered, saying that Larry was on the side of the road waiting for me. At that moment, we flew right past him.

We were on Interstate 264 so I knew that I would have to go down a way to turn around. On my way to turn around, I spotted Cathy pulled over with a flat tire. We whipped in right behind her, and I woke up the hungover investigator and told him to go help this lady change her tire. He complained and asked why I was making him do it. I told him that there was a chance she might know me. After cussing me out, he got out of the car and went to help Cathy. I told dispatch to tell Larry to wait.

After they changed the tire, Cathy thanked the other investigator and offered him money. He declined and she got in her car and started down the road again. I backed up and got Larry while the other investigator immediately went back to sleep.

The chase was back on. It was only a few more miles up the road before all communications with Norfolk would be cut off. We would be officially on our own. I was hoping that all the things that could go wrong had already happened.

Cathy was going west on US 58 at about seventy miles per hour in a fifty-five mile per hour zone. I was pushing the 350 engine in the Camaro as hard as I could to catch up to her. I didn't want to look down at the speedometer; I was scared that if I did, I would slow down. We needed to catch up with her.

The Camaro was handling well with no vibrations, so I just kept the pedal down. It felt like the car might have had more to give, but I didn't want to push it. After a few minutes, we finally had her in our sights again. She took us all the way to Emporia, about ninety minutes from Norfolk.

Once in Emporia, we saw her pull into a shopping plaza. We did the same, but once we got there, we realized we had lost her. The parking lot was full. We had a moment of panic because we needed to physically see her pick up the drugs in order to make our case. I was yelling at Larry asking if he saw her, and Larry was yelling the same to me. At that moment, the hungover investigator sleeping in the back lifted his head, looked around, pointed and said, "There she is" and went back to sleep. And sure enough, there she was.

We watched her park, get out of her car, and open her hatchback. The car parked next to her opened its trunk and took out cardboard boxes, placing them in Cathy's car. There were four or five large boxes that looked like they belonged to UPS, just as my informant had said. We watched the people from the other car load up her trunk, give Cathy a hug, and drive away. We were able to get the license of the other car, a North Carolina tag. North Carolina is only about ten minutes away from Emporia.

The big engine of the Camaro was doing well, but it was not going to let us get back to Norfolk without stopping.

As we were driving through downtown Franklin, we decided to get gas because we knew that our suspect had to drive slower through town. We also knew that if she was heading back up US 58, we would catch her on her way back to Norfolk. Neither Larry nor I were NASCAR pit crew drivers which makes what happened next even funnier.

We got into the gas station and all we had on us was a twenty-dollar bill and a ten-dollar bill. Ten dollars of gas money wouldn't get us back to Norfolk, but twenty dollars of gas would take too long to fill. We began a debate over which one to do. I was pumping gas and Larry was paying the clerk that had come out to help us.

Larry went to the clerk and yelled "Ten!" and began to hand the ten to the clerk. I yelled back, "Not enough!" and continued to pump gas. Larry then yelled at me that we didn't have enough time. As soon as Larry tried to hand the clerk the ten, I told him that we now were at fifteen, so he would need to give the clerk the twenty. Larry pulled back the ten and gave him the twenty.

By this time, the clerk thought that we were trying to rip him off by confusing him. The clerk made some kind of comment like "You guys sure are in a hurry," and Larry yelled back what I had wanted to say since the beginning: "We are in hot pursuit of a wanted criminal!"

The clerk's face was priceless. I started laughing which caused me to go over twenty dollars on the pump. I stopped and looked at the clerk. He told me not to worry about it. He said something to the effect of "go, get your man" so Larry and I jumped back into the 1975 Camaro in pursuit of our weed-dealing grandmother.

As soon as Cathy was back on US 58, she cranked it back up to seventy miles per hour. Here was a woman carrying boxes full of marijuana who wasn't afraid of speeding down the highway. I was liking her more and more.

I had to push the Camaro to keep up with her. We knew we couldn't get too close for fear she would spot us, but every time she passed a vehicle that was doing the speed limit, it would take us several minutes to catch up to her. Ten minutes after the gas station, the "check engine" light came on the Camaro. I showed it to Larry while I pushed the accelerator to pass another vehicle. This lady had no regard for the speed limit. At times I was pushing ninety just to keep up with her.

Larry and I began planning how we would stop her once she got back to Norfolk. From where we were, there were only two ways she could take to get back into the city. We wanted to have units waiting at both entrances when we got back. About twenty minutes from the Portsmouth Downtown Tunnel, Cathy stopped at a 7-Eleven. Virginia State Troopers were parked across the street at a local diner. We pulled into the parking lot, and I watched Cathy while Larry hopped out to talk to the troopers.

Several minutes later, Larry jumped in, and told me that the troopers were going to tell Norfolk we were on our way back. He had asked them to have units on both the Portsmouth Tunnels so we could stop her as soon as she hit the city limits.

Cathy got back in her car and drove towards US 58 like she didn't have a care in the world. She was soon doing seventy. It seemed like she hit cruise control on her way to the police waiting for her at the Norfolk/Portsmouth line. Right before the Downtown Portsmouth Tunnel, Larry was able to reach dispatch who told us that they had units waiting. We gave them a description of her car and our current location. As soon as we pulled out of the tunnel in Norfolk, we pulled Cathy over.

I walked up and looked in the back of the hatchback. If I hadn't known better, I would have thought they were just packages that she was dropping off at UPS. I got to the driver's window and introduced myself. Before I could do that, she simply said, "Investigator Howard." I asked her what she had in the trunk. She replied that we both knew what it was, so let's not play games. She asked me how long we had been following her. When she looked back in her rearview mirror, the investigator that helped change her tire woke up and waved.

The look on her face, like the clerk's, was priceless. Now we had her attention. She was open with us and told me that this was a brand-new car and she wanted to test it out before she gave it to her granddaughter. I asked her if we could search the boxes and she agreed. She told us she was going to cooperate.

I was taken aback by her candor, but she was already three steps ahead of me. She looked at me and told me that I was a week late: Last week she had sixty-eight pounds, but today she only had twenty-eight.

Another investigator immediately took the Camaro to our garage, so we could get Cathy to the office and begin interviewing her. When I got my gear out of the Camaro, the engine smelled like it was melting.

Back at the office, we were able to run the North Carolina tag and found it belonged to another female in Apex, North Carolina. We didn't let Cathy know we had this information; we were hoping to save it for a later date. After advising Cathy of her rights, she told us that she had gone to Emporia to pick up marijuana.

At first, she told us that she didn't know the Emporia connection. She said that she bought it from someone local and that she would put in an order and go wherever they told her and pick up the merchandise later.

This was the game. We knew she knew the woman she met in Emporia. The hug she gave the woman before she left almost looked like the hug you gave a relative. Cathy continued to claim she didn't know her. If she wanted to play that game, so could we.

Right after we got finished booking Cathy, the captain called us back into his office. Larry's sergeant was sitting there, and he and the captain didn't look happy. They asked us to explain what we had been doing all day. We told them the full story: of the trip, the arrest, and what Cathy told us. We added the North Carolina plate too. We wanted permission to go down there and identify the connection.

They then asked us why I didn't tell my partner what I was doing. It appeared that my partner was upset that I didn't include him in the arrest. I explained to the captain and Larry's sergeant that, with all due respect, not only did the events happen too fast for me to properly explain everything to my partner, but that he had a history of wanting to do things the slow way and we wanted to move now. The captain asked if I had any issues working with Larry. I answered no quite honestly. And thus, the legendary duo of Howard and Hill began.

As we were leaving the captain's officer, I felt like I was once again back in the game. The case had taken my mind off my personal life. I forgot about my failed marriage and all my issues at home. Instead, I found something that I could bury myself in. With Larry's knowledge of Ocean View and my good informant, we were unstoppable.

We started planning our trip to North Carolina when the captain walked into our squad room. He asked us how we planned to get to North Carolina. We just looked at each other. The captain said he just got off the phone with the garage. They put oil in the Camaro but it leaked right back out. When they shut it down, the engine apparently sounded like someone had thrown a grenade in it.

He told us that unless we planned on walking, we had no way of getting to North Carolina. I thought for a second that our chance of even getting an "atta boy" for catching Cathy was gone because of the ruined car. Instead he smiled and said we could take his car, as long as we checked the oil and made sure he got it back with a full tank. This might seem like a small gesture, but to Larry and me, it meant our jobs were safe for at least another two years.

We went to North Carolina and identified Cathy's connection. It turned out to be Cathy's daughter. Once she found out that we were indicting her daughter as a coconspirator in the arrest, she came into the office and told us that she wanted to trade her information about the marijuana ring she was involved with for an easier sentence for her daughter. The names she gave were ones Larry and I had never heard before, so we called the Major Case Unit who normally worked cases like this and asked if they knew any of these people. We said that if they did, they'd be welcome to work the case with us. It was getting way too big for Larry and me to handle alone, and we had other things that we could be working on. As we continued to drop bigger and bigger names, they were only too happy to take the case off our hands.

During our second interview with Cathy, she began to complain that I was crazy. She said I was a loose cannon, "a .357 magnum just waiting to go off" were her very words. I didn't mind the reference, but I didn't know where it was coming from. She also accused me of dealing stolen property with other big criminals. She said that because of my relationship with them, they had given me the information about her. It took everyone else in the room by surprise, but I was glad. It meant that I was starting to develop a reputation among the dealers in Ocean View. Little did I know, this was the consensus of *all* the drug dealers in the Ocean View area. It wasn't until later that I found out where all the accusations began.

While working patrol, I had arrested one of the "baddest" guys in Ocean View. He had fought every police officer in the Second Precinct, and I guess it was my turn. Long story short, I won the battle, even though at times it didn't feel like it. There was a huge Internal Affairs investigation over it. After that, I was known as one of the only guys to have ever fought this guy and not been hospitalized. It was the incident that caused me to question whether or not I was really in the right profession.

But what I didn't know was that it also made me into a legend and gave me a reputation that I quickly learned to take advantage of. Larry was known as the cop who grew up in Ocean View and knew where all the bodies were buried, so we became an iconic duo. We were soon known as the "OV Cowboys." We thought this was cool, but what we didn't understand that even though our captain loved us, there were others in the precinct that hated us. Among those were supervisors that only put up with us because our captain liked us. They wished we would make a mistake so they could transfer us. Instead we were making arrests left and right, and other investigators started to look bad because of their slow pace.

We continued to do what we did best: pleasing the captain and making arrests. Not only were we making good arrests together, but Larry and I also had a good time after hours. We both liked to visit the bars. Not really to pick up women, but to watch all the "known outlaws" in their environment. We never bought drinks when we went into a bar; others always bought them for us. Even though we didn't go there with the intention to pick up women, sometimes it just happened.

It became easy to go home with a different woman every night. I formed a set of rules about the women I would or would not leave the bar with—either to my place or theirs. They had to have a full-time job. They had to have their own transportation and they had to be single. I had gotten involved with a couple married women and it never ended well.

We met a lot of investors that came to help clean up Ocean View. Many came with plans to put in resorts where military housing had been. They liked what we were doing and had us over for dinner or took us fishing on their yachts. They were especially interested in us because Larry had grown up in Ocean View. They invited me along because I was his bodyguard, a title I didn't mind at all. Larry knew everyone, and those he didn't know, I found easily in our computer system. I knew how to work all the databases. All I needed was a name.

During our time as the OV Cowboys, we had some noteworthy arrests that got the attention of the news as well as the other outlaws in the area. We took down a guy with five thousand hits of windowpane LSD with a street value of twenty thousand dollars. After the arrest, we were told that at the time, it was the most ever recorded in the state of Virginia.

We got information on a heroin dealer that nobody knew about too. Not one of the usual suspects. We were informed that he was into large quantities of the drug because of the severity of his habit. Once we arrested him, we turned him on several other guys that dealt with the downtown heroin dealers.

We became so popular that we could walk anywhere and every big bad dude who liked to go around assaulting police officers would give us a wide berth. It was always, "Yes sir, Detective Howard," or "Yes, sir, Detective Hill." We were riding a wave that I didn't ever want to end.

We continued to catch flak around the office for our unorthodox investigation methods. We were taking drugs off the street, and they would complain that was *all* we were doing. We never did any long scale investigations, instead Larry and I just kept doing what we were good at.

Eventually, we decided to tackle larger and more organized crime. It was time to show all our naysayers we could run a full-scale operation and still take drugs off the street. All we needed was a group to go after. It didn't take long before we found our dream organization.

Almost two years into our partnership, Larry walked into the office, pulled me aside, and asked me if I would like to investigate one of the local chapters of a nationally known motorcycle gang. This group had local chapters in both Norfolk and Virginia Beach. It was extremely difficult to investigate them because of how tight-lipped they were. But we always heard stories. We heard that they ran methamphetamine, guns, and stolen property through the state and all the way up to New Jersey. They used fear and intimidation to keep their people loyal.

To have an opportunity to take down the local chapter with the possibility of harming the national organization itself was a dream come true. At that point, I believed that nobody could touch our investigative skills. If Larry suggested this investigation, I knew he had something up his sleeve. And I knew it was going to be great.

The whole time I was in patrol at the Second Precinct, I had had dealings with this particular gang. I was always pulling them over for improper equipment violations. I had gone so far as to go to a Harley Davidson shop and ask what was standard factory equipment and what was not, so I could point out all the violations I saw on their bikes. Whether or not I actually wrote them up depended on their attitudes. Long before I entered narcotics, I got to know a few of them. Some of them liked me and thought I was cool, and some of them thought I was an asshole. Of course, since I was now working with Larry in narcotics, they stayed as far away from me as possible.

Before Larry and I began working together, Larry had arrested a brother of a gang member named Ben. He gave Larry some information on some small-time dealers and Larry helped him out during sentencing. Larry had grown up with Ben. Because of this, Ben told Larry that after he got out, if Larry was still in narcotics, he would help him take down the gang. Ben was out, and ready to talk.

We met up with Ben at a safe bar, and it was almost like a high school reunion. Alcohol started flowing and Ben started telling me stories about Larry. I was expecting Ben to go back on his promise but to my surprise, when things got serious, Ben looked Larry straight in the eye and told him that he had been invited back into the gang. That meant he would have access to the clubhouse and all of the meetings.

Ben mentioned his brother's name. That's when it hit me. Ben's brother was not just any gang member. He was their enforcer. If someone needed to be dealt with, his brother was the guy they sent.

I had recently had a run in with him. One night at a local bar, he caught me looking at his bike. It had what looked like an expired inspection sticker, which was one of the things that we liked to bother them about. When the enforcer first approached me, he didn't recognize me, and I thought that he was about to fight me. He was a big dude and I didn't pack a lunch, so I really didn't want to get into it with him. As soon as he realized who I was, he backed off, but for a second there I thought I might have to shoot him.

Suddenly, this situation with Ben was serious. If this gang found out that Ben was helping us, they would kill him without hesitation. They might even try to come after us—reputation or not.

Ben explained that he wasn't officially a member yet. He told us that in order to become one, he might have to help with the distribution of the methamphetamine (meth) they were selling. His job was to take it to known dealers and get the money. The gang would pay him for being a mule.

Because of his status, he would have information on delivery dates, users, sellers, and when they planned to go up north to pick up new shipments. He told us that he was helping because his brother was an asshole, and that the poison they were selling was killing people he knew and loved. Sometimes blood isn't as thick as you think it is.

We knew what we had to do, so we got started.

For several months, we sat on the gang members. We went to their clubhouses and gathered all the information we could. Ben told us they knew we were out there, but that they weren't worried about us because they knew that everyone was too afraid of them to double cross them. Ben was giving us the best information he could without wiretapping a phone. His information was spot-on.

It came time to do what we were now calling a "Cathy" run. This basically meant that we would put a tail on them when they went up north to get their drugs, but to do this we needed help.

During the investigation, my alcohol consumption increased. I wasn't doing much in the line of exercise either at the time. The running thing that had been suggested never happened and my physical condition began to be an issue. I knew I needed to do something about it, but I was so caught up in work that nothing else mattered to me. One morning after a night of drinking, I woke up at my house, with no memory of how I got there. I was still in my clothes and the night before was a blur.

Because of the intensity of the case we were working, I needed to get my life in order. I couldn't afford to go out drinking every night; it was too dangerous. I knew I needed to change, but change was hard. Our investigation took long hours into the night. Normally these nights were followed by drinking and making notes at an after-hours club.

We did two trial runs with Ben on dates, locations, and dealers. The night before the gang members traveled north to buy more drugs, Ben's brother, the enforcer, would go up and collect the cash needed for the deal. We would be watching. Ben wrote down all the routes, the times, and the locations of all the dealers. It was like clockwork as we watched the enforcer do everything Ben told us he would.

We laid out the whole six-month investigation on what we had. The only thing we didn't do was give up our informant's name. We felt that someone might talk in the office, so we made a promise to Ben to keep him out of all documentation and conversations until it became absolutely necessary.

We brought our sergeant with us on the third run as we followed the enforcer getting the money. The sergeant was amazed at how accurate our information was. He felt that on the next run, we needed to set it up to follow the gang north and find out where they picked up their drugs.

Right at this time, we hit the two-year mark with the captain that liked us. He was being transferred to the Second Precinct. He told us that if we ever needed a new home to let him know. He wished us well and told us not to listen to the crowd, but to keep doing our own thing.

We were going to miss him more than we realized. The new captain that came in didn't like Larry at all. I thought that would change when we finally took down this gang. I couldn't have known that all of our work was about to come to a screeching halt.

Our sergeant had given us the green light to follow the gang to northern Virginia so we could locate their source for the drug, follow them back to Norfolk, and then arrest them. It was the same routine we had used when we took down Cathy. This time, we planned on involving a lot more backup, surveillance, and vehicles. The sergeant told us that he would get as many investigators as he could to help.

We knew that the bikers would be leaving at around five in the morning, so Larry and I decided that we should meet up at four, set up our game plan with the other units, and start surveillance with backup. I went home at six the night before and packed a bag in case we were gone several days. This had been a wild ride and it was finally our chance to show everyone just how good we really were.

I was up at three, having gotten no sleep. I packed up the car and drove toward the rendezvous point. Larry was sitting there, his face full of disappointment. He couldn't even look at me.

With his head down, he told me that our new captain had pulled the plug on our entire investigation at the last minute. I wasn't sure I had heard correctly. I couldn't believe that after all the work we had put into this investigation, it was over. He repeated himself and told me that we were done. He said that the captain had heard about us from the other investigators. They told him that we were nothing but cowboys and that we would inevitably screw the whole thing up.

We were told to turn the case over to the state police and let them handle it from now on. The sergeant was in his office and we had to go speak with him. He had called Larry earlier and told Larry that he would have to tell me.

Back at the office, the sergeant told us that we had a good run, but that the new captain wanted us to put in our transfer papers and be out within the next few days. I was pissed, but more than that, I was hurt. We had given all we had to this job. Both of us spent the next two hours complaining to the sergeant, but there was nothing he could do. He had already told the captain we were great investigators and shared our arrest record. We had made powerful enemies in the squad, and they were friendly with the new captain.

This was the issue with not following the rest of the group and having a forced new captain every two years. Just like that, our run in narcotics was over. Even though our friendship continues to this day, I never got the chance to work with Larry again.

The following day, I put in transfer papers to go to the Traffic Division or the Second Precinct to work with the captain who had been good to Larry and me. Several of the guys I had worked with in narcotics had been in traffic, and talked about the fun they had riding motorcycles. Two of my favorite movies were *Electra Glide in Blue* and *Magnum Force*. Since traffic officers got to ride Harley Davidsons with cool boots and leather jackets, I thought it might be a great next step.

The captain and lieutenant with the Traffic Division didn't know who I was and getting kicked out of narcotics was a red flag, so I ended up in the Second Precinct. The move was a tough one with a lot of bitterness in it, but this transfer, and the events that followed, ended up putting me in the right place at the right time.

G etting transferred out of Vice and Narcotics and being sent back to patrol put me in a tailspin. I never thought that I would have to go back to patrol, let alone under these circumstances. Usually investigators only left narcotics if they did something stupid or got promoted.

Word on the street was that we were fired because the police department caught us doing something illegal. The whole situation was a joke. I couldn't understand why they would get rid of two of the best investigators. Others did not see that it wasn't what you knew, but who you knew.

Larry and I both transferred to the Second Precinct, but he was on a different shift. We didn't get to see much of each other.

The captain at the Second Precinct was happy to have me. He was so pleased that he promised to put me in the Fifth Platoon after I had done patrol for ninety days. The Fifth Platoon was an extra unit in which I could do what I did best: put people in jail. Fifth Platoon was the unit the captain hand-picked; they did all the special jobs in the precinct.

Basically, it was a plainclothes unit (except during the summer) at the beck and call of the captain. If we had a rash of burglaries in the Second Precinct, the captain would pull all of us into the area to find the bad guys. Whenever those in the Detective Division needed extra help, they would call us. I ended up working many burglary and robbery stakeouts for the Detective Division. Most of the stakeouts were low priority, but it looked good to the public.

Once, we had a serial rapist in the downtown area. I worked that case for a month, lurking in neighborhoods while looking for other people lurking in the area. Half of the calls the department received for lurking turned out to be either me or one of the others in the unit. If there was nothing going on, we were left to do our own investigations.

During this time, a few things happened that really changed my focus. One of them scared me so much that I almost considered checking into a rehab.

I was on the street for about two weeks when I got into a fight with a guy. He twisted my thumb on my right hand and strained the tendon. I heard it pop when it happened, but I didn't think anything of it. I got back in the fight and finally arrested the guy. There was a little twinge in my thumb, but I thought it had just been turned the wrong way.

When I got out of work, I was changing out of my uniform and as I took my gun out of its holster, my thumb gave way and I nearly dropped it. I realized that whatever happened to my thumb was more than just a twinge and I went to the hospital the next day. The X-ray said it was definitely sprained and the tendon was stretched. I was told that the only way to fix it was by squeezing a rubber ball.

The doctor told me that I couldn't go back to work because I could drop my weapon like I almost had previously, and that if I injured it more, it was likely I would need surgery.

He gave me a doctor's note and I was out for four weeks: injured in the line of duty. I asked him if I could do paperwork at the station. Did I have to carry a gun doing that? I told him that I did, and he repeated himself: Take four weeks off. I was to do therapy and return in a month.

I didn't think I needed the time off. I wanted to go back to work, so I drank instead. Through my bout of medicating my self-pity with alcohol, I had a couple of incidents when I couldn't remember how I got home, and even a few car accidents.

The moment that scared me most was when I woke up in bed with a woman and had no idea how I got there or where I was. I was startled by a big dog licking my feet. The dog belonged to the woman lying next to me.

I think that was the first time in a long time that I prayed. I asked God to just help me get back home and I promised I would change my life. I found my clothes, gun, and keys and went out to my car. I was relieved that it was still in one piece.

I found a street that I knew and eventually made it back home. Of course, as soon as I got back to the safety of my house, I forgot about my conversation with God. I didn't give my life back to Him like I had promised.

Because of that incident and the way alcohol made me feel afterwards, it wasn't hard to curb my appetite. I was out of shape at the time and I made the decision that exercise was going to be my new religion. I contacted my friend, Chuck, the runner, and he took me to a shoe store and picked out a pair of running shoes for me. I almost told him to forget it. They were eighty dollars marked down to forty-eight. I had never paid that much money for a pair of shoes in my entire life. He told me that my body would appreciate the expensive shoes over the box store brand I had already purchased for running.

I started slow. I did everything possible wrong, but eventually I found peace in the runs. Running gave me a chance to think about my day and what I was going to do next. I found out there was a whole group of guys in the department who were runners, so I started hanging out with them. I got as far away from the alcohol as I could. I still had a drink every once in a while, but nothing like I had before. The more that I got into running, the more my alcohol intake decreased.

Chuck had been with the police department, but now he was working for an airline company called Piedmont Airlines. Piedmont was based in Winston-Salem, North Carolina, but had a hub in Norfolk.

Chuck and I had been friends for a while. He was one of the first police officers I worked with after I got released from my FTO. He had this quick wit and could turn a bad situation to good. He had been my best man at my wedding, and I was the best man at his first wedding.

We hung around together for a long time until he started working full-time at Piedmont. After that, I would see him on occasion. He worked in the catering department of Piedmont and would call me if there were any leftover steak dinners from the flights. We would sit around and talk about 'the good old days' and some of the crazy stuff we had done. As soon as Chuck got his full-time position at Piedmont, he took it and never looked back.

Chuck told me that he really loved working for Piedmont. He said that not only did he not miss the police department, but that he could get me a part-time job if I wanted. On one of our runs, I started talking to him about maybe quitting the police department.

After the hurt of getting kicked out of narcotics, I was worried that my career in law enforcement had taken a turn for the worse. I was outspoken, loved to jump into things, and had been told I was too hard to control. I was afraid no one would hire me because of my reputation. If I was going to be forced to stay in patrol all my life, now was the time to make a change. If I liked working for Piedmont, I knew I could apply for full-time. I had nothing to lose. Next thing I knew, I was working as a ramp rat for Piedmont Airlines.

Piedmont had its perks. I met a group of great people there that really helped me out of the funk I was in. I only worked three hours in the early morning—from five in the morning to eight. My days were Tuesday through Saturday with Sunday and Monday off. The station manager took a liking to me because he was a closet police groupie. I think he had wanted to be a police officer but had begun working for Piedmont instead.

He liked to play practical jokes on people and then boast about them. He also liked to listen to all my police stories. He often transferred me to his office to help him track down people that had written bad checks. Even though he was a nice guy, my favorite position was on the ramp.

The five-to-eight shift loaded all the mail on the first five flights that left Norfolk. Most of the time it was an easy shift, but it was rough during the holidays. Not only did the mail increase, but so did the number of people traveling.

The job was mostly physical labor, so it also helped me get back in shape. It also took my mind off police work. Most of the part-time jobs for police officers were loss prevention at department stores, banks, or big events. We were still in uniform and ran the risk of getting into fights. On the ramp, my only fear was of getting run over by a truck or plane. The chances of that happening were slim to none. The other thing I really liked about Piedmont was that I got to fly for free. This gave me the chance to go see my dad.

Donna and I had visited maybe two more times after that initial contact. I can't explain why I went to see him. When I spoke with him on the phone, I felt sorry for him. He talked about how much he missed us boys and how he wanted to get to know us better. I fell for it, and the next thing I knew, I was on a plane.

After just a few hours though, I was ready to jump on the next flight home. I discovered he was a bitter old man who wanted everyone around him to be just as unhappy as he was. He picked on me constantly from the moment I got off the plane. I would tell myself that this would be the last time I would see him, and then he would start planning my next trip down.

Once again, I would feel bad for him and then go see him. The other reason I went to Texas was to see my half-sister Joy. I had forgotten how close we had been growing up. I was always happy to see Joy, so the trips weren't always a total loss.

My mother wasn't happy about my relationship with my father. One day she would question why I wanted to have a relationship with him in the first place and the next, she would tell me she understood that I wanted to talk with him because he was my father. I never knew what she was going to say.

I was with my brothers John and Joel one evening and they asked me about Dad. I told them that he was our father. He wasn't pleasant to be around, but he was still our dad. Soon, we were all planning a trip to go see him. Because I could fly for free, John and

I flew down together. Another time, I met Joel and his first wife and daughter down there after they drove to see him.

Every time I went, my dad did something that made me not want to return. He tried bribing us with Dallas Cowboys tickets. He would tell us stories of our youth when our family was together. The entire time we were together he was always very condescending, and always looking to cause trouble.

One time I went to visit Dad with John, and the first thing he asked when I got off the plane was whether I had gained weight. At the time, I had been working out a lot and had gained muscle, but not really any weight. Until I spoke to him, I had been feeling pretty good about my appearance.

He must not have seen it that way because on the way to his house, he called me "fat boy." I was taken aback, but just shrugged it off. Later at dinner, he said there would be no leftovers because "fat boy" would eat them all. As I got out of his van, he said, "Everyone move out of the way! Fat boy is coming through!" At that point, I told him that "if he called me fat boy one more time, this fat boy was going to kick his ass."

He looked at John and inquired what he had done that I should be angry. John explained that nobody liked being called fat. It was the same as if John had called Dad "stupid." John told me later that Dad just sat there pouting. Dad said he was only joking to which John responded that that wasn't how you were supposed to joke. For the rest of the trip, Dad stayed away from me. He told John I was sensitive, and he didn't want to say anything to upset me. No wonder our relationship was so strained.

After returning to work, the captain called me in and asked me if I was ready to be back. I asked him what he had in mind, and he told me that he wanted to transfer me to the Fifth Platoon. I was up for that. Going into the unit, I was the most senior officer except for the sergeant and corporal.

The corporal and I had worked together in Vice and Narcotics. He was more on the vice side, but we had always gotten along. The sergeant was an old K-9 guy and was also easy to work with. I tried to stay away from the narcotics side and just concentrated on precinct issues. They let me do practically anything I wanted. I made the arrests and that kept everybody happy. They sometimes gave us some bum details, but I completed them with a smile on my face.

I stayed focused on getting myself in shape. I still bounced from relationship to relationship. I had several dates with Donna during this time too. For the first half of the date she would be the person I loved, but by the end she always showed her true self, reminding me why we had broken up.

We had not officially divorced, but I knew we would never get back together. She wanted us to, but I never pushed the issue. I knew that the divorce was coming, and when it finally happened, it wasn't going to be pretty. Between running, the police department, Piedmont Airlines, and all the different relationships, the years slipped away.

The running group at the police department loved to compete in races. They encouraged me to participate to improve my runs. They wanted me to do a 5k and 10k, and then move on to marathons. I told them to slow down.

Running a marathon? Me? I thought they were crazy. I had just reached three miles and they were suggesting twenty-six. I told them to forget it.

My neighbor was a runner and talked me into signing up for the Elizabeth River Run (ERR). He told me ERR was Norfolk's biggest race. It was a 10k (6.2-mile run) that started near the Joint Forces Staff College on Hampton Boulevard and made its way into downtown Norfolk. It seemed like a scenic route through Norfolk, so I thought I might as well try it.

On May 7, 1983, I ran my first race. I decided to wear my cheap K-mart running shoes because they were lighter than the trainers were. In those with red-striped tube socks, K-mart cotton gym shorts, and a ribbed T-shirt, I was a sight to see. My neighbor ran with me the whole way and we finished in one hour and one minute. It was the first time I ever felt the "runner's high" others had told me about.

They were right. I was hooked. I was hugging other runners and talking a mile a minute. At work the next day, people got tired of hearing me talk about the run. I didn't care; I just couldn't wait for the next one.

I was generally able to find a race every weekend, so almost every week, I was out there doing 5ks and 10ks. I did as many of them as I could. After the Elizabeth River Run, I realized I had to change my wardrobe. As I ran that day and saw all the different outfits, I realized that I looked like a hick. I was too cool for that, so my next stop was a running store to buy matching outfits.

I found they were ridiculously expensive. Good running shoes alone were expensive, let alone matching running shorts and shirts, but I had to look cool for my next run. I sucked it up and paid the big bucks for the clothes. I even threw in a couple of headbands so I could really look great.

In my usual way, I completely immersed myself in running. I bought books on running, talked to runners, and tried to run a race every weekend. During this time, I met Jerry Edwards. At first glance, Jerry didn't look like he had the body for running. He talked me into running with him at Seashore State Park, now known as First Landing State Park. Seashore State Park has over nineteen miles of hiking trails perfect for running.

Jerry took me down Cape Henry Trail, which is the main trail from the training center. It's a hard dirt trail that is just wide enough for three people to run side-by-side. It was the most serene place for running I had ever seen. There was no traffic, just beautiful wooded scenery. The only thing you had to worry about was

Maring Corp Marathon 1988

the occasional bicycle, warning you with a friendly "on your left" or "good day" as they passed. Seashore Park quickly became my new sanctuary.

When I went running alone, I did some thinking about my future. I was still in the Fifth Platoon, working part-time at Piedmont and seeing multiple women. My drinking had decreased considerably, but I still felt as though something was missing. I was rarely alone, spending most of my time with my running friends, work friends, or girlfriends. The only time I ever felt really complete, however, was when I was running.

My brothers also started running. This not only gave us some friendly competition, but also gave us something in common. We were still huge Dallas Cowboys fans and occasionally got together with our mom and watched games. We also sometimes did part-time work together for the department after our eight hours was in.

Other than that, it seemed like we didn't have anything in common until we got together. We were like any other dysfunctional family. We all had certain issues, but we always had each other's backs. Sometimes it didn't seem that way on the surface, but deep down we were still "the Howard Boys."

Life was quickly passing me by. Between the two jobs and all the different women, another six years went by. Sometimes I dated women that worked at Piedmont, and we would just jump on a jet and go somewhere for the weekend. I had a different set of women that I met in the department that came over for visits too, no matter what time of day it was. Then there were those I met at bars and spent the night with—only to see them one or two more times tops. As soon as they started talking about wanting a commitment, the relationship was over.

Most of the women I saw were, as a friend of mine once said, "comfortable." They never turned me down and I never made any promises. This guaranteed a good time for both of us. I didn't like to meet parents. I only made appearances for special holidays or birthdays. All the mothers would ask me why I wasn't married yet. I told them I wasn't into marriage.

One girl I dated for a while told her mom that I couldn't say the "L" word. She was right. I couldn't. To some degree, my schedule was to blame. As a policeman, I worked from seven at night until three in the morning. Then I took a quick nap and went to work at Piedmont at five. Afterward I went home and slept.

Since my days off with Piedmont were Sunday and Monday, I limited my going out time to Saturdays and Sundays. On Wednesdays, I would pick up the phone and go down my "comfortable list," calling to see if any of the girls I knew were free for the weekend. If the first one was busy, I called the next one on the list. If all of them were busy, I went out with the guys from work. I knew I could always pick up another girl from the bar.

I was never alone, but I just couldn't commit. I often woke in the middle of the night and wondered if my whole life would be like this. I could have married any of the women I was seeing. I just didn't love any of them. After my failure with Donna, I was a little gun-shy about doing it again. However, I didn't realize that my issues went a lot deeper. All the women I was seeing were always good to me. They never complained about my lifestyle, but I was still miserable. I wanted someone, but just couldn't find the right person.

My brother, John, came to me one day and told me about his wife's coworker. He was worried about me, and thought that maybe

I should meet someone for more than a one-night stand. He said Pat was a really nice girl, but she wouldn't put up with my lifestyle. I told him that I would call her and ask her out. I was a little lost in the relationship department, so maybe this would be a step in the right direction.

One Monday, I decided to go and take a look at her. She worked at an upscale leather shop in the mall that I had visited often. They had the best leather jackets at great prices. I didn't remember ever meeting Pat when I was in there.

I was taking a chance, and part of me was hoping she wouldn't be there. As luck would have it, she was working on a display when I walked in the door. I told her I was John's brother, and she stopped what she was doing to talk to me.

We talked for a few minutes about the store and the jackets, but I wasn't getting a good feeling from her. I stopped talking and turned to leave, but as I did, I asked her if she would like to go and get dinner. I was surprised when she said yes. She lived in Newport News, which was a good ways away from where I lived, so I really didn't think that a date would happen.

It almost didn't. We set up a time and I showed up at the restaurant, and waited there for twenty minutes. I started to leave as she pulled up. She said she had been on her way, but had to turn around because she couldn't remember if she had turned her iron off or not.

She was surprised I was still there. So was I. Dinner went well, but there were no fireworks. Later I would tell John that I thought she was nice, but maybe a little too nice. After dinner, we said our goodbyes and talked about getting together again, but I seriously doubted it would happen.

However, since John had said Pat would not put up with my lifestyle, I decided to prove him wrong. He was right about the fact that relationships were important to her and one-night stands were not. She put me through a couple of tests.

Once she invited me to her sister's house. Her sister was also attractive and the entire time we were over for dinner, Pat watched to make sure I wasn't paying more attention to her sister than her. I passed her test, but not without laughing. I was thinking that if it didn't work out, I was going to ask her sister out.

After several dates and several tests, she invited me to a family birthday party. I thought it was odd that she would invite me to a family function so soon, but I soon found out that if her family didn't approve of me, there was no chance for us.

I didn't expect it, but I fell in love with her family. She had two older sisters that she looked up to. Both had good jobs, and the oldest was married. I had already met her brother-in-law, Joe, several years before. He sold sailboats and I had looked at some in his shop. Joe and I might have only spoken for ten minutes, but once I saw him again it was like we were old friends.

Pat's stepfather had a large house in Denbigh, Virginia. Behind it, he had a large greenhouse where he grew orchids. He was known in the area for them. In WWII he had been a bombardier in a B-25 bomber. He had been shot down twice. He told fascinating stories, yet when you talked to him, he was a really down-to-earth guy. He once told me about when he worked at a photo company. He had taken one of the very first pictures of a bullet leaving a gun and following it to when it hit its target. He had grown up in a fascinating time.

Pat's mom was a sweet person too. She loved to have her family present during the holidays, and made it a point to make everyone feel special. She made me feel welcome the first time I met her. She made some jokes about rules, but eventually opened her home to me.

The only thing about them I didn't like was that they were all smokers. And they weren't just smokers, they were chimney smoking fiends. They lit one as they put one out. Their kitchen looked like the haze in Los Angeles. I would try to stand being in the kitchen with them as long as I could, and then retreat to the family room with Mr. Pate and Joe. Mr. Pate was always in his favorite rocking chair, watching the television with Joe.

I didn't like the fact that Pat smoked, but something about her caused me to overlook it. She had a good heart, a good job, and she wasn't into the bar scene. Most of all, she had the family life I had always wanted. She had recently broken off a bad relationship and was gun-shy just like me. I took my time. I still had a couple of women I was seeing on the side, so I didn't mind taking it slow with Pat.

After we had dated for a little while, I asked her to marry me. We got married at her parents' home. This was it for me.

For the first time in a long time, I had everything I needed. Most of my focus was on my new family. Every birthday, holiday, and a couple of random weekends a month were spent at the Pate home. Pat's other sister eventually married too, and soon there were three sisters and three brothers-in-law. I had a big family that got along together really well. This was how life was supposed to be. I went for several years without even thinking of stepping outside of my marriage.

I was still in the Fifth Platoon and working at Piedmont at the time. I felt that if this marriage was going to work, I had to get better hours at both jobs. I went to my new captain and asked him if he could get me back to regular hours.

My decision with Piedmont took care of itself. Piedmont was bought out by US Air and all part-time employees were going to be let go as soon as the merger went through. It was now or never. I either went full-time at Piedmont or stayed with the police force. To get full-time would most likely require a transfer out of the area. I knew Pat wouldn't want to move away from her family, so I decided to let Piedmont go.

There was another reason I didn't want to get transferred anywhere else. I liked my job at the police department. I got along great with the sergeant and corporal that ran the unit. Sometimes I was a pain in the ass and they didn't always know how to handle me, but most of the time, they just let me do my thing. Every once in a while, they sat me down and made sure we were on the same page, but that was all.

I viewed police work like a game, and I didn't like losing. We had to go by certain rules, but the bad guys didn't. I excelled at finding ways to use the law and still get the bad guys. I was always bending the rules a little bit. I sometimes made my supervisors cringe, but I always came out on top.

Case in point, there was a law in Virginia called "Glazing on Glass." Window tinting was just coming out and was a big deal in other states. In Virginia however, you couldn't have tinted windows on the driver's or front passenger's windows. If I saw a car with tinted windows, I pulled them over and issued a ticket for "Glazing on Glass."

Every time I went into a specific judge's court, I got a conviction. Judge Vernon D. Hitchings, Jr. was a robust judge with a quick wit. Very often if someone tried to show up a police officer, Judge Hitchings put them in their place. He heard an average of two hundred and fifty to three hundred cases a day. Between 1954 and 1977, he had heard over a million cases, which put him in the *Guinness Book of World Records*. I got along well with him. Other cops told me that I could bring in Jesus Christ and His apostles and still get a conviction.

When Judge Hitchings retired, they split up the traffic courts. Our precinct got a defense attorney that everyone said hated police officers, but Judge Leonard B. Sachs was a meticulous judge who wanted every last detail laid out perfectly in a trial. The first time I had a case with him, I carefully watched how he handled other officers testifying in their cases.

He was smaller than Hitchings in many ways. Hitchings was tall and weighed about three hundred pounds. Sachs was shorter and weighed about one hundred and fifty. Sachs sat at his desk with everyone else on the docket in front of him. He would read the docket with reading glasses that sat on his nose, and whenever someone was speaking, he would just look over his glasses.

He got frustrated quickly when officers weren't prepared. He was quick to anger with those that fumbled with their paperwork and couldn't share a case summary in a hundred words or less. When our case was called, I made sure I was ready to give him everything needed succinctly.

One involved a motorcycle gang member that threatened one of my informants. The informant told us that the biker carried a gun in his back pocket. Later that night, we found him cruising around town, and pulled him over. We found not only the gun, but a pair of brass knuckles too, in addition to several knives in his saddle bags. This gave us a multiple weapons charge against him.

When he showed up in court, he had an attorney with him. The attorney inquired about the reason I stopped the guy in the first place. I didn't want to give away my informant, so I told them the suspect's motorcycle had a burned out taillight.

Once he was off his bike, we asked him if he was armed and he said that he carried a gun in his back pocket. We didn't share it in court, but when the guy said this, my partner drew his weapon, and told him that now he had a gun in his ear too, just in case he planned to make a move toward the one in his pocket. After I explained my probable cause, Judge Sachs seemed to be enjoying my case. (I made a mental note to myself to be better prepared the next time I went before Sachs though.)

But back to the original point: The first time I brought a "Glazing on Glass" ticket to Judge Sachs, he was sitting on the bench, looking over his reading glasses at me and reading the charges. I gave him the circumstances, and he looked over his glasses, and told me that he wasn't going to convict the driver.

He explained that the shop owners didn't tell their customer that it was against Virginia law when they got their windows tinted. Shocked. I asked, "What happened to the idea that ignorance of the law was no excuse?" He stared at me for a moment, and then told me that if I ticketed anyone else with this, he would dismiss the charges.

I questioned, "Because they don't know it's against the law, you won't convict?" He responded that he was glad I understood. I thought, *Fine. Challenge accepted.*

A week later, I saw a vehicle with tinted windows. I pulled the gentleman over and explained that the glazing on his windows was illegal and he needed to have it removed. I told him I worked this area regularly, and I was sure I would see him again. I waited two weeks, saw him again with the glazing still on, pulled him over, and issued a summons.

The following week, I found myself in Judge Sachs's court. As soon as he called my name with the charge of "Glazing on Glass," I could see the sneer on his lips. Looking over his glasses, he asked me if he had not been clear on his feeling about this charge. I explained that he had been perfectly clear, and asked for the opportunity to explain myself further. I told him I had warned the driver weeks before I had issued him the summons.

Judge Sachs took a long moment to process what I had just said, looked at the driver and asked him if this is what had happened. The driver confirmed what I said. Sachs looked at me and gave me a genuine smile. He found the driver guilty of "Glazing on Glass" and told him to get the crap off his windows. Sachs told me that if I could work the summons like this every time, he would get me guaranteed convictions. Judge Sachs laid the foundation and I ran with it. I didn't back down, and I could tell he was impressed by my tenacity.

Because the hours of the Fifth Platoon were not good for my new marriage, I went to the captain of the Second Platoon and asked if I could get transferred back to the street. Working in traffic had more reasonable hours and I had a wild desire to ride a motorcycle. By the next month, I was back to patrol and working under a friend of mine, one I had known since I began in the department.

We had worked together in Vice and Narcotics and had been friends a long time now. While I was happy just being an officer, he made rank quickly. He was always fair and had a great police presence. He was happy to have me, so I just worked the streets as an officer until I could get a job in traffic.

Whenever I had spare time, I went down to the Traffic Division to get to know everyone ahead of time. That captain rarely had the time to talk to me, and once again, I feared my reputation was hurting me. This captain happened to be a good friend of the captain that had kicked me out of Vice and Narcotics.

Therefore I avoided him, and spent a lot of time talking to the lieutenant instead. He said there weren't any openings in the Traffic Division, but there was one in Crime Analysis.

Crime Analysis worked in the same building. I had heard of it before, but thought it was a place to retire, not a place for hard workers like me. However, the lieutenant explained that it was a straight day job with weekends and holidays off. He added that it would also gave me an opportunity to get to know the captain better, and I would be right there when the next spot in traffic did open up.

Holidays and weekends off would give Pat and me an opportunity to have a halfway normal life, and more time with her family. In patrol, I sometimes had to work during family weekend outings.

I just didn't know if I was cut out for a day-time job. I had never done that. Even though it would put me near traffic, *real* cops sometimes looked at crime analysis as a wasteful unit, and judged the guys in it the same. I met the corporal that ran the unit. He was an old supervisor of mine, and we hit it off. I thought I'd give it a shot and transferred.

Crime Analysis takes all the crimes that happened all over the city of Norfolk and looks for patterns in them. Criminals are creatures of habit. If they break into a business and don't get caught, there is a good chance they will be back in thirty to sixty days to try again. Study after study has shown this theory to be true. Several of my good friends at the Norfolk Police Department had written a book on crime analysis so they had set up the procedures for the unit.

My job was a number-crunching one. We would sort all the crime reports in Norfolk. The city was divided into planning districts. Multiple planning districts made up car districts. The car districts were in sectors and the sectors were in precincts. At the time, Norfolk had two precincts: First and Second. The First was mostly the downtown area. The Second was the north part, or what people called the Ocean View Precinct. We scanned all the crime, and tried to find a pattern.

I walked into the job thinking it was just for guys who didn't want to work the street anymore. To some extent, that was true, but when I saw that the unit really helped catch the criminals on the street, I was all in.

Once again, I completely immersed myself. I read books and studied every case that came across my desk. I worked the Second Precinct burglaries—both commercial and residential. This position got the most cases. I might only get one or two cases during the week, but when I got back to work on Monday, twenty more would be waiting.

We logged reports by date, occurrence, time of day, day of week, and the type of entry. Doing this helped us see patterns. Once we noted one, we put out a bulletin to the precincts and let them handle it how they saw fit.

I remember my first hit. I had predicted that a place of business was going to get hit during a specific set of dates, and I was spot-on. I was hooked on crime analysis. I now realized that this was an important part of the department. There was a lot I could learn. I was also sure that if the captain of the Traffic Division saw how hard I was working, he would hire me.

After several months there, another officer pulled me aside and told me I was upsetting the apple cart by being too gung-ho. Apparently, I was making the rest of the guys look bad. He told me to slow it down, and make my work last for the week instead of being finished by noon like I normally was. Even on Mondays with twenty reports on my desk, I normally finished my logging by noon. I spent my afternoons studying crime analysis or looking for patterns.

The officer talking to me worked robberies and homicides and had maybe four cases a week. It took him an entire week to log them and look for patterns. Since I wasn't the same, the other guys thought that maybe this wasn't the place for me and labeled me a troublemaker.

I didn't back down. I told the guy to worry about his job and I would worry about mine. I got along with everyone, but I knew they were hoping I would get transferred before I could cause any trouble.

On the home front, Pat and I seemed to be the perfect match. We were the perfect couple at parties and events. Working days with weekends off, most of them spent with her family, made life seem idyllic. I still did a lot of running, and I even built a gym in my house where I spent a lot of time perfecting my "religion." I went several years without letting my old self out of its cage. I focused on work, exercise, Pat, and her family. I signed up for my first marathon and started a whole new journey. I didn't leave time for much else.

Marriage is not fifty-fifty; it's a hundred-hundred. You must both give it your all or it won't work. When a couple of things didn't go my way about sex, finances, or our relationship, I began to drift. The first time a woman came up and gave me the attention I didn't feel I was getting at home, I faltered.

I told myself it was just a mistake and that it wouldn't happen again, but then another woman would flirt with me and I would fall again. I didn't want to lose what I had with Pat and her family, so I justified what I was doing by saying that I wasn't getting what I needed at home. I was starting to revert to my old self.

I never lied about being married, but sadly that didn't seem to matter. It was only a matter of time before I got caught and lost everything. However, life was about to take another dramatic turn.

The thing I had stayed away from all my life in police work was about to challenge me like I had never been challenged before. Politics. And the funny thing is, I was ready.

English Family in 1980s

I n the 1980s the Norfolk Police Department created the Systems Development Unit (SDU). SDU's primary mission was to look at current technology and see how it could benefit the department. They worked hand-in-hand with the City of Norfolk's Department of Information Systems (IS) in the beginning of this endeavor. City employees from IS maintained the department's Criminal Justice Information Systems (CJIS). This mainframe record management system had been developed in the 70s through grants and federal monies. At the time, nearly all seven cities in the Hampton Roads[1] area participated in the project. Because of budget costs and maintenance fees, most cities had their own records management system, so data-sharing usually required phone calls and word of mouth.

IS employees also worked as the liaison between the city's IS and SDU. SDU consisted of Lieutenant Benny Rogerson, whom I had known when he was a sergeant, and one other officer named Leon Melcher, or Mel as everyone called him. SDU applied for a grant to buy IBM XTs and place them in various police divisions that wanted computers to help automate their daily procedures. Crime Analysis fell under this grant, so the second year I was there, we received an IBM XT personal computer.

---

1   The seven cities of Hampton Roads are Norfolk, Portsmouth, Newport News, Chesapeake, Hampton, Virginia Beach, and Suffolk.

These computers came with WordPerfect, word processor; Lotus Symphony, a spreadsheet; and dBase III, database management software. Mind you, nobody in our unit knew how to program; heck most of us didn't even know how to turn it on! Very quickly, it became apparent we were at the mercy of IS. After some brief training, I met some IS members and discussed what we did with pen and paper, asking if they could take either dBase III or Symphony and create an automated system to help us do our work. When Crime Analysis is broken down to its basics, it's just statistical calculations and numerical tracking. It would be great if we could put the information into the computer, press a button, and let it process the information, giving us the best projections for the next crime. IS told us the software we had purchased was no more than an electronic filing cabinet. What we wanted could not be done with this software. Most police divisions viewed computers only as glorified typewriters, so basically just word processors.

Two things happened after that meeting. I began to realize that if we wanted something created on these computers, we had to do it ourselves. IS didn't seem to understand what we did and exactly what we wanted. They told us on many occasions that we didn't understand computers and were asking for "science fiction." Someone once asked how difficult it would be to learn how to write a program with our software. IS scoffed at us. Police officers couldn't program, they said. What were we even thinking? You needed a college degree in computer science to do that. We just didn't understand the complexity of these computers. After that meeting, we were clearly on our own. If we wanted these computers to do anything besides word processing, we had to do it ourselves. *Challenge accepted.*

I started looking into the database software. Our local community colleges offered a course on dBase, so I signed up. Within three months, I created entry screens for the guys in the unit to start plugging in their crime reports. The second class I took on it taught me to complete the process, so in six months I wrote a complete Crime Analysis program that did what we wanted it to do.

All of a sudden I was a little bit of a celebrity. Here I was: a police officer that wrote a program using unfamiliar software without a degree in computer science in less than six months.

Even though the IS Department said it was impossible, when Lieutenant Rogerson of SDU saw my work, he immediately transferred me to his department. I met Leon Melcher (Mel), and discovered he was a bit of a legend himself. Mel had been a crime scene technician and was one of the best in the state. He was one of the only fingerprint examiners grandfathered in when the state began certifying latent print examiners. It was no easy task to become a latent print examiner. Several of our guys took the test multiple times before they were certified. When they had hard cases, they often asked Mel for his opinion. Latent print examiners came in with print cards and asked him to review them. He would break out his personal fingerprint magnifier, and tell them whether or not they had their man.

When I began, Mel explained our role in the unit and where we were in the pecking order with IS (we were low). Little did I know that we were about to start a war between the Norfolk Police Department and the Norfolk's City's IS Department that lasted for almost twelve years. I was right in the middle of it.

Only picture of Dad and all the boys in 1985

Howard Boys on Texas Trip

Lieutenant Rogerson saw my potential in programming and turned me loose. He began by giving me small applications to write. The more I wrote, the more he gave me. Word started to leak that I was writing code. IS stepped in, and I had my first real taste of politics. IS complained that I was not a programmer. Police officers, they maintained, cannot be programmers. They wanted me to stay with police work, but I just kept programming.

I wrote a system for our Special Intelligence Unit (SIU), then one for Vice and Narcotics. I wrote one for Personnel, and then the Detective Division. Some of the police brass, old timers, didn't like the whole concept of officers in SDU. They felt we needed to be on the street doing "police work" instead of what we were doing. They had never needed a computer when they were on the street. It was just old-fashioned police work that did the trick for them. Enough with this stuff they saw in the movies. Yet when departments realized what I could do and how much easier I was making their lives, the requests for computer work just kept coming in, and I kept writing code. These were not just data entry screens either; they were full systems with reports and analytical analysis. It was saving a great deal of time for the police, freeing them from all the mundane information they had to write every month.

After several years, we had so much work that we were able to justify hiring our first civilian programmer, David Rabidoux. Once we brought him on board, we were unstoppable. David was brilliant in coding, but didn't understand police work. However, he was a great listener. I told him what we needed, and he did it. Before we knew it, we became a force to be reckoned with.

In the early '90s, we started working on regional systems. A large multijurisdictional grant was issued to revamp the old data-sharing system used among the seven Hampton Roads cities. SDU was given forty thousand to network all the Vice and Narcotics units in the area. IS was given $250,000 to write a system to share data on arrests among the seven jurisdictions. Since the regional system had been developed back in the '70s, several had pulled out and were doing their own thing. We needed to create a system that shared information among all seven cities. I worked on both the regional mainframe system and assisted David with the Narcotics part of the grant.

In six months, we networked all the Narcotics units together using some free bulletin board software, and the software we had already written for Vice and Narcotics with some new bells and whistles added. Now the Narcotics units were able to identify repeat offenders without having to call other agencies. Once an agency inputted a drug arrest, our program tracked that person's address, and notified his resident city's department that this person had been arrested in another city. Additionally, if another agency posted that they had arrested a person and a second city arrested that same person a month or so later, the original city got notification that this person had been arrested again. Suddenly, seven metropolitan Vice and Narcotic units were getting real-time arrest data they never had before. Narcotics arrests grew. Everyone that saw the system wanted it. The commanders of the Vice and Narcotics units got together and decided to call the project (and the software) the Hampton Roads Drug Arrest System or HARDASS. The name alone made a splash.

At the end of the year, both the IS and the SDU showcased what we had done with our grant monies. The city's IS department had the first part of the day and demonstrated what they had accomplished, and in the afternoon, we presented our truly regional system. Afterward there was a meeting with all the agencies' command staff. The consensus was that they didn't want the IS's product. They wanted ours. All hell broke loose.

The city managers got involved, and the Norfolk Assistant City Manager over the police department threatened to have us fired if we wrote one more program. It was only after all the Commanders of the Vice and Narcotics units stepped in, and advised all the city managers of the effect of what we had accomplished with the Vice and Narcotics system that he came back and apologized.

But there were still casualties. Benny Rogerson, the visionary of the whole SDU project, had been promoted to captain, and was transferred to Central Records. Being transferred to Central Records was like being sentenced to a black hole. You knew your career was over when you transferred there. A great friend of mine, Les Barnard, took over SDU. Les was the last sergeant I had worked for on the streets before I went to Crime Analysis. I had also worked with him while I was in Vice and Narcotics, so even though I felt bad for Benny, I was happy to be with Les again. The city thought Les was safe because he didn't know much about computers and was a great soldier. He did follow orders, but he also listened to us, and soon became a strong advocate of the unit. Still it was politics at its best.

We got a new Chief of Police around 1993. He seemed to be another politician that did just what the city wanted, not what the department he headed needed. He gave heed to City Hall and paid attention to the war between IS and SDU. IS told him that police officers needed to be out on the street, and that it was a waste of resources to have a unit doing IS's job. They told him that all we did was cause distractions to their agenda for the department. We didn't have a clue as to what was good for us, only they did. The Chief fell for it—hook, line and sinker. He called everyone from SDU into his office. He began by telling us that he didn't understand the unit and that he was going to transfer all of us, so we could start doing "police work" again. The civilian in our unit was going to be transferred to IS. We needed to leave the programming to IS and stop interfering with their work. All programming was to stop immediately. We could do maintenance on the systems we had already written but that was it. I saw red, and Les had to kick me under the table to keep me from telling the Chief where he could go. We had been busting our butts for the police department, and IS was doing nothing except demanding more money. This was typical political BS.

Shortly after the meeting while waiting for our transfers, the city was getting ready to pass a new ordinance on false alarms. Many businesses had old, outdated alarm systems that went off at least once or twice a week. The police department would get the alarm calls and respond, only to find the building secure. Then they had to wait for the owner to respond to check on the property. It got to the point that some of these systems were so old that even the owners stopped responding. This process was tying up officers for hours.

Another problem in the same vein was that officers got complacent when responding to the alarms. Because they had been at the business a hundred times before on a false alarm, they stopped checking them. However, later an owner would find a gaping hole in the back wall or that the burglars went through the roof and exited through a door, locking it so it looked like the building was secure. It was very embarrassing to have the owner find these points of entry. Not only was the problem with the alarms tying up resources, it was also putting officers' lives in jeopardy. When I heard about it though, it hit me that the real drive behind it was that the city saw it as a way to generate income.

With the new ordinance, after the third false alarm the business had to pay a fine of $25.00. If it happened again, the fine went up to $75.00. The amount of the fine continued to rise until the problem was fixed. Alarm companies backed it too, as it forced businesses to upgrade their systems. The City saw this as a win-win scenario. The police department showed that we were averaging over 400 false alarm calls a month. This was just for businesses, and didn't include residential properties, which were also included in the ordinance. At $25.00 a pop, that was $10,000.00 a month for businesses only. Take that and increase it to $75.00 per a false alarm and you were looking at around $30,000.00 a month. They'd always tell you, it's not about the money, but we knew they were salivating about getting this project started. There was just one problem.

The city planned to pass the ordinance in June without any way to track it. We were now in the middle of April. They had given the task of tracking all the false alarm reports to Central Records, but Captain Rogerson, who had been the captain that brought me to SDU way back when, stated they didn't have the manpower to track all the new rules of the ordinance. He said it would be a paper tracking nightmare, and needed to be automated, so they could just hit a button and print out those that owed money and how much. He also wanted the fine letters to be printed out and tracked so we could easily know who had paid and who was behind on those payments. (The city was planning to go after those that didn't pay.)

In the end, the Assistant City Manager (ACM) that had threatened all of SDU called a meeting with the Director of Information Systems (DIS), Chief of Police, the Captain of Central Records, several of the IS people that maintained all the old police systems, my boss, Mel and me. You could tell by the way the ACM spoke that he was in a panic. He explained the situation, was looking for solutions, and needed solutions now. DIS started off by acting like it was not an issue. He presented a plan that required six months to set up and more time after that for data entry and only then would they begin working on reports. They were going revamp an old system already in use for tracking paramedic calls, but it would cost the police department the salary of one of their programmers and some new mainframe equipment to accomplish. When he finished, the ACM turned to me. I will never forget the look on his stricken face. Here was a way for the city to generate extensive revenue and IS projected it would be at least six months before they could even begin generating reports on who needed to pay. They were also asking for more money and newer equipment. The ACM's job could have been on the line if he took this bad news back to City Hall, and he looked it.

All eyes on me, I looked at the ACM and the Chief of Police and told them we could have a system that tracked, analyzed, and produced the necessary reports in three months. The DIS laughed out loud and told everyone in the room that this was impossible. This was the reason IS needed to be in charge of all automation, he continued. I didn't have a clue about what it took to put a system like this in place.

I stood my ground. Not only would we be up and running when the ordinance went into effect, but we would be finished with the system in two months and test it for one month to make sure it worked without any issues. The IS people in the room were in a buzz, saying there was no way we could pull it off.

They didn't know that Captain Rogerson had already given me a heads up about all this beforehand. I had already looked over the ordinance and pulled in David. We would take one of our already written systems and tweak it with a new entry screen, so it was ready for data entry. When the ordinance was passed, the police department started writing warning summons to advise owners about what was about to happen. This provided test data to complete all the calculations and reports that were required when the ordinance went into production in August.

Captain Rogerson was grinning from ear to ear; he didn't much care for DIS either. He looked over at the ACM and reassured him that if I said three months, it would be three months. DIS stood and told the ACM he didn't have time to listen to "science fiction," and would be waiting for a request from the police department to get started on the ordinance. After a quick retreat, the ACM turned and asked me what I needed to get started. I told him I just needed a new computer in Central Records and a printer. You could see he was already starting to feel a little better. He now had a viable solution he could present to City Hall.

As everyone was leaving the room, the Chief turned to me, Leon, and Les, and told us he was wrong about us not doing police work. He understood the need for support so the rest of the troops could get their job done. We were a big part of that support. If we pulled off the impossible, he would give us his full support from now on. Captain Rogerson told him that I was that guy that got every dirty job nobody wanted because I would get it done.

When all had left, I went into our office and explained to everyone that this was our opportunity to shine. Failure was not an option. Of course, I knew that even without support I was going to get this done. If I had to work twenty-four hours a day, I was going to get this done. Once again, my police department family got together and gave me what I needed to succeed.

We did what we said we were going to do. In two months, we were testing a fully operational False Alarm Incident Report System or FAIRS as we called it. It not only allowed users to enter information on a summons on places with false alarms but it tracked how many times it had happened in the last month, and whether it was residential or business. It also generated the letters that were sent out to the violators and kept track of who paid and who was late on payments. We even learned new ways to do searches due to the amount of data coming in. Our old searches took too much time. We devised a new way of crunching data, so that the users received instant responses on their searches. When August came, we put it in place. In the system's first month, we hit the $10K of fines that the city wanted. Everyone from the Chief to the ACM were amazed. From that time on, I was called into every meeting in which automation for the police department was discussed. They wanted my opinion on anything computer-related that touched the police department. I was becoming a rising star in Norfolk. We went from two officers, a supervisor, and one civilian to three officers and two civilians, and kept on cranking out the programs. Of course, when you become that rising star, there are those out there that want to knock you down. I had made some enemies, and what was about to happen with SDU was going to really change my life.

Even though my police career was taking off, I was worried about my home life. I was having issues. I wasn't sure if Pat was or not, but I didn't think she understood my needs. I wanted her to change. Since I was in control of my destiny (or so I thought) and we disagreed about so much, this seemed reasonable. Three years into our marriage Pat and I attended counseling. We were beginning to fight more often over sex, money and where we wanted to be in five years. Pat liked life to be safe in every way: no chances, no crazy stuff. She didn't want to go out and grab the world and take charge. I wondered if there was something in her past that caused this. Someone recommended counseling, so I talked Pat into going with me to a marriage counselor. Little did I know that there was something in my past that was also creating issues for us. After several sessions, I thought life seemed better. However, the counselor decided she wanted to speak to us separately. She thought Pat might open up more freely without having me in the room. *What? Leave Mr. Perfect out of a session?* I was the one who had pushed for these sessions. I needed to know what Pat said behind my back. I grudgingly agreed and Pat went to two sessions without me. When we got back together, the counselor encouraged Pat to talk about an incident that had really changed her life.

Pat's biological father had passed away when she was really young and it appeared she had never gotten over it. She loved Mr. Pate, her stepfather. He had been the best thing that could have happened to the family after her father's passing, but she had never gotten over the loss of her real father. In fact, when she felt something slipping from her grasp, she wanted to just push it away because she knew that person would eventually leave her too. I didn't realize it at the time but I had the same issue. I did not want to be left alone either.

Two things happened after that. I made a promise to myself that Pat would never feel that from me, and at the same time, I put together my exit strategy, so I would never be alone. I needed to have someone out there that I could run to when Pat pushed me away, which I considered was inevitable.

After the session, I felt really sorry for Pat. How broken she was. I didn't realize I was much more broken than she was. Since I had become a rock star at work, the offers for little getaways became more frequent. I was the king of my world and I enjoyed the fruit of my position. Even so, I promised I would never let her down. That meant I had to work twice as hard at being careful, so she would never know about my occasional "outside activities." These two ideas were diametrically opposed, but I juggled both of them anyway. I had to.

One of those outside activities happened at a mall I worked at part-time. The mall was connected to a hotel. One day a flight attendant I had known before I met Pat came in for an overnight. She had called and asked me to come to the hotel for a drink. I told Pat I was going to the mall to check on my part-time schedule. At the bar, one thing led to another and we ended up in her hotel room. Afterward I told her I needed to go home. I could not stay. She was upset and started to scream at me. I quickly dressed and left, only to have her follow me down the hallway screaming and threatening me.

The whole way home I begged anybody: God, Mother Nature, anybody, to let me get home before she called the house and woke Pat with the story of our affair. When I got home, the house was quiet and Pat was asleep. I was so worried that I took the phone off the hook so nobody *could* call. I also worried that the flight attendant might call the police and tell them I had raped her. While lying in bed that night, I made myself a promise to just stop seeing other women on the side. That lasted about two weeks. When I realized the flight attendant wasn't going to file a report, I decided I just needed to be extra careful.

When we hit five years together, I had another disturbing revelation from Pat. When we first got married, Pat wanted to have children. I think she thought that if we had children, it would settle me down from some of my crazy antics. We talked about it, and I asked her to wait five years before we had children, so we could have some fun and travel. After that, I would be ready to settle down. I don't think she really wanted to wait but she agreed to the timeline. Sitting at dinner on our fifth anniversary, I looked over at Pat and told her I was ready to start a family. Without missing a beat, Pat advised me she had changed her mind. She didn't want children anymore—not now, not ever. It was off the table. I didn't know if this had anything to do with our problems, but I did want to have children and now the person I was married to told me it wasn't going to happen.

I knew I could leave her like I had left Donna and by my logic I was justified. Heck, Pat didn't like half of my dreams and now she didn't want children. The one major issue I had about leaving Pat was her family. I loved her family. I had my police family and now a real family, and I did not want to give them up. My own family was riddled with issues, but Pat's family was built on a rock. My best friends were my brothers-in-law. We did everything together. We celebrated birthdays, the holidays, and about every other weekend together. We even shared vacations, and bought a time-share with one of them down in Key West.

I was really invested in Pat's family. Pat's parents were my idea of what growing old together looked like. I couldn't think of losing this. Pat wouldn't make a decision without asking her sisters first. Her oldest sister was the voice of reason, sometimes to the point that she was afraid of her own shadow. Pat's other sister was a go-getter and often sided with me when I wanted to take a risk. Her husband was a legend in the business world, and was always looking for new ways to make money. When I decided I wanted to buy a house, Pat's oldest sister looked at the possible downfalls of going into debt, but her other sister talked about the benefits. They both had big hearts and were one of the reasons I never wanted to lose Pat. I decided I would be the perfect brother-in-law, and they would never know about my dark side.

I lived a double life. I appeared to be the dedicated husband and attended all the families' birthday parties and holidays. Meanwhile, I was also seeing other women. Other guys in the department did the same, and I justified it to myself because I was always "honest" with the other woman about the fact that I was married. I would tell them that my real wife took precedence over any relationship, and always would. Most of the time I saw other married women. They didn't want to leave their husbands either, so we both knew the rules.

As for my biological family, I only saw my brothers, John and Joel, at work; we didn't socialize that much together. John and I sometimes went out, but Joel was more of a homebody. He had the first child among the Howard Boys. I remember talking to him on the phone and crying with joy about his daughter's birth. The three of us took a couple of trips to Texas to see our dad; but usually these trips ended by nearly destroying the little bit of a relationship we had. Dad would pick on one of us. As the others joined in, the next thing we knew, we weren't talking to each other for weeks. One time the three of us drove to Texas together. On the way back, John and Joel refused to talk to each other because of a fight Dad started. That fight lasted about six months before we started to all hang out again.

My relationship with Mom was tense at best. My youngest brother, Jeff, played French horn like I did, and had the same musical talent that caused Mom to push him as she had me. I am not sure that Jeff would agree that Mom pushed him to what he is today but she gave him everything to succeed. When I was at Old Dominion studying, I said something about needing a piano. Mom said I could go to a church and practice on theirs. She was not going to buy a piano. If I wanted one, I was going to have to buy it myself. One Christmas I showed up at Mom's only to find a brand-new piano in the living room for Jeff. He wasn't even in college yet, but she knew that he needed to play the piano to be a successful music major. Mom knew how much it was going to bother me but I didn't show it. Later I told Pat how it hurt, but that it was okay because I had her family to come to my aid. I didn't need Mom anymore. I was prepared to just walk away from her and never talk to her again. She got me a sweater and some socks

The Howard Boys: Jim, John, and Joel 1996

that Christmas. Later Pat confided that she didn't like my mother and most of her family didn't either. All of them had gotten the word from Mom that nobody was good enough for her sons.

Back to John and Joel for a minute. John was every bit a policeman's policeman. Everybody loved John, but like me, John fought internal demons that gave him issues with work and wives. We worked a lot of part-time together and did our best to support each other in our messed-up lives. I don't think we were very happy, and I learned not to tell John everything because John and Mom were still tight. I once told John about an affair I was having, and the next thing I knew Mom was throwing it in my face. I knew Mom and John were close, so I just became careful about what I shared with him. Once again, I was alone, and I knew it.

Joel, on the other hand, saw what he wanted and went after it. He wanted to quickly make rank. After a couple of years, he made corporal, then sergeant, and then lieutenant. He was also loved by the department because he was 100% police department material. Before he retired, he made captain. At first, I was just happy with being an officer, but after Joel made corporal, I got serious about police promotions. Mom told me that Joel was jealous of my career, and that was why he pushed himself to make rank before any of the rest of us. I am not sure that was the truth, but I knew that Joel had issues too.

My police career was flying. Even though I was in SDU, a support unit, I was able to get a position in our Crisis Negotiation Team and soon worked my way up to a team leader position. In 1992, I finally focused and took the corporal's test. I really didn't want rank at the time, but I started to think about retirement, and the higher the rank, the higher the retirement pay. Additionally, if I ever wanted to go somewhere in the police department I had to make rank. I had a major that gave me insight on taking the exam, and the next thing I knew I had finished number one on the list. John had finished down around seventh. Mom called me right after the promotion list came out. We had some small talk about life; and then out of the blue, she said, "Don't hate your brother John when he makes corporal before you." I was a little stunned. I asked her why she was saying that. She explained that John was a policeman's policeman and everyone liked him. He had received many awards when he was in Narcotics and everyone had told him he was a shoe-in. Basically, she told me he was a better policeman than I was. I lost my temper, and told her I was a policeman's policeman too. I also had a lot of friends in the department; in fact, I was friends with the Chief. Heck, I met with him all the time, I told her. Then I asked her to do *me* a favor and tell John not to hate me when *I* made corporal before him.

I was a little surprised at the way Mom responded to my outburst. I really felt like she didn't know anything about my career. Of course, that was because she and I had stopped talking. Next she asked me to tell her what was going on, and I gave her a ten-minute dissertation that covered the last five years. She seemed genuinely surprised that I was doing so well. She told me she was sure I would make corporal, but not to be mad at John when he made it first. I told her thanks for the vote of confidence and just hung up.

It was clear that she had made up her mind a long time ago that I wouldn't amount to much. She still had that feeling. I felt sad that we had fallen so far apart, but reminded myself that I was on my own. I controlled my own destiny and I needed to focus on that.

In a few months I got the stripes, which was a real boost. Hard work, keeping my nose clean at work, and doing what I felt was the best for the police department had paid off. I had everyone thinking I was the perfect officer, but behind the scenes I was a mess.

It seems like the more power you gain, the greater your chances for failure become. I decided that maybe it was time for a change. I talked to a few people about asking for a transfer back to the street, but the powers that be wanted me to stay where I was until some projects we had started were finished. I didn't realize it then, but my life was about to come unglued on so many levels, and I really wasn't ready for it.

In 1995 the personnel program I wrote for Human Research (HR) showed our first Y2K glitch. Every five years we had to get new police ID cards. Human Resources (HR) ran a report on the first of each month to see whose ID card was about to expire. The system created a letter to each command so the personnel with the soon-to-be expired cards could go to Central Records and get new ones. In 1995, the new expiration year should have been 2000, but our system only collected the "00" which the computer interpreted as 1900 instead of 2000. During the next month, whenever an HR person ran a report, *all* the ID cards that had been recently renewed showed up as expired. I got a call, and when we looked at the raw data, we immediately realized we had a Y2K issue. I contacted my lieutenant and explained that this would not be an isolated issue. All of our systems were going to crash or produce bad data in five years. We needed to get the bigwigs together and make a plan. Y2K was just around the corner and we were already behind the curve.

We had a meeting with the Chief, our commanding officer, the DIS and his staff. They downplayed the problem until the Chief bluntly asked the director if the systems that kept our arrests, warrants, traffic and other police information would fail or not. DIS said they would. All the software would revert to 1900 instead of 2000. As I sat there, I suddenly realized that every system we had would malfunction. Our mainframe system had been developed in the '70s. The system would translate 00 in a date field as 1900 instead of 2000. It had to be able to compute 2000. We were in trouble, but the director of IS was acting like it wasn't that big of a deal. I knew why. He wanted our department to come begging for help. What happened instead took me completely by surprise.

The Chief called Lieutenant Bobby Crowder, the new Officer-in-Charge (OIC) of SDU and me into his office. Les Barnard, who had made captain and had now been put in charge of Services, which included Crime Analysis and (SDU), and Assistant Chief Bruce Hierstein were also there. The Chief asked me if I would consider being in charge of making the police department Y2K-compliant. I was curious as to why city hall wanted to put me in charge of anything, especially something as important as this. In less than five years all the programs written for them—both mainframe and micro-based—were going to crash and they wanted me? I was the thorn in so many people's sides. I was amazed they wanted me in charge of such a large project.

We were also looking at going to National Incident Based Reporting (NIBR) which was a new reporting system. It would replace the old Uniform Crime Reporting (UCR) which was another can of worms. I told the Chief I had two questions. Were we handling this project on our own, or with the city's IS department? He said IS would be assisting, but we were in charge. We called the shots. The Chief had finally realized that I didn't do this job for glory, but for the officers on the street. He wanted it done right. Then he asked what my second question was, and I told him it was more of a request. Once this project was finished, could he transfer me back to the street? He said he would and I became the project manager for the Y2K project.

On the ride back, I asked Lieutenant Crowder why he thought I had been put in charge of such a huge project. Bobby Crowder was a career officer who always looked for the good, but was also street smart enough to be cautious. He said he didn't think the DIS wanted to do this project. This way if we failed, they could just blame us and that failure would add credence to their never-ending reminders that police officers could not be programmers. I looked at Bobby and said, "Then we cannot fail." The next five years would completely change both my professional and my personal life.

I have to jump around a little bit here, so stay with me. There were some really important things I had learned that I was going to need in our Y2K project. It would take everything I had ever learned in my police career to accomplish this project. I knew from the day it began that it was going to make or break my career. I was either going down in flames for failing or I was going to nail it. I thought I was ready, but I quickly found out how real politics worked. Have I mentioned how much I hate politics?

Early on, I had learned that I needed the proper tools to do my job. I had quickly recognized just how important our records management system (RMS) was to officers on the street as well as the detectives in their investigations. In Vice and Narcotics, I had been the guy to whom the other detectives gave partial names, license plate numbers, or city license numbers. From that, I learned to find the person they were pursuing. I knew how to search the systems to locate anybody. At that time, our RMS was written in COBOL and Assembler and used what they called flat files.

To find someone, you could not just go to one place and run a master search to find *every* place that person appeared in the system. Instead, you had to go into *each separate system* and look for them. To look for a suspect, you might start in the Arrest System, then try the Offense System. If you still couldn't find them, you might check out the Traffic Citation System, then the Property

Assessment System. Most officers didn't take the time to learn all of these, so once I mastered them I became an important asset.

Criminals had to pay their bills too; and if they did something stupid, there would be record of it somewhere, so I tracked names for everyone. The second big system I wrote was an intelligence system. We called it one-stop shopping. If you entered data on someone in any category, it checked them all. Detectives often called to tell me they had entered something years earlier, and just found a connection they would not have found in our other CJIS systems.

So looking at the Y2K project, I knew what we wanted and what we needed. It had to be as close to artificial intelligence as we could get. It sounded like science fiction, but I knew it could be done. The new system needed to be more intuitive and user-friendly.

The second thing I had learned early in my career was that I always looked at police work with an us-against-them dynamic— the good guys against the bad guys. Police officers were supposed to play by a hardline rulebook while criminals had no rules at all. To them, everything was fair game. From great officers, I learned that you could bend rules as long as you didn't break them. You might get your hand slapped every so often and be told not to do that again, but in most cases, you got away with that slight bend. I also found that every saint had a dark side, and every sinner, a good side. I met people in Vice and Narcotics that would probably have been my friends in another universe. Unfortunately, now that we had worked together, I had a long list of officers I didn't trust to invite to my home. I would never trust them with my life.

I had also observed early in my career that people spent too much time and energy avoiding what needed to be done. In the long run, if they had just jumped into it, the project would have been accomplished with little fuss. Too often people wasted time in fruitless disagreements instead of looking for solutions. In the end, it was easier to just get a job done.

This dynamic was marked in the upcoming Y2K project. If the members of IS had simply done what we requested instead of looking for ways to avoid it, the project time would have been greatly lessened in the end. More on that later.

Another factor that most people don't understand is that the police department is a paramilitary organization. If you understood the hierarchy and played by the established rules, you would do well. I knew my place in the chain of command, but I was also able to voice my opinion if asked. Speaking up sometimes got me in trouble, but everyone knew where I stood. I wasn't one for sugarcoating my opinions. I was a police officer through and through. You cut me, I bled blue.

My main focus in life was the department. Our mission statement declared: "We, the men and women of the Norfolk Police Department, shall provide protection and police service responsive to the needs of the people of Norfolk." I was dedicated to that mission, so I was seriously intent on doing everything in my power to help provide necessary computerized services to the men and women that served Norfolk on the streets every day. I understood my part in this and nobody was going to get in my way.

When we began the Y2K project, I quickly discovered another us-against-them. I could write an entire book on this part of the endeavor alone. The civilians assisting in the project were divided into two groups: those that were for the project and would take my lead, and those that fought us at every turn. There were even some in the police department that caused us grief. That was a hard one to swallow. A lot of these guys were friends. It was hard to understand their position. They didn't like change, yet knew what was going to happen if we didn't do anything. I guess there will always be naysayers. It just sometimes surprised me *who* they were.

When the project began, the Chief's office wanted to be advised of our weekly progress, so every Friday we met with the COP, DIS, the primary team, Captain Barnard, and a major from the Sheriff's Department. I usually gave a twenty-minute update on the project. Then DIS would say a couple of things, and if the chief or the major had any questions, we'd answer them. In the beginning, these meetings were over in twenty-five minutes.

However, the DIS mumbled when he talked, to the point that we couldn't understand him. Each week someone would share that he had said such-and-such, and he would tell us we had misunderstood him. That was not what he meant. It got so bad that the Chief required the meetings be taped and transcribed. That way we had the transcripts the following week for clarity. On multiple occasions, the DIS maintained that we didn't understand something, only to have the records show he wasn't telling the truth.

The project was a huge undertaking. Sometimes it was hard to see how it would turn out, but I had a vision and was dedicated to making it happen. I didn't believe in no-win scenarios. From the beginning, when IS told us it couldn't be done, I had accepted the challenge. I had proved them wrong before. I would do it again. I came to work almost every day with a chip on my shoulder. I didn't care though. Most of my fellow officers supported me 100% and that was all I needed. I knew who the enemy was; and even though we disagreed so often and so much, I still needed them.

There were three options to fixing our Y2K problem. Option One was to rewrite all the old systems with a new look: a graphical user interface (GUI) with some new bells and whistles, but we had a big issue with that option. The old CJIS system was written in the 1970s in COBOL and Assembler, which were really outdated. Most of the programmers that had written the programs were retired or had passed away, and most of the code to the programs had disappeared a long time ago. IS didn't want to go down that road, so we looked at Option Two.

Option Two was updating our SDU's present systems to the next level. I liked this idea; IS didn't. In the long run though, I could see what would happen the first time something went wrong. IS would blame the police department, and then run to city management, claiming they told us so, and we would get the blame. Then IS would take over and give us something we really didn't want. In the end, it would prove their point that we never should be writing our own systems in the first place. That wasn't a good scenario.

Option Three was to purchase an off-the-shelf software package that would fit most of our needs. None were going to do everything we wanted, but if we could get something that did eighty percent of the job, we could work on the other twenty percent later. We just needed a program that could be implemented before January 1, 2000 that would give us the basics. We would worry about the rest later.

All our programs were written in a software package called Fox-Pro. We had moved away from dBase III (another battle with city hall) and had excellent results with FoxPro. Moving all our applications to it was discussed. There were a lot of positives with that route. We had several FoxPro programmers in the police department and IS had a couple too. However, one of the main problems we had was that most of these systems had been written specifically for one project. Our first program for Crime Analysis had been written based on a flat file platform. It would take some data conversion to change that.

However, our special intelligence program was written in a relational database platform but was only used for our special intelligence unit. Our false alarm system was also different because of the information Central Records needed. We were so busy putting out fires that we didn't get into the standardization of data fields. We had the basic database structure down: last name, first name, and the other main fields, but there was something unique to each system. To do a whole new FoxPro RMS would almost have been like starting from scratch. Time was a factor and the more we looked into it, the more it seemed this was going to be our Y2K solution.

While we were putting together a plan to write our own RMS, we received an invitation to watch a demo of another RMS package written in FoxPro. We were open to just about anything, so we took a ride over to Hampton and watched the presentation by a company from North Carolina called Open Software Solutions, Inc. (OSSI). It did around eighty percent of what we required. After the presentation I gave my card to the president of the company, denoting our interest. His name was J.A. Savage and he had heard of our FoxPro-based police programs.

In government work, you just can't go out and purchase something. There are always hoops you must jump through. Sometimes I am amazed that anything gets done at all. First, we had to write a request for information (an RIF) to see what options were available to us. We only found two software companies that were even close to what we required. OSSI was one of them. Then we had to write a request for a proposal (an RFP) to both companies. This was a sort of pre-purchasing procedure. OSSI ended up being the only company that had anything close to what we needed. At the same time, we found that our jail was also looking for a replacement for their old system, so we brought them into the project too. Additionally, the Virginia Beach Police Department decided they were going to go with OSSI too. Now we had two jurisdictions in the area wanting to purchase OSSI's software. Soon other agencies followed suit. This was a win/win situation for us. The more agencies that purchased the same software, the easier it would be to share information.

But not so fast. Every time we took two steps forward, it seemed like we also took three steps back. Every time we felt we had a deal, IS stepped in and found something they didn't like. They would complain and the whole process would come to a halt. Apparently, DIS didn't like OSSI, so he continually threw roadblocks in our way. OSSI wanted to get a footprint in the Hampton Roads area. If the two biggest cities signed with them, the others would quickly follow.

The OSSI president declared that the first one to sign with them would get the best deal. Virginia Beach signed a contract with them first. Contract negotiations with OSSI were brutal on both sides. In one meeting, our DIS called the OSSI president a liar, causing the room to explode. A recess had to be called, so cooler heads could maintain a good discussion. IS continued to run OSSI through the wringer. J.A. Savage got to the point where he refused to talk to the DIS. Then he refused to sign the Norfolk contract because IS basically wanted him to financially back the whole project. J.A. wanted to sign with us, but had been beaten up enough. He was about to walk out of the deal when the Chief of Police stepped in. He told the city to clean up the contract. Two years after we first met OSSI and J.A. Savage, we finally signed a contract. It was 1997. We now had three years to get it up and running. Our war with IS was just about to really get nasty.

In 1996 while contract negotiations were going on with OSSI, I got promoted to sergeant. Lieutenant Crowder was transferred out of SDU and I became the new officer in charge (OIC) of the Systems Development Unit. I reported to Captain Les Barnard and Assistant Chief Bruce Hierstein, two of my closest friends and supporters. The stars were finally aligned to get some work done. The Chief of Police was also totally behind us. I thought I had the support I needed to get this project finished now—except for the civilians from IS. I needed to get IS onboard. That was going to be an uphill battle. However, I was also having a battle at home and was about to lose Pat.

Very often I had been going home and telling Pat about my problems. I was drinking and feeling sorry for myself. I hoped Pat would give me the attention I desired, only to end up in an argument, which led to us not talking to each other and sleeping on opposite sides of the bed. I let her go to bed before me, so I could go online and talk to other women I was seeing on the side. The more I drank, the angrier I got with Pat. Once again I was looking for an exit. However, every time I thought about leaving her, I'd have a great weekend with her family and tell myself I needed to find other outlets to relieve my anger. I needed to stay with the family.

I was still running, but also went to the gym three times a week. The gym scene was nothing but a soap opera. It was easy to pick up women, but you got to hear everyone talking about who was sleeping with whom as you worked out. On several occasions, I forgot the workout, and hooked up with one of the female gym rats instead. They were simply adding my name to their lists of conquests, just like the guys did. It was unhealthy, and I was afraid that things would get back to Pat. Even though she never went there, she knew a few people who did. I spoke to Pat about taking the money I was using for a gym membership, and building my own in the house. One of my brothers-in-law was getting rid of a home gym with a pulldown bar and a couple of other pieces. I purchased a bench and a bunch of dumbbells, and I was in business. Now instead of going to the gym, I just went upstairs. This kept me home, helped me get rid of some of my frustrations, and reduced my drinking too. I was hoping this might bring Pat and me closer. We seemed to be drifting farther apart.

It got to the point when we had no physical relationship at all. This drove me even further into other women's arms. I found out much later that Pat was seeing someone too. One night, she didn't get home until nearly four in the morning. I heard her come in and go to the guest bedroom. In the morning, I got up and went to work without talking to her. Later that day, I called her on the phone and told her that since we both apparently wanted different things, if she wanted to separate, I wouldn't fight it. We could split everything down the middle and go our separate ways. She agreed, and just like that our marriage was over. Within a month, she had moved out of the house and took the relationship I had with her family with her. We had been married almost ten years. For the first time in a long time, I felt really alone. Filled with anger, I told the world to go screw itself. I told myself I was better alone. I was in charge of my life, and I was tired of not getting what I wanted. I had no excuses anymore. All my time went into my job, working out, running. In other words, I put everything back into me.

When the City of Norfolk and OSSI finally signed the contract, we got the software and started testing it. It became quite clear that we were running a beta copy of the software. We were a little confused by this. We figured that since Virginia Beach had already purchased this software, most of the bugs would have been discovered and fixed by now. Virginia Beach knew we were coming on board, so they decided to let us have first crack at it. They wanted us to find all the bugs, so they could benefit from our work. At first, IS was hot on accusing J.A. Savage of tricking us into thinking the software was ready to roll from the outset. Even though I was a little concerned about the software issues, the problems also gave us the opportunity to have J.A. change things so the software would be better tailored to our needs in the end. I was happy we got the job of testing. I thought it was a win for us, but IS couldn't let it go. For over two months, IS brought it up at every COP meeting, saying OSSI had lied to us.

That was when the internal fighting really began. Criminals learn how to deflect at an early age. In fact, all of us do. We get caught doing something wrong red-handed, and we point to one of our siblings and say, "You know, John did this, and that is much worse than what I just did!" IS became Master of Deflectors and royally wasted our precious time. Every time we asked them to do something, they did one of several things. They might explain that we didn't understand the fundamentals of data storage in the CJIS systems, or point out that the data we were asking for was way too big for them to be able to do something with it. Of course, when all else failed they just pointed a finger at OSSI, repeating their tired claim that if the software had not been so messed up, we would already be done by now. None of these responses helped us make any headway.

Here's an example. We wanted to convert our old CJIS data into the new system. OSSI immediately said they were not in the business of converting data; this huge task fell on us. They balked because they said that we had over one million different names in our arrest system alone. The project was just too big. Nobody in their department had any experience in converting data. It was way beyond their pay grade. At the COP meeting that week, IS pleaded their case and I was asked my opinion. I said I would need to look at the data, but was sure we could do it. DIS jumped in, and quickly pointed out my obvious lack of understanding of the intricacies of data conversion. *Challenge accepted.*

I had converted data before, so I knew a bit about it. When I talked with our team, and then other police and IS members that supported the project, they also concluded that my theory was sound. It could be done. Because of IS's statement that I didn't comprehend the logic behind flat files and that there was still this issue of over one million different names in the arrest system, I needed to debunk several issues. First there was the deal with the one million records. Every time IS said that it caused me concern. One million different names amounted to a *lot* of people being arrested in Norfolk, so I went back to my office and did the math. It didn't add up.

The CJIS system was put in use around 1977. If we had one million records by 1997, it meant that we had added that number of arrests in 20 years. And these were new names, not frequent flyers. When I divided one million by twenty years, it came to fifty thousand new people every year. Next we looked at it by the day. To get that number, we had to arrest 137 new people a day or 5.7 new people per hour. I quickly called the sheriff's major assigned to the project, and asked him about this. He replied that they often didn't process six people a day, much less six an hour, but he would check and get back to me.

While waiting for his answer, I will explain another factor about a flat file system. Every time you were arrested and entered into the CJIS system, a "new" record was created. I looked up a local drunk that was arrested on a weekly, sometimes daily, basis. I counted how many times he was in the system. He had over 800 arrests. That's when I realized that IS was counting each of these as *new* names. The major called me back and told me my hypothesis was right. We did not arrest that many people. IS's logic was flawed.

I entered our next weekly meeting with a huge smile on my face. I couldn't wait to pass around the figures that I had printed on this. After we talked about how things were going, I brought it up. I explained that we needed to go over the conversion again. DIS quickly cut in, once again claiming that I just didn't understand the complexity of data conversion. After all, with a million names in the arrest system, they couldn't envision even trying it. He said it was a dead issue, one that did not warrant any further discussion. I passed out my data and walked them through it. When I explained that I had called the major, it was clear their figures were way off.

There was a moment of silence while everyone digested this new information, and then DIS exploded. My numbers were incorrect, he said. I had only included the arrest system and there were other systems in CJIS too. I quickly pointed out I was using his numbers. He had been the one claiming there were one million *new* arrests. He had brought this to the Chief's attention. As usual, he said we didn't understand him. He claimed he had been talking about the *whole* CJIS system, not just the arrests. This time, everyone just laughed. He'd done this too many times to be taken seriously. The Chief said the whole room understood him. I quickly pointed out that even if we did include every section of the CJIS system, the math would still be flawed. There was no way we were processing six new names an hour in all the systems. If we did, we would have had one of the highest crime rates in the country.

As I looked at the head of IS, I knew our war was just heating up. I may have won this battle, but I knew I had better watch my back. He was going to be after me with a vengeance. The Chief told him he needed a better number. The DIS said they would take a look at the files and have a number by next week. Then the Chief asked me if I thought we could convert the data. I explained that we could. The DIS stood up, sneered at me, and told the Chief that I still didn't know what I was talking about, but if I would lay out the procedure on how to do it, he would have his guys handle it. Before I could answer, he abruptly left the meeting. As everyone filed out, the Chief stopped me and told me to be careful how I handled the DIS. We needed to get this project finished and we did need them. I explained that the police department was my major concern. I wasn't a politician but a soldier. The Chief smiled, and said, "Be careful."

I was fuming inside. *I would take the director of IS down. He had lied over and over again and was still lying. Most of his team didn't support us; we had to fight with them all the time. We had to waste energy on all this stupid stuff. I had enough of his smugness. I wanted him and his group off the team. I worked better alone anyway. All the support and resources I needed were in the police department. If they would just get out of my way, we would be finished by 1999 with a year left over for testing. Be careful, my eye! Hell, it was full steam ahead. I would be prepared for their next attack. I'd crush them.* By the time I got to the office, I thought my head was going to explode. I slammed my door and planned my next shot.

After some discussion with IS, we decided to convert the warrant data file. They told me that it was one of the smallest of the archives and would be easy to check afterward. They estimated a new number of records (about 750 thousand) in the whole CJIS system. I still thought those numbers were too large, but I'd deal with that later. I laid out the plan for the conversion. IS was going to give the project to one of their own programmers. I was happy with the choice because he was one of the IS people I could depend on. He had a background in FoxPro, so he understood the data structures. He was on board. We set up our first trial when I got a phone call saying he had been told not to pursue it. IS had found a problem with the data and we needed to have another meeting before we continued. I asked him if he could tell me what the problem was, and he told me he didn't even know. He had been ready to run the conversion when they told him to stop.

I called the person that was in charge of the IS side of the project and asked her why we were not converting data. She repeated that they had a problem with the data and needed to sit down with me after the COP's meeting and discuss it. I asked her again what the problem was, and she told me that she would lay it all out at the meeting because she wanted the Sheriff's Office involved in the meeting. She added that everyone had enough work to do as we were still debugging OSSI's system. A deflection, and she played it well. *Forget about the data issue for now. Let's blame it on the fact that OSSI's software was not ready for real time.* I saw through the ruse, but I ignored it. I just got ready for the next battle and it turned out to be a big one. The DIS was going for blood.

At Friday morning's meeting, everyone was present: the Chief of Police, my captain, my assistant chief, the major from the Sheriff's office, the director from IS and the lead team members from IS. I explained that we had been ready to do our first conversion on the warrant file when I received a call from the team leader that said we needed to discuss data issues before we continued. I turned it over to her. She passed out a fifty-page document printed on both sides with names. She said that when they did a sample run of duplicate names in the system, they came up with this report. Before they could continue, this information had to be corrected. Otherwise our data would be bad.

The report showed that even though someone's first and last name would be the same, their date of birth would be off by a year (criminals lie!). One entry would have a social security number, but the other entry wouldn't, or one might have the social security number and date of birth correct, but one name said Jim and the other record used James. The major immediately commented that we didn't need bad data in our new system. This needed to be corrected. The DIS had a big smirk on his face. I thought, *Well done, pal, but this isn't over.* I asked the team leader who was going to correct the data and she replied that someone in the police department would have to do it. Most of the information was from police arrests.

At first I erupted, claiming it was just another ploy, but the Chief lifted his hand, signaling me to calm down. We'd look at the data. I remembered his earlier warning, so I didn't respond. The DIS put the burden of cleaning up the data on the police department. Once we fixed it, they'd convert the data. Meanwhile we could also focus on debugging the new system because we needed that fixed too. It seemed like a further waste of energy, so I suggested that we convert the data and then correct it in the new system, but the major thought it would be best corrected first. I was outranked, so I backed down. After the meeting, the Chief pulled me aside again, telling me to be careful. They were looking for a way to discredit us and we needed to make sure that if we went against them on this one, we were in the right. I told him I understood, and would take a long look at the data they provided.

I went back to the office, set up a meeting with Captain Rogerson of Central Records, told him what had happened, and asked if I could get some help with correcting the data. He told me his staff was already short but if the Chief authorized the overtime, he would look into it. Right now just wasn't a good time. I knew his feeling for the DIS. He gave me his Rogerson grin. He agreed that this was a ploy to delay the conversion. After all, it was not odd that a suspect lied to us. Heck, if they gave us even half their personal data correctly, it was a win. This was just another way for the DIS to run the show. He wished me the best of luck, but told me it would take months to complete the corrections.

I went back to my office and closed the door, thinking I might call a couple of buddies and get hammered. *What a waste of time over a couple of pages of duplicate entries.* Looking at the report, I realized they had done it again. They brought us pages of names, but in the grand scheme of things, how much did these names matter? For a novice, fifty pages of names front and back was a lot, but I had caught them at this game before. They were just up to their old tricks. I sat down with my calculator and the report. By the time I was done, I was really ready to go out drinking, but not to drown my sorrows. I was going to celebrate.

I couldn't wait until next Friday's meeting now. I was in a great mood all week. We continued to test the software and I communicated with OSSI about our findings. The IS team thought I had accepted defeat, and was happy about not having to convert data. Friday couldn't get here soon enough. On Thursday, I pulled the police team in and showed them my figures. I wanted to make sure I was correct. I was. They all wanted to go to the meeting too—just to see DIS's face. I promised pictures.

My office was located at a different building than the Administration Building. I went down early with my own report. It was only one page. I met up with my assistant chief and captain. Both looked at me and asked what I was doing. They knew me long enough to know the look I had on my face was trouble. It was the same as the satisfaction I felt when someone was going to jail. We laughed and I told them to get good seats for the fireworks. Both had words of caution because of the tangible animosity present between the director and me. I told them I was just going to quote the truth. The truth always had a way of setting you free.

At the meeting, the DIS and his team bounced into the office. We were nearing the final testing of the software, and we felt it was becoming a solid product. It would soon be ready to test it to see how it would hold up. I think the Chief thought something was up. He later told me I looked ready to pounce. I asked the major from the Sheriff's office what an acceptable amount of bad data would be to do the conversion. What percentage would he feel comfortable with? 20%, 15%, 10%? I told him there would never be 100% perfect data. He knew that and everyone in the room did too. So what would he consider an acceptable number so we could reach it and go ahead with the conversion? He said he could easily accept 15%. He understood the way people lied to the police. When I passed out my one-sheet report I told everyone that this was a correction of the fifty-page report IS had brought earlier. In actual fact, the data that needed to be corrected was less than .5% of the 750 thousand names IS said they had in their records. I asked the major if that was acceptable.

There was total silence in the room as everyone looked over the report. The major broke the silence by asking the director about my accuracy. Not looking up, he mumbled that he thought my numbers were correct. The major wondered why this data had not been converted. We could have already started testing by now! Finally the Chief firmly told the DIS to get the data converted. This time, it was the Chief that abruptly walked out of the meeting.

The DIS had not looked up from the report but when he did, he stared at me like he wanted to jump across the table and choke me. Then it was gone. It was replaced with a resolve I had seen many times before. I may have won another battle, but this war was not over. He told me to reconnect with their guy so he could get a couple of files converted before the next meeting. Then he got up and left. After the other members of IS left, I found myself sitting there with the major, my captain, and my assistant chief. All three instructed me to watch my back. The look on the DIS's face was the one of disgust that a criminal gave you right before he hit you with everything he had. Even though I had won a big battle for the police department, I wondered what the cost to my career would be. It wouldn't take long to find out.

pulled the police team together and told them what had happened. There were congratulations all around. I explained that
this was not a time to let our guard down. We had to make sure
we were accurate with our procedures for converting data. While
we were going over our findings, I got a request for a meeting the
next day from the IS team leader. She wanted an all Y2K-team
member meeting. She explained it was about the warrant file and
how I wanted it converted. She wanted to make sure that everyone
was on the same page and there were no misunderstandings. I told
her I thought that was a great idea.

As I hung up the phone, I knew something was up. We needed
to be prepared. We spent the rest of the day doing that. We went
over the procedure several times, went out to lunch, then got online and played a rousing game of Doom for the rest of the afternoon. At the end of the day, I was the king of my career but still
the pauper of my relationships. Pat had all but moved out and I
was going home to an empty house. Even after the big win over IS
that morning, the phone call after the meeting had put me on alert
to the point that I felt like I needed to head home and get ready
for Monday. I played out all kinds of scenarios over the weekend
in my head. But none of them prepared me for what they tried to
pull Monday morning.

One of the things SDU had been put in charge of during its
existence was moving most of the Norfolk Police Department from

the downtown area to an industrial area ten minutes away. The command staff stayed downtown but First Patrol, Detective Division, Vice and Narcotics, Central Records, and SDU moved into the new building. Shortly after we moved, our Dispatch moved into the other half of the building, so the whole complex became the Emergency Operations Center (EOC). Because we were in charge of the move, we gave ourselves an extra-large office space, which became the topic of many conversations, and placed a large meeting room next to our room. We even had our own entrance. The meeting room was used by everyone in the building, but because of its location, it was very convenient for us. On Friday I called and reserved the room for the Monday meeting. IS beat us to the room and brought donuts, pastries, and coffee. A peace offering?

The team filled the room: about six from the police department and six from IS. The IS team leader started the meeting by saying they wanted to offer a slight variation on Friday's decision of moving the old data to the new system. Because of the errors they had discovered in the data, they felt that we shouldn't just depend on the new system for warrant lookups, but should run dual systems. Only new warrants would be put into the new system and the current warrants would be kept in the old one. This way the old "corrupted" data would not be put in with the new "perfect" data. The IS department felt more comfortable with this process. They were afraid there would be a "false arrest" due to bad data otherwise. That one little statement started a heated debate between the two teams.

It seemed that everyone from the IS team had something to add. As usual, they played their "the-police-department-doesn't-understand-what-they-are-asking-for" card. Every time an IS team member gave their opinion the police team looked at me. They did not support this new idea and were hoping I wasn't going to agree with it. Several of the officers expressed their opinion, but the IS team kept pounding that this was the way to go. I probably let the airing of the opinions between the two groups go on a little too long. It was getting heated with no real solutions in sight. Finally, the IS team leader stood up and addressed the group. Looking at me, she stated that unless her team got a letter from the Commonwealth Attorney's Office absolving them of all liability of the possibility of a false arrest because of bad data, they were going to have to refuse to convert the data.

The debate came to a screeching halt. There was total silence. All eyes turned to me. I waited a second before I said anything. I had plenty of ammunition, but I wanted to make sure that I didn't lose my temper. This was a setup. A sweet donut and pastry-filled setup. Of all the scenarios I had played in my head, I had never expected this one. This had taken a very ugly turn, and I was not sure how I was going to handle it. This was a mutiny. If I lost my temper on the IS team, they would run back to the DIS with a tale about how mean I was to them. They would declare that they couldn't work with me as a leader. On the other hand, I knew that the police department would revolt if we tried a dual system. We were trying to get rid of the multiple systems we already had. Several things came to my mind: *Wow, I didn't see that coming. Bravo IS team, for thinking up this one. But how dare you walk into our project and give us an ultimatum like this one? How dare you threaten to halt this project over bullshit!* I could see they thought they had their ace in the hole.

I asked the IS team leader to sit down. At first she hesitated, I could see she was physically upset. I politely repeated my request. We needed to talk this out. When she sat down, I asked the police team to leave the room. There was a mad rush to the door. They could see this was not going to be pleasant and they didn't want to be there. I took a deep breath and looked at the IS team. I explained that I would not go to the Commonwealth Attorney's Office and ask for such a document. Then I gave them my ultimatum. I made sure I kept my anger in check because one bad sentence and I knew it would come back to haunt me. I began by explaining the value of each team member. It would be a great loss if we were to lose any of them, but here was the deal. They could get on board with the conversion or request a transfer from the project. There was not going to be a dual system; we were moving away from that. I didn't know where they came up with the idea that they could get sued over a bad arrest because of erroneous data, but that was not a reality. Unless they considered what they were doing unethical, illegal or immoral, they needed to get back to work. They could give me an answer now or by Wednesday, so I could present it to the Chief on Friday. And thanks for the donuts and coffee.

As I came out of the room, I was met with resistance; the PD team was pressed against the door. I told them what happened. We just needed to be sure we were ready for what was about to come our way. I was sure this was not over, and I didn't want to be caught off-guard again. None of us had seen that ultimatum coming. Before that day, the PD team had not realized how big the battle was between them and the IS. Now they saw it. The IS team consisted of some really good people. Most had been good friends of mine at one time. The IS team now spoke to the PD team behind my back about how difficult I was. If I would just get out of the way, they said, we could get this project done. For the first time today, the PD team finally recognized the truth.

There were a lot of people that thought I was crazy. I was an "us-or-them" type of guy when it came to getting things done. If you were not for us, you were against us; no happy medium. Most of the PD team was new to what I had been dealing with since I had been transferred to SDU. I was known as hardheaded and I refused to back down, but I had watched how often the PD was treated like a bastard stepchild. So if I had a chance to change things for the better, I did. I was not distracted by people that smiled in your face while stabbing you in the back. I was for the police and the citizens of Norfolk, and it was in your best interest to stay with me or get out of my way. The PD team finally saw what I was up against. At that moment, we became a true team.

I called Les and told him what just happened. He asked me if anyone went to the hospital (Les knew me really well), and I told him no. Of course, I did tell him I used some of the negotiation techniques I had learned from him. That got a laugh. Les knew what we were against. On multiple occasions, he had threatened to choke the living crap out of the director of IS. Of course, he always said that behind his back and out of earshot. Les was known for his negotiating skill and proud that I handled it the way I did. He asked me if there was anything he should do. I explained that even though I was sure it wasn't over, the team was good. I went on to explain that the PD team now realized what we had been dealing with for years. His last words to me were: "Watch your back and keep your head down." *Maybe I should start wearing my bulletproof vest again.*

Ok, some history here. From 1986 to 1993, there were five separate shootings across the country in which a U.S. Postal worker had gone off the deep end, went to work and killed coworkers, and most of the time, killing himself. This is where the term "going postal" originated. It was used all the time to describe a disgruntled employee. The police department was full of them. Even though we never had one hit the Norfolk Police Department, I am sure there were a few that thought about coming in with guns blazing. The only problem with that was that all police officers were armed too. You might take a few out, but there would be return fire. I have seen many officers go off the deep end, often killing their mates, and sometimes themselves, but I had never heard of a situation in which an officer walked into work and opened fire.

Imagine my surprise when I walked into the office on Wednesday and found a frantic phone message from one of my only friends in IS, asking me to call him immediately. I dialed his number and he picked up. "Was it was alright to talk?" he asked. He had my attention. I closed my door and asked him what was so important. He said that after the meeting on Monday, the IS team had come back telling everyone that I was about to lose it and "go postal" on them. They told the director that not only was I under a lot of stress, but they were afraid for their well-being. After their meeting, my friend overheard the DIS calming their fears by saying he would talk to the Assistant City Manager (ACM) in charge of the police department (the same one that we had a love-hate relationship with), and see if maybe it wasn't time for IS to take over the project. It was getting deeply political. As I said goodbye, I reassured him that his secret was safe with me.

I got off the phone and immediately called Les. "Could I come and see him and Assistant Chief Bruce Hierstein? We had a problem." He told me to come down after lunch. I sat in my chair and wondered, *Was I really that crazy the other day or was this just another ploy to get me off the project?* We had come so far and now I was being accused of being unstable. In some areas, I might be, but I had a clear vision of where we needed to go with this project. Maybe I was too hard on the civilian IS team. No. Now I was pissed. These people were messing with my career and the PD's need for a Y2K-compliant system. I wasn't going to take it. I just needed to talk to Les and Bruce. If they backed me up, screw IS; I really wanted IS off the team altogether. *But what if they may agree with the IS team?* That would be a hard pill to swallow. If that happened, it was time for me to put in my request to be transferred.

It was difficult to do anything during the morning. I pulled the team in and told them about the call. I asked them their opinion about my attitude on the project and IS. You have to understand police humor. They were ready to "lock and load" and take IS out. I had my team behind me, but I needed an IS team that supported the project. The PD team kidded that maybe I needed to talk to a shrink, or they might take my real gun away and give me a rubber one so the IS team felt safe. This was my family once again coming to my assistance. This was why I loved the police department.

As I prepared for my meeting with Les and Bruce, I realized how tired I was. I was home alone most of the time right now. Even though I had contacted some of my old girlfriends, I really missed Pat and her family. My ex-brother-in-law's dad had passed away. He had been a fireman from Milwaukee. He had moved down to Virginia when he retired. Sometimes we got together and exchanged war stories. We would have a couple of beers and laugh about old times. He was one of the best. I was invited to the funeral, and was looking forward to seeing Pat's family again; but when I got to the funeral, the family sat together and since I wasn't considered family anymore, I had to sit by myself. It felt like it wasn't just a funeral for my friend but for my whole family. I was afraid I'd go into a tailspin again, so I decided that physical fitness would be my religion. It had always helped me relieve stress before, so I viewed it as my new savior. I was alone again and I needed to take care of me.

I headed downtown to the Police Administration Building (PAB) to get more support. I was a little concerned about the meeting. By now, I knew politics. I might get told I needed to play nicer and give up something to get the project done. I walked into Bruce's office, and Les was already there. Bruce offered me a chair. Their faces showed true concern. *Maybe I bit off more than I could chew. I began this project full of piss and vinegar, but were they going to tell me I had to learn to go with the flow now? We could afford to lose a battle here or there, but we must eventually win this war. Politics.*

I asked them about how I was managing the project from their perspective. Was there something I was missing? Something I wasn't doing? Was I wrong in my approach because I was so adamant about my vision? I told them about what had happened, and told them I had received word that the DIS was going to our ACM to tell him his employees were afraid to work around me. This was the ACM that had threatened to fire me before I helped him out in the false alarm crisis. The IS team had told everyone I had lost it, and they were afraid that I might "go postal" and kill them. Bruce and Les just looked at me and started laughing.

Bruce told me that when I got the job leading this project he knew that I had the police department's best interest at heart, and there was no one else more perfect for the job. Don't change a thing, stay the course, and get it done before the year 2000. I looked over at Les and he just smiled. I felt a huge load roll off my shoulders. They had my back; I was renewed. Bruce asked me how the PD team was holding up and I told him they were great. They had now seen the real IS and finally understood how it was an us-against-them deal. I wasn't crazy and making that up. I sat back in the chair and relaxed. Then the jokes started flying. Watching Bruce and Les was like watching an Abbot and Costello. They went after each other, and before long we were laughing so hard it was almost impossible to catch your breath.

After a good laugh, I saw Bruce look up; standing in his doorway was the Chief of Police. He asked if he was interrupting anything and Bruce waved him into the office. The Chief said he had just had lunch with the ACM. He had told him some disturbing news: that I was losing it and might need to be taken off the Y2K project. Bruce smiled and asked the Chief to come further into his office and pointed at me behind the door. He told the Chief to ask me if I was doing okay. Surprised, the Chief asked if I was okay. I jumped up from the chair and answered the question with a question. I asked him if I was doing a good job for him. Did I need to change my attitude or the way I was running the project?

I suddenly remembered when he first came to the PD and our first meeting when he suggested a transfer so I would start doing real police work again. At that time, he didn't understand the importance of having officers in a computer unit. Then I remembered all the times I had been put in my place because IS "wanted the best for the department." I thought of the many times they had said that I (as a police officer) "couldn't possibly understand the complexities of computers" or be a programmer. *Would I see the politician I had seen in him so many times before?* I was afraid he was going to tell me to play nice and let them win every once in a while. I was wrong.

The Chief began by reminding me that when he first came he had not understood why we needed an officer like me in SDU. Now he did. It was crystal clear. I was looking out for the department, and doing real police work. He now understood the importance of having officers like me in SDU. He needed me to continue what I had started and finish the job. Don't worry about the politics; just get us ready for Y2K.

I walked out of Bruce's office feeling ten feet tall. Screw my private life; I was where I was supposed to be. I had the full cooperation of the Command Staff and nobody better get in my way. I got back to the office and called the IS team leader. She seemed surprised to hear my voice. I didn't tell her I knew about the plot to get me removed. I asked her if her team had made a decision. She hesitated; they were still talking it out. I told her that I had just left the Chief, and he had agreed I was doing the project the way he wanted it done, so I needed an answer as soon as possible. I needed the data converted. If she and her team were not going to do it, I needed to find someone who would. There was a moment of silence and she told me she would get back to me.

Friday's meeting was interesting, to say the least. The Chief laid down the ground rules. If the IS team could not meet the needs of the police department, there needed to be some changes made and made now. I could see the defeat in the IS team's eyes. There were no arguments, just compliance. At the end of the meeting, the Chief told the IS team leader and me to discuss where we were going next and decide if changes needed to be made.

The IS team leader had been a great friend of mine for many years. She had known my first wife and Pat, and we had talked about family on many occasions. During the regional project, my grandfather had passed away. She was the first person I told and the first person that gave me a hug and told me it would be okay. Her husband was a police officer too. Great guy, good police officer, one of those guys you were happy to have as your backup. However, this project had driven a wedge between us.

We sat there in total silence after everyone left. I finally broke the silence by explaining our three options. She could take over the project, and I would surrender command if the Chief allowed it. She could work with me on the project or she could request a transfer. These were the only choices. She was angry and stated that the IS department thought I didn't have a clue as to how to run the project. She thought the Chief, Bruce, and Les would agree with her but now she saw she was wrong. I asked her if the whole IS department thought I was wrong or just the director. She teared up and started to cry. I told her she didn't have to answer.

I told her I respected her friendship, her leadership, and her ability to create unity among the teams. I wanted to do this project with her, so I volunteered to be the fall guy when the director said he didn't want to do things our way. She could tell him that if I didn't get my way I would make trouble. I had a reputation for that anyway, so he'd believe it. She told me everything had been difficult with the new director. Nobody trusted him and morale was low in the group. We had been a team for a long time, but now there was this war between us. She really wanted to quit. I encouraged her to stand fast. We needed her. I promised I would be more understanding, but it had to be done the PD way. We needed her and her team to complete the project. And just like that, she became my friend again. We decided to work together. She would advise me when the director was going to push a different agenda. I had to be careful when she gave me information though. She didn't want to lose her job.

That was a major breakthrough. By the next week we were converting data and testing it in the new system. I will never know how much the chief had to do with getting our project back on track, but I was grateful. From then on, everything went smoothly. It appeared that we might finish the project ahead of schedule. There were still small skirmishes between the director and me, but things had changed. He and I actually got together and talked now. On more than one occasion, I conceded to his wishes. However, I knew I had won the war.

While I was on top of the world at work, my private life was a roller coaster. Two of my friends from the police department and I decided to begin our own "He-Man Woman-Hater's Club" inspired by Spanky and Our Gang, which we all watched as kids. We went out every Friday, tried to meet women, and saw where it would go next. We all needed therapy. I found it easy to pick up women, but the other guys did not. I loved them as brothers, but we had issues. Sometimes my real brothers also got together and went out with me. By now, all of us had gone through at least one divorce, so we were walking disaster areas. Joel met a really nice girl, Terry, and it seemed that their life was going well. John had met a girl that was driving all of us crazy, so sometimes it was difficult to get all of us together. Most of the time we either met for lunch or worked a part-time job together. We often talked about our past, and the conversation always seemed to get around to Mom and the fact that I needed to contact her.

Eventually hanging out with the "He-Man Woman-Hater's Club" was just as depressing as staying home alone. The group grew, and the next thing we knew female officers and clerks from the PD had been invited, so now we had our own little "posse." Sometimes after a night of drinking, I found myself with one of them, and hated myself in the morning. You were never supposed to mix work with pleasure, but this showed just how lonely everyone was. It was strange. Nobody cared who was sleeping with whom. It was a continual string of one-night stands.

One night, we went to a bar that had live music. A young secretary from work came with us. She was married, but her husband was in the military and out of the state. While watching the band warm-up, I recognized a sticker from a local record shop on an amplifier. Right before Pat and I had separated, I had seen that number on one of our phone bills. I had called it and it was the record shop's number. Pat told me one of her closest friends worked part-time at the shop. As the band got ready to play, Pat walked in and came right over to the musician that had the sticker and kissed him. It all came to me at that moment. Pat had been having an affair with this guy while we were still married. I couldn't say anything because of my own transgressions, but it was still a shock. Somehow it had never occurred to me that it went both ways.

Everyone in the group (except the new secretary) knew Pat and saw what had just happened. Some of the guys wanted to pull the musician off the stage and beat him up, while our female partners wanted to yell at Pat. They asked if I wanted to leave. I shook my head. I was okay, and truly it was what I deserved. After a few drinks, the young secretary had been filled in on my moment of truth, and decided I was not going home alone that night. Of course, after we got up in the morning, I found out she had a six-year-old boy, and he was going to wonder where Mommy had been all night. I didn't know how much lower I could get. I needed a change.

Out with the gang one night, I ran into a homicide detective friend that worked with my brother Joel. He had commented that I looked like I had been working out. I told him that physical fitness was my new religion. He invited me to a gym, explaining that the owner of the gym was a great guy and did a lot for his customers. It wasn't like the other fitness places that just wanted your money. Many popular gyms lured people in like they were the most important person in the universe until they signed a two-year agreement; then they were ignored. This was a month-to-month gym, so if you didn't like it, you could just stop going. Even though I had a nice setup at home, I thought I'd give it a try. I went down the next day, and it was exactly as he had described it.

Walking into Flex Gym, I noticed that it was clean, but there were only a few people working out. Not like the glitter gyms I had been to before. There were pictures all over the walls of bodybuilders. I didn't know if this was a good gym for me yet. I wondered if you had to be a "gym rat" to work out here, but looking around, it dawned on me that most of the crowd was over sixty. No "gym rats" anywhere to be seen. It was a smaller gym, but it had everything I needed.

The next thing I knew a huge guy, close to 350 pounds and not in shape, walked out of a small back office. He approached and gruffly asked me what I wanted. Slightly taken aback, I told him a friend of mine had recommended this gym. He snorted and asked my friend's name. I told him and he asked if I was a cop. I said I was, and he replied that they had their quota of cops for the month, so I could just turn around and walk my ass out the door. I must have given him my "I ain't afraid of a 350-pound fat guy" look. No matter how big he was, I could still outmaneuver him. He looked at me very seriously, and then burst out laughing. A bigger-than-life laugh. He moved toward me and I thought myself it was good I hadn't said anything stupid. He was a lot quicker than I thought. He put this enormous paw of a hand out and shook my hand, introducing himself. This was my first encounter with Al Walke. We talked for a few minutes and Al walked me around the place. I told myself my friend was right: this was a great little gym. It became my third home for the next three years. Between work and the gym, I found the support system I needed. I didn't need a relationship to mess things up.

I was there three days a week and it didn't take long before I met a couple of other guys to work out with. I didn't like going home alone, but Pat had left me with two cats, so I often went to work, ran, went to the gym and then hung out with the gang on weekends. I still had my list of ladies I could call if I wanted companionship, and my issues over losing her family continued. I missed them more than I did Pat but both ex-brothers-in-law didn't want to stir the pot. Pat had a new boyfriend, and it would just make things uncomfortable to include me in the family circle.

It didn't take long to begin to meet the female gym rats. Denise had her picture on Al's wall as Ms. Body Builder of the Year for 1997. She was brash and straight to the point. She told me the first night we met that she was going to have me. I was attracted to her forthright boldness. She was very different from any other girl I had known. Denise was a nurse at the hospital in a unit that was one step above ICU. If you woke up in her unit, you had died at least once and they had brought you back. It was a place full of people that most would have given up on, a place of miracles. Both nurses and police officers have that same morbid sense of humor, so we hit it off, and the next thing I knew I had a new girlfriend.

She knew a lot of the detectives because of her patients. Gunshot or serious stab wounds usually ended up in her ward. She knew many officers so we had a lot in common. She liked to show off her body and liked having me on her arm, so we became the talk of the hospital *and* the police department. Very outspoken and strong-willed, she sometimes shocked me, and reminded me of a bit of my first wife. But every time things seemed like they were going south, she turned on the charm, took me out, bought me drinks, and spent the night. Then everything seemed okay again.

Work was moving along. I did a presentation for city management about the Y2K project and our progress, and the next thing I knew I was on a first-name basis with all the city managers and being invited to dinners with the bigwigs in the city. I invited Denise to one of these dinners, telling her it was semi-formal. She knew detectives and officers from the hospital, but had never heard of any of them being invited to something like this. Dressed to the hilt, she made quite a splash. Before the evening was over, the city manager, chief of police, and several other men of the city had made a point of asking about my new friend. She flaunted herself, enjoying her newfound notoriety. I was done. I just wanted to be out with the guys having beers.

After the dinner, she suggested moving in together. I explained it was too soon. A week later she told me that they had found major damage to the structure of her townhouse, and everyone had to move out for six months until they could fix it. She spoke about renting a place, but was trying to trick me into letting her move in with me. She was worried about having to pay for two places, she said. I fell for it. A week later, she had moved into the house with me. In the back of my mind, I was thinking this was a bad idea. It was. The next six months became a living hell.

We lived at the gym. It became the normal routine: we worked out, got food and alcohol, drank and slept. She took over the house, telling me how to eat and what to eat. One night she yelled at me for eating an apple. Carbs were out; we could only eat protein during the week. If she worked hard on her body, I needed to do the same with mine. Then she didn't want to hang with the gang anymore because there were loose women in the group. At the gym one night, she falsely accused me of staring at another girl and made a big scene. The gym was my second home, and I told her I wasn't going to stop working out there. She accused me of not caring about her feelings one night and wouldn't let me go to bed until I apologized. Apparently she didn't know me that well. I went to bed anyway, only to be wakened by her standing at the end of the bed screaming at me about what a jerk I was.

Then I found out that she had lied to me about her townhouse. There was nothing wrong with it. She had rented it out to a friend and lied to me about the damage. That night I told her I wanted her out of the house as soon as possible. I was afraid she would tear up the place, so I asked her if she could find a place to stay until she found a permanent home, From then on, I was her number one enemy. She informed me that she was going to ruin my career.

Since we were both well-known at the gym, we scheduled our workouts so we didn't run into each other. During the holiday season, Al put on the Christmas party of the year. There was food, booze, and a small gift for each member. It started at seven and ended at eleven at night. As soon as the date was set, everyone was talking about it. Because of the situation with Denise, I decided I would go early and leave early so Denise could arrive at nine and stay till they closed. That way we could both have a good time, without worrying about what the other was doing. I was more worried about her creating a spectacle.

I arrived at seven, and it was a party. More food than at large Sunday buffets, the beer and wine were flowing, and everyone was dressed to the hilt. I ran into a girl I knew and she asked me where Denise was. I told her we were not seeing each other anymore, and had decided to go our separate ways and still be friends. As we continued to talk, Denise came in the door. Of course, she looked like a model off the runway, flashing her big smile and hugging everyone. I looked at my watch and saw that it was only 7:45. Worried about her causing a commotion, I bid the girl I was talking to goodbye and moved over to speak to some of the guys.

About twenty minutes later, the girl I had been talking to told me that she knew the real reason we had broken up. Apparently, Denise had burst into the bathroom and demanded to know what we were talking about. When the girl said it was none of her business, Denise yelled at her, accusing her of trying to go home with me later. Denise went on telling her what a disgusting person I was and how I would do it with anyone. Then she stormed out. I was sorry this had happened, but the girl told me not to worry about it. She was seeing the real Denise and it wasn't pretty. Once again I was warned to watch my back.

Because it was the holiday season, there were parties constantly, and I seemed to be invited to them all. From December 1ˢᵗ to the 24ᵗʰ there was a party every night. I tried to pick and choose which ones to attend because Denise might be there. A detective friend called, saying he had heard we broke up, and asked if he could introduce me to his girlfriend's roommate. I hated blind dates, but what did I have to lose? We had both been invited to a party hosted by the city's medical examiner, so he planned to introduce me to her there. I was a little concerned because Denise might be there, but figured that if I went early, I could get in and out and not see her.

It was another party to top all parties with plenty of food, booze, and all sorts of crazy stuff going on. I found myself with a group of friends, and of course, they wanted to know what had happened between Denise and me. I always took the high road because I didn't see any sense in causing more trouble. When my friend got there, he was with a crowd. There were multiple women with him and I wasn't sure which one was my date. He spotted me, walked over, and introduced me to Wendy. She had big hair and a great smile. Born in Iowa, she had just moved here, and was living with his girlfriend over on 64th Street off Atlantic Avenue. I knew the area well because it was near the Seashore State Park entrance. She told me she was staying right next to it. I ran at the park a lot. Wendy looked at the group, said she needed a cigarette, and the next thing I knew they had gone outside to smoke. I knew it was my time to leave and headed out the door.

Another one of my strict rules about the women I dated was that they couldn't smoke. I couldn't stand smokers. I had to put up with them all the time in the police department, and that was enough. I wasn't interested in a smoker. I would have bet money that Wendy and I might be friends, but life has a way of throwing you curveballs.

Before I start talking about Wendy, I need to bring you up to speed on other things that were going on in my life. After Denise split, I started working on me again. During our year together, she had taken a lot of me out of me if that makes any sense. I had stayed in the relationship way too long because of the physical aspect of it, but I needed to be me again. Work was going well, but I needed to find myself again.

A running buddy of mine from work, Bruce Dutcher, asked me if I would like to do the New York Marathon. Every runner wants to do the NYM. Bruce had grown up there and his parents still lived twenty minutes from the city, so we could stay with them, cutting the cost down to just the marathon entry and gas. I was in. At that time, they used a lottery system to get into the marathon, and we were mutually surprised when both our applications were pulled. This gave me my next mission and I was focused. My goal was just to train for the marathon.

Next, I needed something to boost my manhood. I had been driving a Ford Contour, a little four-door and decided it was time to man up, so I went and purchased a Ford F150 truck. It was a beauty. It had all the comforts of a luxury car but still had testosterone written all over it. It was probably not the smartest thing to do, but it did help my ego. I was feeling better about myself in everything but relationships. Nothing new there.

Dating services were the new thing so I decided to join one, even though we viewed them as a bit of a joke. The very next night at another Christmas party I ran into the detective and his girl-friend again. They asked me what I thought of their friend, Wendy, and I told them I did not date smokers. I really did not see her fitting into my world. They were looking for someone to show her around because they had helped her move to Virginia. They mentioned that they knew I was getting over Denise, and I told them I would think about it. I said I would meet her for coffee and see how it went. I did not tell them I had signed up for a dating service. Besides, I was still meeting other women out with the gang, so if Wendy was not the best girl ever, coffee was going to be it.

I had always been (and always will be) a music lover and movie junkie. My parents raised me on the classics so I grew up knowing Mozart, Bach, Beethoven, and Strauss. I always got straight A's in music class. Of course, this made me look like a sissy at the time. Because of being in the band and orchestra, I went from classic orchestra into more modern music of which my dad did not approve. Once I began listening to rock 'n roll, I went downhill musically in my parents' estimation. If I could have had long hair and worn sandals, I would have, but I couldn't. I was living on a farm and going to a small school in Texas. I would have gotten my butt beat. I expanded from Blood, Sweat, and Tears and the Beatles to other groups like Creedence Clearwater Revival, Moody Blues, James Gang, Pink Floyd, and Led Zeppelin—all devil music by my parents' standards. As I mentioned before, I also liked movie soundtracks.

I often went to the drive-in with my parents. My dad loved war movies and at the drive-in, we got to see a doubleheader. I saw *PT-109* with Cliff Robertson and *Merrill's Marauders* with Jeff Chandler. In Glen Rose, we also had a small movie theater open on Fridays and Saturdays. John Wayne, Rock Hudson, Gregory Peck and Kirk Douglas were always the favorites there. I remember seeing *Giant, The War Wagon, The Wild Bunch* and *Marooned,* a flop of a movie but with special effects that made me want to go to space. Most of the movies were clean (maybe not *Giant*), but come the weekend, everyone went to the movies. One of my all-time favorites was *To Kill a Mockingbird.* Even though it had been made in 1962, they brought it back for a special showing. Seeing movies was my way of escaping my home life. I dreamt of one day being an actor or singing in a musical. One of my favorites was *The Music Man.*

I had a bunch of movie-going quirks. I had to get there early because I had to sit in specific seats: I wanted the last row in the middle. That was my seat. If I could not get it, I knew I was not going to have a great movie experience. I also liked to see all the previews so I could decide which movies I could look forward to. I was known as the movie critic of the police department. I knew the directors, producers, and had my favorite movie composers, James Horner, Danny Elfman, and Hans Zimmer. I could tell a composer just by listening to the movie preview. Back then, we did not have a new movie out every week, so I saw just about every movie out.

Every Christmas I went to a movie. A new one always came out on Christmas. Since my family did not get together on Christmas, it was a good day for me to go to the movies. On Christmas in 1997, *The Postman* with Kevin Costner was coming out. I had heard it was his next *Dances with Wolves* and I could not wait to see it. The composer was James Newton Howard, another one of my favorites, so I was geeked out for this movie. As a promise to my detective friend and his girlfriend, I asked Wendy if she wanted to see a movie on Christmas day. She was alone and I was alone, and this would give me an opportunity to check her out.

I called Wendy and asked her, and she said sure, why not. I explained my movie eccentricities: how I needed to be there early, have my favorite seat, liked the previews and enjoyed the first showing of the movie in a theater. She said she was fine with my idiosyncrasies. I told her I would meet her at the theater. I didn't want any smoke in my new truck, so I gave her directions and she said fine, she'd meet me there. I breathed a sigh of relief. I had met my obligation. I had invited my buddy's girlfriend's roommate out. I was sure I would not like her, so we would have one safe date and be done. What could go wrong with a movie, right?

Christmas came and I was excited about the movie. As I got ready, Wendy called and asked me to pick her up. She was new in town, and afraid she might get lost. I tried to give her clear directions instead, but I could hear the panic in her voice. This was before having a GPS in our phones, so I went and got her right away. It occurred to me that I might miss a couple of the previews, but figured we would make it on time for the movie. Because of heavy traffic, it took me longer than expected, and by the time we got back to the theater, the movie had already started. I was a little pissed but there was always another showing. On the way, she told me she liked comedies. I noticed there was a new comedy getting ready to show, so we ended up seeing *Mouse Hunt* with Nathan Lane and Lee Evans as our first movie together instead of *The Postman* with Kevin Costner.

While waiting for the movie to start, she told me a little bit about herself. She was single and had never been married. She had worked for a startup phone company and bought stocks from the company. The company had done well, and her stocks doubled. She wanted to live near the water, and when her good friend moved to Virginia, she decided she was tired of the cold winters in Cedar Rapids. She had cashed in her stocks and sold her house and moved too. She was close to her mom, Wanda, and the move was hard on them both, but she talked to her each morning. I wondered if her mom had something to do with me having to go and get her. You know how moms can be. Wendy made it perfectly clear she was not looking for a relationship. She had just escaped a bad one and was more interested in getting herself back together. Sounded good to me. I was not looking for a relationship with a smoker, so it was perfect. She said people had told her about me, that I had a couple of brothers on the police department. She asked me about my family and why I was not spending time with them on Christmas. I told her it was a story for a different time.

I planned to get through the movie, take her home, and call it an evening. Now the movie opens up with a funeral. It's raining and there is no one even attending. While they are taking the casket up the steps of the church, they drop it. It slides down the steps, hits the road, breaks open and the corpse flies out. Wendy let out a snort, a scream, and a big laugh that startled me. Everyone in the theater (six people) turned and stared. I just shrank down in my seat. Thank goodness this was a short movie. I couldn't wait to take her home and drop her off.

After the movie I took her back to her apartment. Seeing that the gate to Seashore Park was open, I told her I ran there all the time. She said she had not been there yet. Since the weather was good, I asked her if she wanted to take a walk. As we followed the path, I told her about my dysfunctional family and why we did not get together on Christmas. My brothers had other families they wanted to be with on Christmas; we met later in the week. It was a Howard tradition to never have Christmas on Christmas Day. We had a pleasant enough afternoon, but then she lit up a cigarette and I decided one date was enough. When we said goodbye, I left without making any further plans.

Work was going better than I expected. We were still having some disputes between OSSI and the IS department. Programs kept crashing and they were loading updates every day. I saw it as an opportunity to tailor the programs to our needs, but IS saw it as a delay. The IS team and the PD team were getting along much better. Fewer issues were raising their heads, the conversions were going well, and life was good at work. I was at the gym almost three times a week, found some great workout partners, and avoided Denise like the plague. I knew her schedule so that was easy.

I got really serious about my marathon training. I cut alcohol to one night a week and that was usually with the gang, of which Wendy had become a permanent member. Over time, I began to spend more and more time with her. Eventually I felt I could overcome my aversion to her smoking because of her charismatic demeanor. Pat had smoked when we first met and quit after five years. Pat's smoking had caused many arguments and had been the reason I did not date smokers, but every time I had an opportunity to be near Wendy, I wanted to be with her more.

I was still with the dating service and seeing several other girls on the side. Wendy would ask me about my dates. I thought that was strange, but she always said she was not ready to date anyone yet. I just took it that our friendship was growing, but nothing more. I often called her after a date to talk. The dating service sent me a profile for a possible date. I would read it, and if I was interested, give them a call. Sometimes I got turned down, and they were often surprised I was not mad. Several of the ladies I talked to told me that most of the men from the dating service demanded they went out with them, as if it were an escort service. Eventually I realized the sham in the service. Most of the ladies had definitely lied on their profiles. One said she was a runner. When I met her, I could tell she was not into physical fitness. When I asked about running, she told me she had bought some shoes and was thinking about starting. As soon as my dates ended, I called Wendy and asked her to have a beer with me. Then I would tell her about the night.

While out with the gang one night, I ran across a girl I had dated when Pat and I had first broken up. She was rich and bought me a lot of nice clothes. While we were together, I had gone away on a business trip and got home a day early. I drove by her house to surprise her and saw another police officer's personal car there. I called her, said I got back early and would like to go out. She said she was sick. I could tell by her voice she was lying. The next day I confronted her. She told me she liked police officers. While I was away, she did not think I would mind her having another one over. I wasn't interested.

When she saw me, she came right over to us and pushed her way to me. She told me she had changed and wanted me to come over to her house. When I got there, it was full of pictures of us when we were together surrounded by lit candles. It almost looked like a shrine. She said she was finished with chasing police officers and wanted only me. I explained that I was not ready for a permanent relationship; I was not seeing anyone seriously right now. I appreciated the offer, but she needed to give me some time. Then she got mad and told me to get out of her house. I called Wendy and we got together and had another couple of beers.

Wendy and I seemed to always hang out together—with friends, the gang, and I even took her to meet my mom. Everyone had the same question. What was wrong with her? I could not give them an answer. She was perfect in so many ways, but she smoked. She had the perfect disposition, a great smile, and she was very pretty. When we were hanging out, I'd tell her my plan to go out with another woman, and she would tell me to call her if I needed someone to talk to later. We met at least twice a week over beers, and talked about what was going on in our lives. But there was no physical interaction between us.

On New Year's Eve I stopped by her house. She had been drinking with the owners of the apartment above her. I was on my way to another party and just wanted to wish her a Happy New Year. She was quite intoxicated and we started making out, but I knew it was the alcohol speaking so I put a blanket on her and walked out the door. Later she told me she appreciated that I did not take advantage of her.

In late January of 1998, Denise called. She had bought me a Christmas gift and wanted me to come and get it. I did not think it was a good idea, but she turned on the charm. I was weak and work had been rough the last couple of days, so I conceded. I stayed the afternoon. She cooked dinner. While we were eating, she told me her psychiatrist thought it would be a good idea if the two of us went to a session together. She thought we could work out our problems and get back together. Her psychiatrist wanted to help us. I was shocked, and just a little bit scared. This whole get-together had been a setup, and I had fallen right into it. I told her I would think about it, got my things, and left. A day later I told her it was a bad idea. I was not going to any psychiatrist and did not plan on getting back together. She started screaming at me, threatening to ruin me as before. She called me a devil. One day, she said, I would regret not being with her. I hung up, cursing myself for getting back into this mess. I called Wendy and told her I really needed another beer.

Denise called that night around ten and told me her therapist said it was okay for her to call me and have me come over and console her. I could not believe what I was hearing. I told her I was not coming over. She insisted that it was okay. She was so lonely. I asked for the therapist's number. I wanted to check with her about this. She gave me the number and I called. A woman answered the phone. I explained who I was. Immediately she told me it was not ethical for me to call her about a patient. I could feel the tension, so I told her the situation and she warmed up. She told me it was *not* a good idea for me to see Denise, and that if I needed anything else to give her a call.

I told Denise what the doctor said, and she started talking about killing herself. I had been around her enough to know this was just another attempt to get me to come over, so I went into crisis ne-gotiation mode and talked to her for about two hours. I told her I would call her in the morning. She needed to get some sleep, and I made her promise she would be there in the morning for my call.

She said she would. Toward the end of the call, I felt better about the situation and bid her goodnight.

At 2:30 in the morning my phone rang. I didn't recognize the number, but answered anyway, thinking it might be work. One of Denise's friends screamed at me and called me all kinds of names. Denise had called her, saying she had taken a bunch of pills and was going to kill herself—all because I would not go over there. She asked me where Denise lived, so I gave her the address and told her not to call me again. I was getting ready to call dispatch when my phone rang again. It was a corporal that worked with my brother, asking me if I knew Denise as they were at her residence. I told him I did, and asked about the attempted suicide. He said it looked staged.

Several calls had already reached them that night. When the paramedics arrived, the door was locked, and there was no response. They got inside with the help of police and found pills on a table and a nude "non-responsive" female on the bed. As soon as they started working on her, she came around. She told the paramedics she had taken a particular number of the pills, but they told her that if she had, she would have been unconscious by now. On the way to the hospital, she wanted to speak to the police supervisor. She made sure to tell him that she would not have done what she had if "she could have just killed me." She spoke of me with venom. I thanked him for letting me know, and they left a copy of the report on my desk.

Even though that was not the end of Denise, it was the end of Denise and me. She often called my office at night, continually threatening that I would get what I deserved—and soon. When I told her I was going to get a restraining order and make sure her bosses knew about it, she stopped calling. She never really talked to me again.

I thought that kind of craziness was over, but one night I was out and met a girl I had known many years before. Our relationship was purely physical. She had her crowd and I had mine, and every once in a while we spent a night together. This was one of those nights.

The next morning, I opened my front door and found clothes all over my porch. I immediately recognized them as those one of the police groupies bought for me. Thinking she had just left them there for me, I picked up a shirt and found it was shredded. In fact, all of them had been shredded with a knife and left on the porch. I quickly went to my friend's car to see if it had been damaged. It just had pieces of paper full of insults about me taped to it. It seemed I had a problem here.

At the office, my voicemail was full of hateful calls from her too. I left her a message, warning that if she tied up our phone lines again with such hate-filled messages, I would be forced to charge her. She showed up at the house later that night and told me that she would never call me again. I wished her the best, closed the door, put my gun away, and thought, *I really need to change the women I am with. This was getting way too crazy.*

Of course, I called Wendy and asked her if I could come over. When I got there, she was bouncing off the walls with excitement. She had landed a job and was starting the first of March. She wanted to go back to Cedar Rapids before then to visit her mom. She did not know when she would have another opportunity for a while. I thought, *Cedar Rapids, February, it has got to be cold up there. No way would I want to go there in late February.* I was right about that too. Wendy said it was snowing and temperatures were right around zero at night. It warmed up to a whopping twenty degrees during the day though! Then she asked me a question I will remember forever: Would I like to go with her, and meet her family and friends? It would be fun. One part of my brain said, *Hell, no!* and the other said, *You just had two crazy women threaten to harm you, things are going well at work, maybe you could use a break. And you like Wendy. This will give you time with a sane woman who doesn't want anything from you.* Then I heard my mouth say, "Sure, why not? Sounds like fun." I did not sleep well that night.

I got the time off and we decided to take my truck with the understanding that there would be no smoking. Her mom had already figured out the time we should get there and our route. If she did not hear from Wendy by then, she said she was calling the state troopers. She did not know or trust me and suspected I might hurt Wendy and leave her on the side of the road. She'd never know how often I was tempted to leave her on the side of the road. She drove me nuts.

Taking a trip with Wendy was a trip. She could not sit still. She sang (and danced) with the radio and wanted to stop at every Cracker Barrel. Then there were the constant smoke breaks. At rest stops on I-80, it was brutally cold. I'd run into a restroom and when I would come out, she'd still be smoking. I would jump in the truck and turn up the heat full blast to warm up. Wendy would finish her cigarette, put it in the trash, and head back to the truck. I would lock the doors and tell her to air out. Being as good natured as she is, she would stand in front of the truck and dance around to clear the smoke. Even though I thought about keeping her out of my truck, I was falling in love with her crazy antics. I loved her company.

We drove straight through. I had never seen so much snow in all my life. There were large semis on the shoulder of the road, one nearly covered in snow. There were cars in parking lots completely buried in snow. Wendy told me that some people just left their cars until the snow melted, and that could be weeks. I wondered how people lived like this. I knew why I loved Virginia.

I took quick naps while Wendy drove. I did not trust her driving so did not sleep very long. I did not trust the conditions. After almost twenty hours on the road, we finally made it to Cedar Rapids. I now understood why Wendy had moved to Virginia Beach. Even though Cedar Rapids was a genuinely nice place to visit, it was just too cold.

I was nothing like Wendy's mother had pictured. Wanda was a deeply religious woman that worried about her daughter's lifestyle. While there, she told me that Wendy had a habit of picking up "strays": guys that did not have homes and had told Wendy some sad story. In the end, Wendy got hurt by them—emotionally or even physically. Wanda did not get into the specifics, but alluded to the fact that Wendy's childhood had been difficult. Her father left Wanda for another woman and then died. She thought Wendy was mad at the world. While taking all this in, I saw there was a Wendy I did not know. I wondered if she had also been abused as a child. I planned to spend our twenty-plus hours on the way back to Virginia digging a little deeper into her life.

Eventually Wanda liked me. I was well-dressed, polite, and good-looking. I had a great job in which I was invested, drove a nice truck, owned a nice house, and had a great smile. I was the best-mannered of all the Howard Boys. Heck, even my credit score was excellent. Little did she know of the demons I fought every day, and how they could turn on her daughter as they had on others so many times before. My private life was a mess. I was running from two women at the time, and her daughter was right in the middle of it. I fit the description of one of those "strays" Wendy was known to pick up. I just appeared to be more together on the outside.

My youngest brother, Jeff, had moved to Minneapolis, four hours from Cedar Rapids. Since it had been years since I had seen him, Wendy decided we needed to drive up and visit. On the way I told Wendy every little dirty secret about myself. It was a true confession; I did not leave anything off the table. I do not think I had ever told anyone everything; but for some reason instead of me feeling ashamed of what I had done, I felt a relief. I kept trying to read her body language, watching for signs of rejection. She just listened and did not judge. I even told her I was an asshole and always hurt the ones I loved. That did not faze her one little bit.

She answered by confessing herself. I could see that we were two messed-up people. She had been abused as a child and a teenager by a relative. She had just as many issues as I did. Even though she seemed like one, she was not a wallflower. She liked to party just like me. By the way I handled myself, she had considered me a stuffed shirt at times, but we both learned a lot about each other on that four-hour drive.

We spent the night with my brother and his wife and the next day went to the Mall of America. When we drove back to Cedar Rapids, we spent the next four hours going over everything we had talked about before on the trip up. We were both trying to make sure we were on the same page. I wanted to take the relationship up a notch, but with no commitments, of course. Wendy did not run from the offer. Deep in my mind, I knew that if we moved to the next level, I would probably ruin it. I had a way of doing that. As usual, I still had other options on the side. I was not ready to settle down. Wendy said the same. We agreed to a friends-with-benefits arrangement, which I knew was the kiss of death. Therefore, I started planning my exit strategy.

Meeting Wendy's family was also a trip. Her older sister, Crystal, was critical of me and always right on every subject. She and I would never get along. I was pleasant and polite to her because of Wendy. Her sister wore the pants in the family and controlled Wendy's brother-in-law, Brent, like he was an unfortunate necessity. He had a decent, stable job and provided for Crystal and her two daughters from a previous marriage. Brent was easy-going and very naïve.

While Brent and I were sent on an errand to pick up something from a local grocery store, he pointed out the new police station. I asked him where the old station was and he did not know. He'd never been there. Crystal bragged about how Brent had been a thirty-something virgin when they met. She had told the family she was going to break him in. Crystal also habitually put Wendy down. She commented that she was not streetwise and was easily manipulated. Whenever she said that, she gave me dirty looks. She clearly did not know her sister. This family was nothing like Pat's. I would not be buying a time-share with them.

I met Wendy's foster-brother Scott too. Scott knew of Wendy's past bringing home "strays" because he was one. He had been adopted by the family. When I first met Scott, I liked him, even though I did not agree with his lifestyle. He walked around me like he was sizing me up. It was almost like the alpha male sniffing a new male in the herd. He was very skeptical of me, but I could tell he was the smartest, streetwise, of the group. Wendy and I went out with Scott and his life partner, Mike, for drinks. While there, Scott interrogated me with perfect precision; it was the kind of questioning in which one wrong answer would show weakness. Scott kept that watchful eye on me, waiting for that mistake. I did not give him one; in fact Scott, Mike and I became good friends. If Wendy and I broke up, Scott, Mike, and I could continue to be friends.

Before we left, Wanda pulled me aside and told me she appreciated the fact that I was taking care of Wendy. She was going to pray for us. Wanda reminded me of the kind of mother that died a bit each time Wendy left. I promised I would keep an eye on Wendy, but in the back of my mind I knew that one day Wendy would be calling her mom and telling her what a jerk I was. Twenty minutes into the twenty-hour drive back to Virginia, I was already starting to panic, wondering how I was going to get out of this relationship. I knew that once Wendy really knew me, she would leave me. Screwed-up relationships had been scattered along the way for as long as I could remember.

During the trip home, Wendy gave me many reasons to tell her that I just wanted to be friends and nothing more. She could not get comfortable in the truck and kept moving around. At one point she had both of her knees on the floorboard of the truck with her chest and head on the seat trying to get comfortable. Then there were the shot glasses.

Cracker Barrel had a shot glass with the state seal on it in every state. On our way to Cedar Rapids, she bought one, so she was on a mission to find a shot glass from every state on our way back. This required stopping at every Cracker Barrel along I-80. I wanted to get back home, but every time we saw a Cracker Barrel sign, Wendy begged to pull over, so she could see if they had a shot glass of that state. The first couple of times was cute, but it swiftly became annoying. Do you know how many Cracker Barrels there are between Cedar Rapids and Virginia Beach? Too many. Plus it was hit-or-miss on the shot glasses. Many didn't even have them. After three misses, I lost my temper. The clerk behind the counter saw the problem and gave us a list of the phone numbers for all the Cracker Barrels in the country according to their exits on the interstate. That list saved our relationship. When we saw an exit sign for a Cracker Barrel, Wendy called to see if they had the shot glasses. If not, we continued down the highway.

After we got home, the craziness seemed to go away. Work was good, I was seeing a couple of different women, and Wendy was right there when I just needed a place to recoup. Her roommate had moved in with the detective friend, so she had her apartment to herself now. It was nice too. It had lots of extra amenities: pool and hot tub and location right next to the entrance to Seashore State Park. A friends-with-benefits arrangement never looked so good.

Wendy said she wanted to stop smoking, but needed my help. She knew I was into working out and good health. She wanted to know if there was a supplement she could take that would help her when she quit. She had one last smoke fest with one cigarette after another, and then she was done. Not only did she quit, she also lost weight and started to go to the gym with me. I introduced her to Al at Flex Gym and he fell in love with her. He wondered what was wrong with me. Why was I not grabbing her up?

I had explained to Wendy that physical fitness was my religion, but I do not think she got it. One day at the gym she kept talking and talking until I finally looked at her, and told her to be quiet. I was in my house of worship. No talking was allowed. We stopped working out together shortly after that, but Al took over and kept her in the gym.

All this time, I was also training for the marathon. Wendy wanted to bike ride with me on the long runs, so I bought her a beach cruiser. She rode while I ran the long runs for the NYM. She also carried my drinks and sang to me along the way, which always cracked me up. Sometimes she just talked to me about things she wanted to do, and places she wanted to go. She understood though that once we got to a certain distance, she could only ask me yes or no questions. It was the best training I had ever done for a marathon.

We once talked about her moving in. She did not know if she wanted to stay at the apartment by herself. The owners had rented the house above the apartment to two young fighter pilots at Oceana and they were always having parties. It was becoming too busy and loud up there. When I invited Wendy to move in as a roommate, I found out our arrangement meant more to her than it did to me. It was getting harder and harder for her to listen to my stories about spending time with other women. She felt like she was in second place, and it was starting to weigh on her. Wendy meant a lot to me, so I had to think about where I was going with our relationship.

One night at a local grocery store, the "L" word slipped out of my mouth. I was telling her how much she meant to me and I told her I loved her. I don't know how it happened. I looked up and tears were streaming down her face. At that moment, I thought that maybe I had finally found the woman that would save me. As much as I wanted it to be true, I knew me; and so far, nobody had ever been able to save me. What would make her any different?

CHAPTER 14

Things started moving faster with Wendy and me. Maybe a little too fast. I met Wendy in December of 1997 and by April 1998 we were a major item. We were the talk of the town. People invited us all over the place like we were rock stars.

More than anything I loved Wendy's free spirit. She would do anything for the fun of it. She wanted to go to any place I had ever been and experience it with me. We hung out with all the popular crowds, went to all the popular parties, and she was loved by all. I never met a person that could charm others like she did. I kept searching for that one fault that would push me out of the relationship, but couldn't find it. Someone would suggest we go to the beach at two in the morning and watch the sunrise, and Wendy would be the first one to sign up. She was afraid of nothing.

She was also one hundred percent behind me in any dream I had. Every time I thought about taking a chance on something when I had been with Pat, it put her in a tailspin. When I had wanted to buy a house in Virginia Beach, Pat did everything she could to discourage me. Not Wendy. She would ask if I was able. If I was, I should go for it. The sky was the limit. She loved to show affection and never turned away an opportunity to be intimate. She would do anything for me.

Her mother and one of her nieces came to Virginia Beach right before the 4th of July. Since beach traffic was at its all-time worst,

I invited Wendy and her family to stay with me. Every time we hugged or kissed, her niece would tell us to get a room. At one point, we went to a mall to get out of the heat. I joked around that we needed to go to a jewelry store and act like we were buying a diamond for our engagement just to get a reaction out of her niece, but so many things fell in place that day that I ended up really buying one. That afternoon, I proposed to Wendy. Her mom started praising God for the union. (I told Wendy I wasn't interested in her mother's God and would appreciate if she didn't push her religion on me.)

Wendy's mom was a charismatic Christian. She believed in speaking in tongues and that the Holy Spirit came into people's bodies and made them do strange things. I had nothing against Wanda, but every time she lifted her hands and started going into a trance, I asked Wendy to ask her mom to stop. The evening I proposed we planned to go out to dinner to celebrate. As I walked past the spare bedroom, I saw Wanda on the bed, rolling back and forth with her hands up, praising God. At first I thought she was having a seizure. I told Wendy, and she yelled at her mom to knock it off because she was scaring me. She quit and apologized, but she couldn't contain her excitement over our marriage. She truly felt that God had put us together. I was happy that God could be happy with our plans but to me, God had nothing to do with this relationship. I took care of my own life.

On the 4th of July we drove to Windsor, Virginia where my mom and stepfather lived. Wendy couldn't wait to tell my mom the great news. My real reason for going to my mom's house was that the school across the street had the best fireworks in the area. Telling my mom about our engagement was not on the top of my list. After the way she had treated all my ex-wives, I was sure she wouldn't be any different about Wendy. I expected to leave her house that night frustrated and angry. However, I was pleasantly surprised. Mom was so friendly toward Wanda and Wendy that I felt uncomfortable. She positively gushed to Wanda about how much she loved Wendy. She said she was really happy for both of us. Wanda exploded about how it was "God's plan" and all the years she had been praying for the right person for Wendy, and it had finally happened. Now not only was her other daughter married to a really nice guy, but Wendy too had found one that was safe, kind, and stable.

Bob made friends everywhere and was his usual charming self. He just laughed and agreed with everything Wanda said. Mom, on the other hand, continued to smile and nod her head like she couldn't agree more, but I just knew something was up. I was just waiting for the other shoe to drop. But it didn't. Instead we had a night of celebration, great fellowship, and fireworks. I just couldn't get over how friendly my mom was being. When we left, she hugged everyone. On the way home, Wendy and her mom were talking about how great the night was. *Hmm, maybe Mom had turned a corner and changed. Maybe she really was happy for me.* Still, I had that nagging feeling that this was all a show for Wanda and Wendy. Later she would share her true feelings.

It didn't take long for my mother to come back to her real self. Once Wanda returned to Iowa, the wedding planning began. Wendy and Wanda decided the wedding would take place in Cedar Rapids, as all of Wendy's friends and family lived there. Because it was her first wedding, Wendy wanted it to be big and perfect. I kept telling her we should save the money, and invest it in our honeymoon, especially with my history. She thought I was funny and continued planning the big event. I saw how important it was to her, so I conceded. I really didn't care. This was my third marriage. I was simply hoping it would be better than my last two. I told Wendy to let me know the day and time, and I would be there in the tux she had picked out for me.

I was home alone with the day off when my mom called. She started the conversation with my name—my first clue that something was up. If my mom just wanted to talk, she typically began with: "Watcha dooo-ing?" It was her way of letting you know she really didn't have anything to say, and just called to talk. But this call was different. She began with "Jimmy." It was always the precursor to a shot across the bow. She went on: "The other night Wanda said it was God's plan for you and Wendy to get married, but you do know that Satan has a plan too, right?" I asked her what she was trying to say. "Well," she began, "if I had a daughter, I wouldn't want her to be marrying a guy like you." I stupidly asked her to repeat that, which she did with relish. Then she added, "This relationship and the wedding were the Devil's plan, not God's." Thanks, Mom!

And there was the woman I knew so well. I had wondered the night of the 4th if there had been an alien abduction, but no. She was back. I took some time to answer. I didn't want to explode on her or hang up. Instead, I demanded an explanation. She tried to backpedal a little by saying she knew I would take that "the wrong way." I asked how I was supposed to take it. But Mom didn't miss a beat. She said that "if she had a daughter, she would want her to marry a Christian, and I wasn't a Christian." Still reeling from the attack, I continued to press her about her original statement about Satan's plan. She told me I was taking it out of context, and I wondered aloud how I was supposed to take it any other way. I fired back with a heated defense: I was a nice guy; I had a good job; I had never, ever hit a woman, not even when I worked the street; I didn't gamble or drink as much as others. Most mothers would be happy to have their daughters marry a guy like me. At that moment, Wendy walked in. She could feel the tension, and had heard my raised voice from outside.

Mom backed up. This conversation wasn't going the way she had planned. She knew she had thrown the first punch, but instead of folding, I had punched right back, so what now? She did what she always did. She changed the subject. "Why did I want to marry someone so much younger than me?" Wendy was thirteen years younger. I asked her if she wanted grandchildren. Wendy wanted children and so did I, so her age was perfect. I don't think my mom was prepared for that. It blindsided her. She wanted more grandchildren. She was quiet on the other end. After a few minutes, she realized that this wasn't going her way, so she told me she would pray for us and hung up.

I got off the phone and told Wendy about the conversation. Wendy erupted. It was the first time I had ever seen Wendy that upset, and it wasn't pretty. This was the first time she saw evidence of the difficult relationship I had with my mom, and she didn't appreciate it. She said it was none of my mother's business, and she was no longer invited to the wedding. I realized it was going to take a few minutes for Wendy to calm down. I was wrong. It actually took a few *hours* for Wendy to put my mom back on the invitation list; but for the first time, I had seen a side of Wendy that concerned me. I put this flare of anger in my folder and hoped I wouldn't ever see it again.

Events really started moving faster then. I didn't have a chance to catch my breath. Even so, I was worried about my past. After seeing Wendy's anger, I was concerned that I was going to use that as my reason for building an exit strategy. How long would it take before I began to look for another relationship on the side as I had in the past? Then Wendy became that charming, let's go have fun, and forget about your mom person again, and I relaxed. I was back to loving someone that wanted to push me to be my best. It was so refreshing to have someone that laughed at all my jokes, shared my dreams without hesitation, and jumped at anything I asked her to do. Every time I said let's go, she grabbed the car keys, and we were out the door.

It was now the end of July. Wendy wanted to get married in her mother's church in Iowa, but when she called there, she found that they only had one open date for the rest of the year, and that was one week after the New York City Marathon. Once again her mother claimed this was God's perfect timing, and therefore His plan. How much better could this be? Even though I was concerned about the speed of all the arrangements, I started to think this marriage was really meant to be. Maybe this time it would be different; maybe the third time *was* the charm. Maybe I could break the Howard curse and be happy for once. Joel had done it with Terri, his second wife. It appeared that after John's third marriage, he and Debbie were firm too, so maybe it was my time.

My training runs for the NYCM got longer and longer. Wendy was right there by my side, riding her bike, singing songs and telling me stories. She knew what it took to push me through the long runs. My training went so well that I thought this might be the first marathon in which I wouldn't walk for a part of the route. I always seemed to hit a wall at twenty miles, and have to walk/run the rest of the way. But this time, with Wendy's help, my training was almost perfect. I did a twenty-mile training run and felt so good that I pushed it to twenty-two miles. Wendy continued to carry my drinks and encourage me. I pushed my feelings of being alone in a closet, and closed and locked the door. I wanted to throw away the key, but didn't know how, so I placed it somewhere I could find it if needed.

Wendy spoke to me about inviting my dad. It would be the first time that my dad would be at one of his son's wedding. I thought it was a good idea, but knew exactly what would happen. It would be considered a slap to my mother's face. I had to let it leak out ahead of time. I didn't want her and Bob flying to Iowa and then find out Dad was there, so I told my brother, John. John always spoke to Mom so I knew he would let her know. He did.

As soon as the invitations went out, my stepfather called, questioning our inviting Dad. He told us that they would not be coming if he was there. I told him I was sorry about that, but we were not going to dis-invite him. In fact, the first persons to RSVP were my dad and his wife.

Several weeks later, my mother called. She had talked to her sister about the situation, and her sister said that "Satan himself would not keep her from the birth of a grandchild, a birthday, or a wedding so suck it up and go. If she did not, she would regret it for the rest of her life." As Mom was describing what her sister said I could hear in her voice that she wasn't going to let my dad defeat her again. It was time to put on her big girl pants and face one of her nightmares. I felt proud of her for her decision. It brought me back to those days when she had worked three jobs and pushed me hard, forcing me to look ahead instead of dwelling on the past. I told her that Wendy and I were pleased that she was coming. Wendy and I both felt we had done the right thing in inviting both parents.

Work was moving so smoothly that I felt that I was just in the way. We brought in another sergeant to help with the transition. We were not only moving rapidly toward being Y2K-compliant but we were also moving away from the old way of reporting a crime (Uniform Crime Reporting or UCR) to the new way (National Incident-Based Reporting System or NIBRS). The quickest way to explain the difference between the two is that UCR looked at only the *major* crime committed. For instance, a rape case included kidnapping and also a felony battery because of the physical attack on the victim. In UCR, you only listed the rape without listing the other elements of the crime. NIBRS wanted the officer to list *all* the elements in a crime together, so in one event you could list three crimes. It was a major change from the old way of reporting, and implementing it required plenty of extra help. Sergeant Joe Ribeiro became the lead person for that project. He was a breath of fresh air and would replace me. I could see the light at the end of the tunnel: life after the Systems Development Unit.

Before I knew it, the weekend of the New York City Marathon arrived. This was one of the best marathons ever. Wendy and I rode up to New York with Bruce Dutcher and a workmate of ours, Don Lancaster. Bruce's parents hosted us before and after the marathon. They welcomed us and made us comfortable in their house. You can forget whatever you have heard about New Yorkers being rude and unfriendly; they were anything but. I could see where Bruce got his personality.

Bruce was a great tour guide, and showed us around New York. He told me he used to ride his bike down to the city, and sure enough, he knew every parking spot and street like the back of his hand. His parents let us use their van, and he drove in and out of the traffic like he was a taxi driver. We hit the NYCM's Expo, the World Trade Center, and the Empire State Building in less than five hours. Later that night, I was bragging to his parents about Bruce's NASCAR driving ability in the city. He kicked me under the table. As I saw the concern on his parents' faces, I remembered we had been using their van. I changed my tune a bit. Smiling, I told them he had been a careful and courteous driver. Later he told me that his father knew how aggressive he really was, but we did need to use the van again tomorrow.

The NYCM was the best marathon I ever ran. I had done the Marine Corp Marathon, and thought it was the best, but that was before New York. The people of New York come out in force and cheer you on the whole run. Bruce knew how to work the crowd. Family members stood on the side of the road with signs, cheering on their spouses. They usually had that person's name on their sign. Bruce would run up to them and tell them they had spelled his name wrong. Their expressions were hilarious; we would laugh and continue on, buoyed with the celebration of the NYCM experience. As we ran into Central Park, the leaves were falling which gave you the impression of confetti. Because of Don Lancaster and his uncanny way of making it through New York, Wendy was able to see us twice during the marathon. It was strange; my life seemed to be back in order. Work was going well. I was on top of my religion of physical fitness, a proven fact since this race went so much better than I ever thought it could. Mom's voice was echoing in my head, *Keep looking forward, forget about the past.* Maybe I really did need to let the past go and focus more on the future. Wendy was becoming my best friend. That had never been the case with Donna or Pat.

On the way home from the marathon, we dropped Wendy off at LaGuardia Airport so she could head to Iowa to finish up with the wedding preparations. I had to take care of a couple of things at work and then planned to fly up with my brother, Joel, his wife, Terri, and my Vice and Narcotics partner, Larry Hill and his wife, Louise. My foster brother-in-law Scott was going to take us out for a bachelor party. We told him we wanted to go to the roughest bars in Cedar Rapids. The first one was in Czech Village. They warned us that there were fights there every night. Just like old times maybe? We put on our game face and headed toward the door, only to hear singing. Everyone was swaying back and forth to the music and toasting each other. Joel, Larry and I just looked at Scott. This was the toughest bar in Cedar Rapids? He shrugged. The waitress saw our puzzled looks and explained that there was a soccer game going on and everyone was in a great mood. We ordered the first round of drinks and gave Scott a razzing about how tough the bar was. He promised that the next one would guarantee a fight. Next thing we knew a second round of drinks appeared and the waitress told us they were on the house. I realized at that moment that Cedar Rapids, Iowa was really the America that had been forgotten in the Tidewater Area. The rest of the night we saw bar after bar. There were no strangers; everyone was welcomed like a long-lost friend. I am sure they have their problems, but we saw none that night.

The next day was the wedding rehearsal and the moment of truth: Both Mom and Dad would be there. This would be the first time in twenty-eight years that my parents would be in the same building. Even though I had talked to my dad on multiple occasions, he had never shown any animosity against Mom, but that wasn't the case with her. Every time she mentioned his name, it had an edge. She despised Dad and had never forgiven him for what he had done to us. I understood that. There were moments that day when I felt I had made a big mistake. I made sure Larry and Joel were close by in case one of them produced a weapon. But it didn't happen. They were both cordial to each other, introduced their spouses, and went to their side of the building. I saw this as a good sign, yet every time my dad moved, I found out later, my mom thought he was going to his vehicle to get a gun and come in and kill us all.

The day of the wedding went without a hitch. It was a cloudy November day in Cedar Rapids. After the wedding, Wendy and I went to a hotel in a limousine where the reception was to be held. I remember thinking how cool it was that there were snow flurries and my parents had not killed each other. A strange combination of thoughts, I know, but I was at peace. I had married my best friend, brought most of my family back together, and maybe I really was king of my world. The reception was at the same hotel where most of the guests were staying. Joel and Larry kept running up to their rooms for vodka, and bringing it to my dad. He was having a good time, joking with everyone and even dancing with his wife, Winnie.

Mom and Bob didn't drink, were pleasant to everyone that spoke to them, but kept mostly to themselves. During one of my conversations with her, Mom told me how uncomfortable she was. They were going to leave soon, and go to their room. I begged her to stay, but she reminded me that Dad was crazy. It was only a matter of time when he was going to pull out a gun and start killing people. I realized at that moment that she still lived in the past. We had so many fights about looking forward and not backward, but at this moment, we were back in Glen Rose and that incident was still fresh in her mind, and a big part of her life. I gave her a long hug, kissed her forehead, and told her everything would be okay. She turned and walked away. I know she was hoping I would feel guilty for asking Dad to come. Not this time. I watched her and Bob grab their things and leave. I felt sorry for her at that moment, but not guilty. This was a celebration for Wendy and me, and I was going to enjoy every moment of it.

Wendy and I headed back to Virginia Beach with just enough time to change the winter clothes out of our suitcase to summer clothes on our way to Key West for our honeymoon. We had rented a bed and breakfast two blocks from Duval Street, and there was nothing she didn't want to do. I always wanted to go over to the Dry Tortugas National Park, but never had because of the cost. We were there the first day, and registered to go over to Fort Jefferson.

Every night we walked Duval Street, checking out the local bars and having the time of our lives. Each night our conversation turned to what we would do when I retired. Perhaps we could come down here. I could get in this police department and we could live the island life. Wendy never said no. Wendy fit so well in Key West it was almost scary. No matter where we went, she made friends. No one was a stranger to Wendy.

Once we were walking down Duval, and I wanted to get a drink so we ducked into this bar. As soon as we entered, I realized I was the only heterosexual guy in the place. Wendy felt me tense up, and asked if I wanted to leave, and I told her no. I would get a drink and then go so we didn't offend anyone. While there, a patron looked at us and yelled, "Newlyweds." Without missing a beat, Wendy smiled and asked how he knew. He said he could just tell, and asked where we were from. Wendy fired right back: "Virginia Beach!" It turned out that he was from Richmond. If we had not had dinner reservations, we would have stayed there all night with our newfound friend, talking about Key West and all the craziness.

Our cabdriver on the way back to the airport was from New York. He told us that he and his wife had come down for vacation and instantly fell in love with the Key West lifestyle. They moved down and bought what they could afford, but it hadn't been what they expected. They hadn't really been happy ever after. His logic made sense to Wendy and me, but Florida still had this allure for us. Even so, I did not think we would be down there in the next few years. However, to Wendy the sky was the limit. Anything was possible. Her attitude was refreshing. I felt like my life had finally changed for the better. Perhaps I could lock away my old fears. Being the master of my fate was finally paying off and life was great.

We got back to Virginia Beach and life just kept getting better. Work was going well, Wendy was thinking about getting a job to help financially. I had been using a nutritional product for years, so I had Wendy begin looking at their business model. She was

great at meeting people, but hated to be rejected. She started working for a chiropractor that appeared to be interested in helping us
with the nutritional business, but when that fell apart, I felt she
needed something more. I understood her frustration. We tried the
nutritional business for about six months, but when I saw how it
affected her, I didn't think it was a good fit. We still took the prod-
ucts but the business just wasn't in her blood.

Wendy never said no to anything I wanted to do. I took her to
a boat show because my ex-brothers-in-law were both into boats.
She fell in love with the idea of living on a boat and traveling up
and down from the Chesapeake Bay to the Keys, and anywhere else
we wanted to go. A great deal on a boat came our way and bam, we
were boat owners. One of the marinas in Norfolk catered to police
officers and gave them a huge discount. We helped keep the place
safe in return. We got a slip and when we partied in Norfolk, we
stayed on the boat instead of driving back to Virginia Beach. My
best friend Larry Hill got his boat docked near us, and Wendy and
I started enjoying the boat life.

We joined a boat club, and the next thing we knew we moved
up from a twenty-six-foot-single-engine to a thirty-foot-twin-en-
gine with air-conditioning and room to sleep six people. It became
our home away from home. We worked hard during the week and
partied even harder every weekend. It seemed we didn't have a worry in the world, but the weekends were becoming more and more
of a blur, full of parties, outings, and alcohol. I wasn't complaining
though. Wendy was always the life of the party, and I was the lucky
guy who got to go home with her. Life was good. I thought it was
going to just get better, but there was a dark cloud on the horizon
that neither of us saw coming.

I was on call all night on New Year's Eve 1999 in case Y2K took the whole world down. No drinking, I needed to be completely sober just in case, but the year 2000 came and went without a single hitch. By two o'clock in the morning, we were able to relax. The world had not come to a screeching halt. The new criminal justice system was up and running, so I felt my job was done. When I got back to work on the first of January, I put my papers in for a transfer back to the street. My captain talked to the chief of police, reminding him that he had promised I could go back to the street when we finished the conversion. At first he wanted to say no but a promise was a promise, and Chief High was a man of his word. I requested a transfer to the Second Patrol Division (where I started) and felt like I would end my career there. The transfer was approved and after twelve years with the Systems Development Unit, I was finally back on the street. I soon realized there was no greater job than being a sergeant on the street.

I was given a large sector with ten officers on my platoon. The first corporal I had reminded me of a Vietnam movie. I was like the stereotypical fresh new lieutenant sent to a seasoned platoon complete with a gruff veteran sergeant who had to take the green lieutenant under his wing and teach him how it was on the street. In some ways that was true. Times had changed since I had actually worked the streets, but I had kept my toes in the water with part-time jobs here and there, and staying involved with the Crisis Negotiation Team. (I began as a negotiator and moved my way up to be a team leader, so I hadn't lost all my street smarts in my time away from the streets.) However, I was a little surprised by how much harder the youth in our society had become. A large majority of the crimes, including stolen cars and burglary, were committed by juveniles. There were many calls of kids wreaking havoc. It saddened me. Most of these kids had no idea where their fathers were, and their mothers were either working several jobs or involved in crime too. I decided to focus on my troops and not the street.

I found out quickly that my predecessor had been a micromanager. The officers on the street would not make a decision without calling me first; so at first, I was being bounced around, backing up officers on calls. Once I found out they were afraid of their shadow because of their previous sergeant, I had a squad meeting. I told them they were all over the age of twenty-one and had been sworn in as a police officers. They carried guns and had the power to arrest people, so they needed to grow up and handle their calls without constantly calling me to make sure they were doing it correctly. Three months after my little pep talk, I was called into the captain's office. She asked me what I had done to my platoon. I asked her what she meant. She said they had exploded in the last three months, getting more work done than ever before. I told her I treated them like adults and turned them loose. She told me to keep up the great work.

Several months later my first corporal got transferred and a corporal that I had known for years took his place. George Brehm had worked with my brother and was well-liked by everybody. He was a no-nonsense police officer, but fair with the troops. He was a breath of fresh air, and for the rest of my career, he made me look good. The rule was that corporals and sergeants were not supposed to ride together. I often took my patrol car to the marina, and George would pick me up. Then we would ride around together, check out calls, and reminisce about the old days. We did do some police work too. There were several times when we backed up other officers. It was great being a patrol sergeant. When George was off and I was working the three-to-eleven shift I would connect with another friend, Russel Grimes, and we would travel around the district. Russel was also a sergeant so we could do just about anything we wanted without anyone saying anything to us.

Once there was a bad accident at Little Creek Road and Shore Drive, so they called for a supervisor and someone to assist in processing the accident. Traffic was backed up. I headed toward the scene, expecting another supervisor would get there first, but I was first. Since several officers looked to me for direction, I started barking out orders. Russel pulled up and asked me if I knew what I was doing. I walked over to his car, leaned in, and told him I didn't, but asked if I looked good. I looked marvelous, he said. That was all I needed to hear. I might not know exactly what I was supposed to be doing, but I looked the part. Life was good as a street sergeant.

At home Wendy and I hit a snag. We both wanted children. We had talked about it and decided we would wait five years and then start trying. Even though we had only been married for two, I could tell she really wanted to get started on having a family. She explained she had a history of polycystic ovary syndrome (PCOS), a common hormonal disorder. Since she might not be able to have children, she wanted to talk to doctors now so that when the time was right, we could. She went to the doctor and gave me a call. It was almost definite that we would not have any children because of her condition. She was devastated. I told her that the most important thing was that we had each other. We would just live our life as boat people and travel the world. She liked the idea, but she also really wanted to have a baby. She told me that the doctors were still running tests. When we were ready, there might be different treatments we could try. I told her I would love her—children or no. Eventually we decided to look at different fertilization methods. The doctors explained that it might take a while for it to take effect, so they started running tests to see which one was the best alternative.

In October of 2000, I hit my twenty-fifth year with the Norfolk Police Department. It felt good to know that I could leave with a full retirement. I wasn't planning on going anywhere but it was nice to have options. With my computer background, I considered working for a public safety software company. I wasn't looking because I was having so much fun in the Second Patrol Division. Wendy got a job with a software company as an event coordinator and was doing really well. I really felt that I had finally made it.

Near the end of October 2000, Wendy's place of employment was going to send her to Las Vegas for a conference. She had to go early to make sure everything was set up and invited me along. We just had to cover my airfare and meals. Sounded like fun. I'd never been to Vegas. We had been to the doctors and they planned to begin fertility drugs when we returned. They noticed her hormones were a little high so they gave her something to help level them out. They told us not to get our hopes up; but with the right treatment, it might be possible that we would be able to have children.

During the setup in Vegas, Wendy noticed that her breasts were really sore. I blamed it on the drugs they had given her to level out her hormones, but it got to get to the point that she slept with a pillow to her chest. If I even came close to brushing up against her, she screamed in pain. The trip went well, but she was still complaining on her way back, so she decided to call the doctor.

She called as soon as we got back, and he told her to come in so they could run some tests. The doctor guaranteed that she wasn't pregnant but they wanted to check to make sure. I was at work when I got a page to call her. When I dialed the number, all I heard was an excited buzz and word "pregnant." I hung up the phone, thinking I had the wrong number. I called Wendy again and she asked me why I hung up on her. I told her there was a crazy woman on the other end, screaming she was pregnant, and I thought I had the wrong number. It was her, she said. She was definitely pregnant. The reason her hormones had been high was because she was pregnant: three months. It was great news.

George was sitting at a desk across from me and congratulated me. I told him thanks but at the moment I had mixed emotions. A child was a huge responsibility and I was afraid. And now we would have to curb all our parties on the weekends. We would have to curtail, even cease, the lifestyle I had grown to love. What had happened to my five-year plan? We were only in our second year of marriage. I had to start thinking about being a responsible adult. Was I ready for that? George had two children. He told me that the moment he held his first child, his whole life had changed—for the better. Once I held our little baby, nothing else would matter. I hoped he was right, but I was not as happy about the news as Wendy was.

Later that evening Wendy and I talked about all the things that needed to be done before the baby came. I think she could tell I wasn't as excited as she was. I explained that it had caught me off guard but everything was going to be fine. I had planned to wait for at least a year, so I was surprised. Even so, I was happy that she and the baby were fine. That was all that was important to me. In the back of my mind, I felt that need to run. Apparently the lock on that door I had locked was faulty after all. In a matter of months I would be right back where I had been before, and once again would almost lose everything that was important to me.

W hen the chief transferred me to the Second Patrol Division, he requested that I still attend some of the SDU meetings, especially those that pertained to regional data-sharing. The seven Tidewater cities desperately needed a vehicle to share critical data. All of the cities trusted and valued my opinion because of my work in Systems Development and the successful narcotic's data-sharing project. At one of the regional meetings, a company by the name of Templar demonstrated their data-sharing solutions. OSSI was originally the chosen one for the project, but that had eventually fallen through for many different political reasons. I attended the Templar presentation and the CEO, Floyd Holden and the CFO, Ryan Owens, of the company asked if they could talk to me afterward. They told me that they had heard about my expertise and wondered if I would be interested in working for them. Since I had just reached retirement, I thought this was my opportunity. I told Wendy and she advised me to check them out.

A lot of government projects develop a software system, and once the project is completed, that developed software is out there for the public to use. The software Templar claimed that they had developed had actually been developed in one of those projects. Floyd and Ryan had both worked for the military, saw an opportunity, and jumped at it. They thought they could sell it to police departments with the right people. The key to this system was a data driver called Open Database Connectivity or ODBC. It did not matter what your data was stored in, they could retrieve the data using ODBC, and then share it with other departments over the Internet. I told them we had done the same thing in our Y2K-conversion. They asked Wendy and me to come to Alexandria and discuss the possibilities of me becoming one of the team. Two weeks later, Wendy and I were in Alexandria with the management of Templar wining and dining us.

They put us in a nice hotel near downtown Alexandria and brought me in for an interview. Later that afternoon, they invited us out for drinks and dinner. We talked about their vision of helping law enforcement share data. This was right where I wanted to be. They had received several grants to do two major projects: one right here in Tidewater and the other working with the Florida Department of Law Enforcement (FDLE) and several other Florida agencies. They told me that if they brought me on, I would lead both projects once I learned the ropes. I loved it. Helping police share data so we could catch criminals was the reason I had joined the police department in the first place, and now I was going to help departments around the country.

Wendy and I were invited to their Christmas party where I met most of the employees. Every time I spoke with someone new, they told me that management was talking about how great it was going to be having me with the company. I was going to guide the company to that next level. At the party, Floyd started talking to me about money. Templar was going to offer me a salary three times as much as my pension, putting me at a level I never expected. He told me that there were several things that needed to happen first. I had to retire, sell my house, and move to the D.C. area. The more

I spoke with them, the more I felt that all my hard work over the years was finally paying off. The Norfolk Police Department had been exceptionally good to me, and now it was time to take everything I had learned, and move on. This was my next chapter, and I couldn't wait to get started.

Yet there were things at home that were starting to come unraveled. What if I slipped back into my old ways? The pregnancy had really thrown me for a loop. First I had been told that it was almost impossible for Wendy to have kids and now she was several months pregnant. There were concerns with the pregnancy because of Wendy's pre-existing condition too. We found out that we were going to have a girl, and even though her checkups all came back positive, we were still concerned and that caused more stress. I didn't know how to handle my feelings about this overall. I still wanted to go out with the gang and have fun, but now I needed to get ready for a baby. Even our trip to Alexandria had been stressful. I had wanted to go out and sample some of their nightlife, but Wendy couldn't drink and seemed to tire quickly. I didn't want to go out alone.

Midway through December, Wendy told me she was homesick and wanted to go back to Iowa for Christmas. She did not know it, but her even mentioning leaving me alone on Christmas pushed me into a downward spiral of depression. I was angry that she would even suggest being away from me on Christmas, but this was always how Wendy dealt with stress. She would say she was homesick and plan a trip to Iowa. In several stressful situations, she had done this now. At first it really didn't bother me because I took it that she really was just homesick. This was her first marriage, and

I was sure it wasn't easy. I wasn't the easiest guy to be around and I knew it. But to leave me on Christmas was a huge deal.

When I had left home, I made a decision that birthdays and Christmas would be a big deal in my life because they were never a priority in my childhood. One year my dad actually forgot my birthday. I didn't know until later that he came home after work without a gift. He and Mom had a big fight, and my dad stormed out of the house, driving to a local thrift store to get me a present. After dinner, he joked about it being my birthday, and told me my present was under the seat in his car. Excited, I ran to his car, wondering what could be so cool that he would leave it in the car. I found an executive desk set, still in the paper bag from the store. A pen, mechanical pencil, ruler, stapler, and a stapler remover. I acted like it was the best gift ever because I knew if I complained he might get mad and hit me. It was unbelievable.

Wendy and I had met right before Christmas, and her mother was concerned because I wasn't having Christmas with my family. I explained that Christmas wasn't a big deal to the Howards. I didn't tell her that it was to me though. I had decided that all my birthdays and Christmas would be fantastic—with whomever I was with. And now Wendy was making plans to leave me alone.

It didn't take long before friends of mine were calling, asking if everything was okay. I told them I had to work or I would have gone with her which was a lie. They felt sympathetic and would have invited me for Christmas dinner, but I politely told them no. I was afraid I might show how angry I was that Wendy would leave me on a special holiday. I also knew that this time next year we would have another person in our family. I just buried myself in my work and getting the house ready to sell. If Wendy wanted to run away to Iowa and have the baby, let her go. I was making my own plans, and maybe being alone in the D.C. area wouldn't be as bad as it seemed. Besides, it had always been easy to find someone else to fill the void. I just didn't realize how easy it was going to be.

Because Wendy was leaving, I took a last-minute uniformed part-time job on Christmas Eve. That night a woman made a pass at me. At first, it excited me, but initially I ran away from the woman. We closed the shift that night together and the compliments kept coming. I was able to get away from her that night, but knew that if things didn't improve at home, I now had an alternative. The woman told me she didn't want a lasting relationship—just some married guy that could come over, satisfy her, and go home. The whole time she was said all that, she was smiling at me. I enjoyed the whole show because of the situation between Wendy and me. I knew that if I didn't get away from her though, I would eventually screw up.

I made it home alone, and Christmas morning Wendy called and told me that her coming to Iowa for Christmas was a big mistake. We talked, and I felt better. I was glad I had not gone home with the woman who had been flirting with me, but before the day was over, I was thinking about calling her just to have some drinks. Maybe to help my bruised ego. I knew it would be a big mistake, so I talked myself out of it. Wendy would be home soon, and I could forget about her and move on with my life.

But before Wendy got home, I did call her and had dinner with her. She told me about what she was looking for. If I were ever interested in a casual fling, I had her number and should call. She said all the right things, but I kept her at bay, still hoping that Wendy and I would work everything out and I could prove to myself that I had changed. Maybe I really was ready to really settle down like most of my friends. Most of my married friends had good relationships with their wives and children. I wanted that. Yet my mind kept dwelling on the timing of the pregnancy and Wendy leaving me on Christmas. Now it appeared that I was going to have to handle the move from Virginia Beach to Alexandria by myself too. Had Wendy lied to me about the whole "I might not be able to have children" thing? Maybe she thought this would bring us together. These constant, little whispers assaulted me.

Once again things moved fast. We got our house in Virginia Beach ready to sell and went to Alexandria to look for a new one. We found a townhouse the first day out with the real estate agent. It was close to my new job and in a great neighborhood with a park right across the street, so we made an offer. Later that afternoon, the agent called and told us our offer had been accepted. We put our house on the market in Virginia Beach and had a bid on it the next day. It looked as if things were going our way. My new "friend" faded from my mind. The phone calls were further and further apart, and it appeared my new life would be my focus. Then life got complicated and boundaries obscure, and I got lost again. When I spoke to Wendy about these new issues, she seemed absorbed in her own world. I was at a loss.

I put in my retirement papers for the police department, which would give me fifty percent of my last three years' salary. I was content with that until the new Norfolk city manager announced a new retirement. It would be a higher percentage and retroactive. This meant that if I stayed for one more year, I would go to sixty-two percent instead of fifty. I went to Floyd at Templar and explained the situation, suggesting a solution to do both jobs. I could work Monday through Thursday and then return to Norfolk and work Friday, Saturday, and Sunday and be back to work on Monday morning. Floyd told me he would work with me, but when we had to travel I would have to make other arrangements with the police department. I told him I had no problem with that. Now I had to get the police department to agree to do the same.

I got together all the supervisors that worked my platoon, and gave them an offer: If they would help me with my situation, I would work all their weekends until the new retirement kicked in. Every supervisor was in. I began to work at Templar from Monday through Thursday, and every Thursday evening, I drove to Norfolk and worked a long weekend. After three weeks of working seven days a week, the schedule began to take its toll. The more I worked, the more frustrated I got. I enjoyed my work at Templar, and the police department was treating me well about the extra time off, but my home life was in shambles. I knew this arrangement was hard on Wendy, but I felt like I was doing all the hard lifting. *Why couldn't she just appreciate what I was doing? I was doing it for us, after all.* We didn't communicate and it started to wear on both of us. On one of my trips to Norfolk, the woman I met earlier contacted me. I broke and chose once again to find solace in the arms of another woman.

I started working at Templar in January 2001. It was like nothing I had ever experienced before. The office managers came around once a week and asked what sodas, drinks, or snacks you wanted. Then they went to the store and got them for you. But for all the little perks, they expected you to get your work done, even if it took all night. I was placed in charge of the two biggest Templar projects. The first one, which had been in motion for some time, was the Florida Department of Law Enforcement (FDLE) data exchange. We were working with four departments as the pilot project: FDLE in Tallahassee, Fort Lauderdale Police Department, and Broward and Miami-Dade Counties. FDLE was in the lead and really wanted to see this thing take off. I was introduced to the project lead, Tom, and when he found out that I was newly retired from law enforcement, he was reassured that the project was going to start moving in the right direction. There were plenty of concerns because there had been a lot of hype about the project but nothing to show for it. When I introduced myself to the other project managers from the other counties, I sensed they really didn't trust us, so I could see I had my work cut out for me.

The second project I led was the Hampton Roads Data Exchange Project (HRDE). Since I knew most of the players in this project, there was a comfortable feeling from the outset. Meeting with the two team programmers and the leaders of the project, I asked them to make a list of things they wanted. I would go back to Templar and prioritize the list and we would go from there. It was like coming home, but I had to be careful that I didn't call in sick at the police department and then show up at an HRDE meeting. It became the running joke. Was this a sick day? Did I need a note?

I began to live a double life. One with my "friend" Megan in Norfolk and one with Wendy in Alexandria. It wasn't fair to Wendy. She was going through a pregnancy without me, while Megan had no ties or issues other than making herself available. Wendy and I realized we wanted the same thing, but sometimes just didn't communicate with each other the right way. Most of the time, it would end in a fight which made me want to leave and head back to Norfolk. I would talk about our issues, but Megan would tell me that I needed to stick around, at least until the birth. She told me that holding my daughter for the first time would change my life. (Second time I heard that.) I really didn't think she meant what she was saying. She liked what we had and didn't want anything else. So I just played the cards and lived my double life.

Working at Templar wasn't perfect. I had watched Floyd from a distance while I was learning the ropes. We were going to be traveling a lot together so I wanted to get a good feel for him. It didn't take long to see that he was very opinionated and narcissistic. He wanted everyone to agree with him and know he was the boss. He had asked my opinion on a couple of things, but when I responded he went out of his way to put me down and make it look like I was wrong. I didn't care. I had worked with guys like him before. I would just stand my ground. Later I would go into his office and stroke his ego for a bit, and then we would be good again. He was a pilot in the Air National Guard and anytime I could get him to talk about flying, he beamed. Everyone in the office knew of his issues. At times, I felt sorry for him, but then he would make someone in the office almost cry and I would do my best not to hate him instead.

I noticed that he didn't like the way I got along with the other employees and the project leads. He sometimes put me down in front of them to make himself look better. Most of the leads had worked with him for some time, and they knew what he was like; but I could tell that the more we worked together, the more they didn't like his attitude.

At one point we did a presentation for FDLE and other sheriffs. There were over fifty sheriffs and team leaders in attendance. Floyd did a thirty-minute presentation of the company and the project, and within ten minutes started getting flak from the audience. He was trying to impress them with his intelligence, but they saw right through it. He got more and more frustrated; and the more frustrated he got, the more the audience turned on him. Tom from FDLE saw what was happening and called for a break. He took Floyd aside and explained he needed to just let it go. We should let me go through my part of the presentation now as that was the actual nuts and bolts of what the officers wanted to see.

Floyd sat down, fuming, and mumbled something about the stupidity of the crowd. It wasn't his fault, he said, that they didn't understand his technical mind. He was happy to let me take over. They were just going to crucify me. That did not happen. I started talking in policemen language and showed them what we wanted to do as far as sharing data among the departments. I talked about the information centers and the restricted data they shared with agencies, explaining that we wanted to go one step further: we wanted to share all data. If there was a field contact with a person in Pensacola, we wanted to share that information with Tampa or Miami or any of the county agencies. All information was basically the same, and we had ways of taking it from one agency and sharing with anyone. By the time I finished, the whole room wanted to jump on this project. Tom came up after my presentation and assured them that I was leading it. They were really excited about where this was going. The whole time this was going on, Floyd sat and stared at me like he couldn't wait to rip me apart.

After the presentation, several people spoke with me about ideas, technical questions, and just friendly conversation about my career. Meanwhile Tom had pulled Floyd aside, and was having a private conversation with him. I never found out what was said, but that afternoon Floyd had nothing to say to me. He spoke to the programmers that had come with us, but I could tell his ego was hurt from the conversation with Tom.

On our way back to DC, Floyd smugly informed me that he was going to the American Airlines Admirals Club and too bad that he could not get me in. He said he would meet me at the gate. I knew what was happening, but knowing his type, I knew he would show up at the gate and feel bad about what he had done and offer to buy me a drink on the flight home. Sure enough when he got to the gate, he was in a much better mood (and with a much higher blood alcohol content). He put his arm around me, apologized, and wanted to buy me a drink and talk about the Florida project.

While working on the Tidewater project, I was able to see old friends and spend time with Megan. Our relationship was still one of convenience. One time I took Wendy with me to Norfolk. We were getting together with friends at a party, and I saw Megan across the room. Even though I knew she worked with the City of Norfolk, I didn't realize she knew a lot of the people I knew. I was shocked and petrified when she walked up and said hello, and then introduced herself to Wendy. She complimented Wendy on the way she looked, glowing and pregnant. I told Wendy how I met Megan and the two of them started talking. I didn't understand what was going on, but later Megan told me she wanted to get to know Wendy better. I told her I wasn't sure it was a good idea, but Megan told me not to worry about it.

I should have worried about it. Megan and Wendy became good friends. Every time they would talk, I just knew that something was going to slip out eventually. If I objected too much, I got that don't worry about it look. I tried to keep Wendy and Megan apart, but it was getting harder and harder to keep the lies going. I told myself that as soon as the year was up and I could retire from the department and the Tidewater project was over, I would leave Norfolk and Megan behind. At the time I knew that this was at least a year away, so I just needed to roll with it. It did not get easier.

Work at Templar took a turn that caused even more stress. I started bringing my running equipment with me so I could run in the afternoon. Templar's office was in Old Town Alexandria and I had found a few trails around the area as I was always exploring new places to run. One of the programmers asked if he could run with me and then another programmer asked, and the next thing I knew, we had our own Templar running club. One afternoon when we were getting ready to go out for a run, Floyd came out to my desk and told me he wanted me to learn all the modules of the software. I asked him if I could start on it the next day. He said no. He wanted me to do it now and be ready to explain the modules to him tomorrow. I was surprised by his request until I realized that he was jealous of the "running club" and this clever ruse prevented me from going. I told the guys to run without me. After everyone left, I asked Floyd what was going on, explaining that I had gone to the lead programmer about the documentation on the modules and he wondered why I wanted them. When I had told him that Floyd had requested me to learn them, he quickly said it wasn't necessary and he would talk to Floyd. Floyd exploded on me, saying I shouldn't have asked the lead programmer. I should have found them myself and studied them. He stormed out of the office, cussing as he walked out the door. For the next couple of days, Floyd avoided me.

We were to do a conference call with FDLE on the project so I went to the lead programmer and asked him if he had anything for me to report. He gave me a list of reasons why the project was behind and all of them were FDLE's fault. I started going down the list with Tom and every time I pointed out something that they needed to get done so we could move along, Tom told me it was done. They had already relayed the information to the lead programmer. After the third one like this, I got the lead programmer in the room with me on the call too. He maintained that he was the cause of the delay. He told Tom he was sorry for being behind, that he would try to do better next week. After the lead programmer left, there was an uncomfortable silence between Tom, the other people on the call, and me. I apologized to Tom saying that I did not know what had happened, and Tom told me, in no uncertain terms, to never lie to him again. I assured him this would not happen again and he said something that made me stop and think about Templar. He told me this was the same old stuff that they have been facing for two years. They were hoping that I would make a difference but it didn't appear that way. I promised Tom I would not let it happen again.

I went to Floyd's office and told him about the faulty report. Floyd listened, and asked me to shut the door. He told me that we don't lie to customers; we just don't tell them the truth. I needed to learn how to manage my projects. Sometimes that required not telling them the whole truth. We needed to always look good and keep the finger pointing at the client. I couldn't believe what I was hearing. We do not lie to our fellow brothers and sisters in law enforcement. Floyd told me that in due time I would learn the process. I told him he had the wrong guy if he thought I was going to lie to my fellow law enforcement officers.

One weekend, I was working in Norfolk and I told Megan that once the retirement kicked in, I wouldn't be coming back as much. I left Norfolk that Sunday and was heading back to Alexandria when I got a call from Wendy with good news. Wendy and Megan had been talking, and Megan was looking at a job in Alexandria. She asked if she could stay with us until she found a place. I couldn't believe what I was hearing. Why didn't Megan say anything about this while I was with her? I contacted Megan to verify what Wendy said, and Megan said that Wendy felt it was a great chance for her to get out of her job in Norfolk. She could come to D.C. and start fresh like us. Megan planned to help around the house as Wendy was starting to find basic chores harder and harder to do. They thought it would be perfect. My mind was screaming, but if I protested too much it would have raised red flags. I was too tired to fight about it. Within a month, Megan had moved in with Wendy and me.

At first it seemed like the perfect situation. Megan helped Wendy with everything in the house. If Wendy needed something, Megan was quick to get up and get it for her. If Wendy complained that her feet hurt, Megan rubbed them. However, when Wendy wasn't looking, Megan would grab me or get a quick kiss. At first it scared me to death, but the more it went on, the more I enjoyed it. Why not? Wendy was tired all the time and Megan wanted to please everyone. It seemed perfect, but I was just fooling myself.

In May of 2001, my life took a turn which probably saved my life and our marriage. Wendy started contractions on May 29th and thought it was time. However, the doctors did not agree, so she went through two days of pain until the doctors told her to come in to induce her labor. On May 31, 2001, Jessica Leah Howard came into my life and nothing has ever been the same. My friends were right. The first time I was able to hold Jessica I found out what unconditional love really felt like. I would do anything for this perfect little child. For the first time in my life, I found something I could die for. I made up my mind that I was going to do anything to keep our marriage together for Jessica. Nothing was going to separate us. There was a perfect storm on the horizon, but I didn't care as long as we took care of this precious gift.

One Thursday in June I got ready to head out to the police department and told Floyd I would see him Monday. He called me into his office and told me he didn't hire me for part-time work. He told me I needed to make a decision about which company I wanted. I asked him if he remembered talking about this before. In two more months, I would be finished with it. He told me he didn't remember any such conversation and expected me to be here all next week. I couldn't believe it. I had sold my home in Virginia Beach, bought a new house here, moved my pregnant wife and had a child. I was stuck here now. And he didn't remember the conversation. Since Jessica's birth and the craziness of the house, I didn't want to be going back and forth anymore, but I wanted to get the full retirement for my family. On the way to Norfolk that day I realized I needed a plan to stay in Alexandria, and try to survive until August when I could retire.

While working in Systems Development Unit, I was in a car accident that tore up my shoulder. I went back to work and told them I was having problems with it again and needed to go to a doctor to make sure it was okay before I retired. I found a doctor in Alexandria that gave me a note that said I was injured and shouldn't be back on the street until we made sure I was fit for duty. I planned to never go back to the police department unless they actually needed me. I was upset with the plan though. The police department had been good to me. All the supervisors had helped me work out a weekend schedule, and now Floyd had issued an ultimatum. I wanted to leave the department on good terms. It was only for two months and in August of 2001 I turned in my retirement papers and said goodbye to the only real family I had since 1975.

Once I was working full-time at Templar, I thought things would smooth out between Floyd and me, but they just kept getting worse. There was a big fight over the Florida project and it was rumored that FDLE told Floyd that if he came down again, they were going to arrest him for his constant lying. They said they'd see me, but not Floyd. I didn't know if it was true, but Floyd stopped going on the Florida trips. I did some training in Sarasota, Florida, and fell in love with the area. I had always vacationed on the east coast of Florida, never the west coast. The Gulf of Mexico was beautiful. A group from that area told me that homes weren't expensive. The cost of living was lower and there were no state taxes. Perhaps this was the place for us. I went home and told Wendy, and she was all for it. My work was rough, and now Megan and Wendy seemed to be having issues too. Wendy told me to say the word and she would move.

The Tidewater project also took a nasty turn. I was told we had a million-dollar grant and that the seven cities in the project were willing to throw monies into the project. We were told to find out what they wanted and get started. I took two programmers to a meeting with all seven cities represented. We asked what they wanted. Every time they would ask for something, I asked the programmers if it could be done. They never said no. The seven cities were ecstatic. I was working on the project, so they knew I wouldn't lie to them. They would get the data-sharing system they had been wanting for so long. There were high-fives and pats on the back when the meeting was over. I thought this would be the greatest accomplishment of my life. Until I got back to the office.

The next day, Floyd and Ryan pulled me into the office and asked me what the hell I was doing, promising the world to the seven cities. I was shocked. They were the ones that told me to go down there and promise them anything because of all the money we were getting for the project. They told me the programmers came back, saying I was promising them things they couldn't do. I asked for the programmers to come and tell me that to my face. They had agreed at the Tidewater meeting. Floyd and Ryan told me that they had already talked to the programmers. This whole misunderstanding was my fault. The money was being used at a faster rate than they thought. We could not do half of the stuff I had promised. I asked what had changed between last week and today, but they just told me I wouldn't understand. I needed to take the list the seven cities wanted and prioritize the items, so we could do as many as we could before the money ran out.

Going back to my desk I asked the two programmers what happened. They were clueless. They had both come into work that day all excited about the Tidewater project, and told Floyd and Ryan how well it went. They were talking about all the suggestions the users had made and how it would make the software a better package. One of the programmers said the look on Floyd's and Ryan's faces had been stern. They told them that they would be talking to me when I got in because I had promised too much and they needed to put a cap on this right now. How dare Jim go down and promise the farm anyway? Both programmers told them they thought that was the plan, while Floyd and Ryan said it was not.

One of the office managers came and told me that Floyd and Ryan had spent some of the monies from the project on personal items. Ryan had bought some property and Floyd was ordering a new BMW. When the programmers came in, excited about the project, both Ryan and Floyd got nervous and called me into the office.

On September 6 of 2001, Wendy took Jessica to Iowa to visit her mom. This left Megan and me alone. Megan started talking about me leaving Wendy and coming with her when she moved into her own place. She told me she would help me get Jessica. She would testify that Wendy was an unfit mother. I explained that wouldn't happen, but Megan said it was just an idea. I asked her what happened to her earlier resolve to stay unattached. She had changed her mind, but she wouldn't push me. She understood if I wanted to stay with Wendy as long as she could have me every once in a while. Now I needed an exit plan with my relationship with Megan. I wasn't going to leave Wendy and take the chance of losing Jessica too. I knew if Wendy found out what was going on she would leave me.

Tuesday morning, September 11, 2001 started off great. Wendy and Jessica were coming home and I was going to leave work a little early to go get them at the airport. Five days away from the little one had been too much. I couldn't wait to see her and Wendy. At work I stayed busy by putting paperwork together for one of the projects. We always had the television on for the programmers. I didn't watch it. Around 8:50 in the morning, the office exploded. I walked around to the other side where the programmers sat, and looked up at the television. The North Tower of the World Trade Center was on fire. Someone said a small plane had flown into the building. I stood and watched for a few minutes. I knew I needed to call Wendy. If she heard about the crash, she might be a little scared to fly. I wanted to make sure she was okay because I wanted her and Jessica home.

I called Wendy and she told me that they were just about ready to walk out the door for the airport. I didn't mention the World Trade Center and she didn't seem to know about it, so I told her to have a great flight. I would see them soon. She was excited to get home. I hung up and went back to making copies for the project when the second plane hit the South Tower. The whole dynamic in the office changed when we realized we were under attack.

Everyone in the office had some contact with someone in D.C. Anne, my immediate supervisor's husband, worked in the Pentagon. Floyd and Ryan were in the Air National Guard. Several of the employees had military backgrounds and had been stationed in the area, so when the second plane hit, phone calls began. One of those calls was Wendy. All flights had been canceled. She and Jessica were going to be in Iowa for a while. My heart sank, knowing that this might take more time than I wanted. I told her to hold tight. As soon as I figured out a way, I would get them home.

All work came to a halt as we watched the horror unfolding on the television. We had a large TV in the conference room, and nobody could walk away from it for fear of missing something else. One person said something about a plane hitting the Capitol or the White House. One of our marketers made the smart statement that "D.C. airspace was tighter than a tick's ass." No sooner had he said those words when we heard the first report of the Pentagon getting hit. *So much for that theory.* We immediately turned to Anne and asked if there was anything we could do, since her husband worked there. She said get him on the phone. One of the office managers asked for the number and started calling. It took a while, but we finally got through and he was fine. He said they had planned on staying and working on the situation but had to move out of his area because the smoke was too much. From our office we could see the smoke from the fires at the Pentagon.

We were told we could go home but most of us stayed. As the news continued, the name Osama bin Laden started to float around as the architect of the attack on America. His picture was shown constantly on the TV, and of course, it was noted that he was a radical Muslim. Pictures of radical Muslims were shown dancing in the streets because of the attack on America. We all knew we were at war, but had no idea of the magnitude.

One of our programmers, Eish Dhillon, who was Indian and a Sikh, slipped out of the office and went to the bathroom. He came out without his *pugdi* (or turban). Instead he was wearing a scarf. Sikh believers always wear a head covering in public. Eish Dhillon was one of the best guys working at Templar. The look on his face told me volumes. I pulled him aside and asked if he was okay. He was sure there would be a backlash against people that looked like him. I told him he could come over to my place for a few days until it calmed down. I had his back. He appreciated my friendship but knew his family would want him home. I told him to call if he needed me. He thanked me and said they would be okay.

As the towers fell, the Pentagon burned and United Airlines Flight 93 crashed near Shanksville, Pennsylvania, it hit me that I was no longer in the fight. I had stayed busy all day because that was me. I couldn't stand still while a crisis was going on. I pictured what this would have been like if it had happened in Norfolk and I was still with the department. My brothers and I would have gone downtown to help. That was just how we were, never afraid to get into the fight. I was a little lost that day. I wanted to go to the Pentagon and see if I could help. I had a good friend that was a supervisor for the Arlington Police Department, and I knew he was there. I wanted to go somewhere and get back into the game.

But a little voice in my head kept telling me there was trouble ahead for me. I needed to get ready. I didn't know it but within the next few months I was going to be pushed into a darkness I had only experienced once before. I kept thinking I was the god of my destiny, but I was about to find out that I had no control over my life. I was about to lose it all.

JIM HOWARD

We spent the rest of that day at the office watching the television. Everyone was in shock. More information was being reported about the United Airlines Flight 93 that crashed in Pennsylvania. Reporters were saying the jet was on its way to Washington when the passengers rushed the terrorists, forcing the plane to crash. People in the office had friends and relatives that could have been on that plane, so it took many more phone calls before we knew we had not lost someone related to our office. Wendy and I talked several times on the phone about how I was going to get her and Jessica home from Iowa. It was decided that if flights were grounded for the week, Scott would drive her halfway, and I would meet them.

People sometimes tell you that unless you see something for yourself, it is hard to get a handle on it. I can say that about the Pentagon. The photographs did not do justice to the damage done there. Driving by it brought tears to my eyes. We had been attacked, and I felt that I was not part of the solution. I was not protecting my country. I couldn't even protect my wife and daughter. Megan was now working in downtown Washington so Wendy was worried about her. She began calling her, and then me. Everyone was fine. We both just wanted Wendy and Jessica home. During my drive home, I made up my mind that it was time for Megan to move out, so Wendy, Jessica, and I could get on with our lives.

Megan clouded the issue too much; she needed to move on. When I got home, Megan was on the phone with Wendy discussing the wonderful reunion they would have. Megan assured Wendy that everything was fine at home. Megan was now the manipulator of both of us.

By the time I went to work the next day, Wendy and I had decided that I would start driving up on Friday afternoon, get there by Saturday morning, and meet up with her, Scott, and Jessica. We would be back Sunday. We didn't want to rush. I had driven past the Pentagon and gone into downtown D.C. only to see Humvees with machine guns on them. This was a country at war. When I got to the office, Floyd was pacing the office floor. He told me we were going to have a meeting as he had a plan of how we could help the country. I was thinking, *This is great! Put me in, coach. What can I do?* Trying to busy myself before the meeting, I couldn't help thinking that maybe I had Floyd all wrong. Maybe deep down he was a patriot, and I had misjudged him. He was in the National Guard; maybe he was going to tell us he was signing up. It didn't take long to blow that fantasy out of the water.

By the time everyone got there, Floyd could barely contain himself. We all went into the conference room, and he stated he wanted to have a retreat this weekend. We needed to wear comfy clothes and be ready to work. He wanted to find a way to capitalize on the attacks yesterday with our software. The government would want systems that could search the Internet (and other places) to find our enemies. They would want software that could search law enforcement databases for possible suspects. I was taking notes. After a while, I stopped and read it all over again. I looked around the room. Everyone was in shock. This is what he wanted us to do? Capitalize on the attacks? Did he just really say that?

Without missing a beat, Floyd continued, "Think what we can do now! There will be grants out there for research. We could develop new systems. We could make a lot of money on this." Don't get me wrong, I liked his idea, I just didn't like the way he was presenting it. It was his money-making focus that was appalling. Everyone in that room wanted to help in the situation, but we wanted to help to save lives, not make money. This was just typical Floyd. He went on and on about how this would be a great moment for the company, trying to get everyone to sign on. Of course, when he realized that nobody was enthused about his epiphany, he got frustrated and told everyone to go back to work. He said he would let us know the time of the retreat later.

I waited a few minutes before I went to Floyd's office. I wanted to give him a chance to calm down. I knocked. He asked me what I thought about his idea and I told him it had been hasty. The flames were still burning at the Pentagon and in New York and he was talking about capitalizing on it. We needed to wait. I also told him I wasn't going to be available for the retreat. I was going to get Wendy and Jessica because all the flights were still grounded. He said I needed to be there. Why couldn't I just put them on a train? I wasn't even going to suggest that to Wendy. Jessica was a little over three months old, and Floyd wanted me to put them on a train? Wendy would have had a fit. Wasn't going to happen. He looked down at his desk and said this was an all hands-on deck retreat. I had to find another way to get them home.

That was the moment I realized I had made a big mistake. This was not the type of company for me. If they didn't care about the employees and their families or the customer (I had already seen that), I was in the wrong business. If this was the corporate world, I didn't want to be part of it. I went back to my desk, and decided I wasn't going to be at the retreat. He could just fire me. I had bad supervisors in the past, but even they never acted like this.

Once you were accepted in the brotherhood of law enforcement, you looked out for each other. I remembered when an officer had a death in the family that was across the country. Worried that the vehicle they were driving would not make the trip, they were at a loss. One of the sergeants heard about their plight, and offered his new Cadillac for the trip. That's what we did: took care of family. Officers would give a day to help out when other officers had illnesses that drained their sick leave. That was what I was used to. I had taken it for granted.

I didn't understand why I was so taken aback by Floyd's inattention for his employees and their families. He acted this way all the time in the office. I guess I thought he would change in light of what was presently happening in our country. But no, all he could think about was capitalizing on a crisis.

Fortunately, I didn't have to drive to get Wendy and Jessica. The flight ban was lifted and I picked them up at Dulles. After getting them home, I rushed to the office to find Floyd there alone. I asked where everyone was. Apparently, no one had been happy with his plan. They all thought he was being an ambulance chaser. There were still people missing in New York and in our own backyard, and the consensus was that this was not the time to take advantage of a situation. For a sliver of a moment, I felt sorry for him, but it passed in an instant, swiftly replaced by my disappointment at not being there when the employees voiced their opinion. In spite of everything, I still wanted to work there. I believed in the mission of the company. If we could start sharing information all across the state of Florida and in Virginia, I was in. I could handle Floyd's idiosyncrasies as long as I kept my eyes on the goal of the company: helping police departments share data.

At the end of September, I had my first evaluation. Anne took me out to lunch to discuss my job performance. I wish I had recorded it. She raved about how "Templar was lucky to have a valuable employee like me. I took charge of the projects and they could see progress. There were looking for a long-term relationship with Jim Howard and Templar," she said. Needless to say, I went home that night telling Wendy I was going to be at Templar for a long time. She was all smiles. She had contacted the office that day and asked if I could have a couple of days off because she had gotten us airline tickets to Florida for my birthday. She told them that I had raved about Sarasota when I went down there so she had looked up hotels in the area and was going to surprise me. Later she told me that she had spoken to Floyd and he had wished us a great trip, sure it was okay for Jim to take off.

On October 5th, the day before the trip to Florida, Wendy couldn't keep the secret any longer. She told me about my birthday trip. We were heading down to Lido Key, outside of Sarasota, and staying on the beach. Even Megan was going to help with Jessica so we could go out alone one night. My car was in the shop, so Megan drove me to work, telling me to relax, everything was going to be okay. I was excited about the trip, but still worried about when the truth would slip out what was going on between Megan and me. I decided to relax and enjoy the trip. I needed a few days off.

As a police officer, you develop a sixth sense that warns you when things just don't feel right. Another term for it is "atmospherics." The mood of the baseline changes due to some sort of outside or foreign individual that doesn't fit into the narrative. When I walked into the office I felt that I didn't fit in; I felt like an outsider. The office manager greeted me like her puppy died instead of with her customary warmth. Some of the programmers that ordinarily welcomed me were so focused on their computer screens that they didn't even respond when I said good morning. I wondered what Floyd had done now, but did not want to pry, so I just went about my day. I knew that I would hear about it later. A bit later Floyd came into the office, glared at me, and hastily went into his office. Anne was close behind him, following him. A few minutes later, she asked me if I could come into Floyd's office.

At first I thought this was a part of Wendy's surprise. Floyd motioned me to sit down. I took a seat, looked at Anne, and asked what was up. Floyd informed me, without so much as a good morning, that it was time I cleaned out my desk. My services were no longer needed (or wanted) at Templar. I thought he was joking. I asked him why. He just responded that if I didn't know, he wasn't going to tell me. I looked over at Anne, and asked, "What was all that crap she had just fed me the other day? What happened to 'Templar was lucky to have a valuable employee like you'? What happened to our 'long-term relationship'? Was that all bullshit?"

Anne couldn't even look at me. Floyd just ordered me to pack my stuff and get out. He was going to give me two weeks' severance pay if I didn't cause any trouble, but he didn't have to give me anything. I was dumbfounded. I looked over at Anne again, but she kept her eyes down. I had some choice words to say to Floyd, but don't remember what was said after that. I walked out of his office, and nobody would look at me. I heard one of the office managers crying. Boxes had already been placed on my desk so I could pack my stuff. I tried to log onto the computer to delete some files I had brought with me from Norfolk, and found I had been locked out of the system. I told them I needed to get my files, so they let me in. Once I packed my stuff, it dawned on me that I didn't have a ride home. Anne said she would take me.

On the ride, Anne apologized for what had just happened. I asked her what had happened, but she couldn't give me an answer. Floyd just said that he didn't like the way I got along with everyone. He was not happy that I could go to Florida and he could not or with my surprise trip there. I looked at her and said, "So his ego is so fragile that he is firing me when I have a newborn?" She couldn't answer. I asked her if she knew about the surprise vacation. She did. Wendy had talked to her and Floyd, but she had known nothing about him firing me until last night. He had called her, but he wouldn't tell her why. She said that Ryan was afraid I might shoot up the place because they all knew I carried a gun. Ryan had taken the day off just because of that fact.

I sat in silence and disbelief the rest of the way home. I didn't know what I was going to tell Wendy. As we pulled up to the house, I realized I didn't have my house keys. I rang the doorbell and Wendy answered. Wondering why Anne was there, she greeted us with some alarm. I told her I had been fired. Anne couldn't even look at her. I made my way into the house with Wendy still asking what happened. Anne was carrying one of my boxes into the house, so Wendy turned to her and asked her what was going on. Anne teared up, put the box down, and told Wendy she was really sorry. She had not been told why I had been let go either, but she was sorry. She suggested that if I did some consulting work for Templar, maybe I could get along. I told her to tell Floyd to go… and stopped myself. I could see Anne was about to lose it. Once again she told us she was sorry and left.

I was in shock. *What had just happened?* I went from being excited about my "surprise" vacation to unemployed in a matter of hours. I needed to take care of my family, had a house I couldn't afford, bills that needed to be paid, and not a clue what I was going to do next. Wendy sat next to me. She took my hand in hers. Firing me was their loss, she said, we were going to Florida to have a good time. When we got back, she was sure I would be able to get a job with my experience. I looked at her, and for the first time in a long time, I saw the Wendy I had fallen in love with. The one that had faith in me. I could do anything I wanted. All I had to do was get out there and let people know I was available. I would have a job in no time. That was the attitude we were going to carry into our vacation.

Even though we all had a great time in Lido Beach, recent events hung heavy whenever I had a moment to think. During the night I lay awake trying to figure out what had happened and what to do. Was Floyd's ego that fragile that I posed a threat to him? Or was my own arrogance my downfall? I never bowed to his ways and often fought him. I couldn't stand his lack of ethics, or the demeaning way he treated others. Maybe he had done me a favor. I would get back home and start making phone calls. I would find a new job.

Wendy told me we were financially good for about three months. I was trying to look at this in a positive light, but it was hard. In the past twenty-eight years, I had always been king of my world with a steady job. Getting my feet knocked out from under me stung.

We got back from Florida, and I had three months to get a new job. I was sure I would land one in less than three weeks. I called the two project leaders with whom I had been working, and told them what had happened. Both wrote letters of disapproval to Floyd. The one from Virginia Beach thought maybe I tried too hard to please users from an organization that was constantly found to not tell the truth on issues. He put that in his letter. Tom from FDLE was worried their project would not be completed at all. He had no faith in Floyd. I asked if I could use them as references, and both said I could. Surely I would find a position quickly. I just had one problem that wasn't going to let that happen.

Wendy and I heard of a job fair. I dusted off my résumé, put on a suit, and headed to the event. There were always large crowds of people waiting to get into a fair. Eventually someone always came out with a megaphone and told the crowd that if they didn't have at least a bachelor's degree, there was no point in coming into the building. Experience was great, but the vendors wouldn't even talk to you without a degree. I was shocked. Most of the people waiting to get in did not have the experience I had. I had written programs, run projects, and moved a large police department into Y2K-compliance, a two-million-dollar project. It didn't matter. If you didn't have a sheepskin, they didn't want to see you. I watched as others like me got in their cars and left.

I was devastated and angry. I wasn't going to be able to find a job that paid me what I had been making. Now I was really ticked off at Floyd. On dark nights, I sat and pondered ways to get back at him. I had never been so angry with someone before. He had not just hurt me, but my entire family. I had a little one now. Just before I was fired, Floyd got his new BMW. My friend and old police partner had once shown me his elk hunting rifle, saying a bullet from it would go through an engine block. I dreamed of borrowing that rifle and putting a bullet through Floyd's new BMW. I knew I would never do it (or I thought I would never do it), but as the months went by and I still didn't have a job, it was a good thing I never ran into my old partner.

After three months without a job, Wendy said I needed to make a decision. We couldn't continue to pay for two vehicles, the boat we still had in Norfolk, and some other bills. She had contacted the people that had our Ford Explorer loan. They would work with us, but nobody else would. To protect our assets, Wendy recommended we file for bankruptcy. That sent me over the edge. I had perfect credit and had always been proud of the way I handled my debt. To go bankrupt was lower than low, something I had always promised myself I would never do. However, we had to file. It was another low point from which I didn't think I could recover, but then I would have ten minutes with Jessica, and realize I needed to be there for her, so I would get up every morning, read the ads, and hope for a break.

One day Wendy showed me that Pinkerton and Burns, the famous security agency now known as Securitas, was having a job fair. Another hit to my ego. Having been at the top of my profession for so many years, I felt that I couldn't get any lower than private security. I felt like the retired head chef of a five-star restaurant that was about to start flipping burgers in a fast-food joint now instead.

Hat in hand, I took my résumé and went to the Pinkerton and Burns job fair. I handed the lady at the desk my résumé, and they ushered all the applicants into a room for a recruitment video. The whole time I was sitting there, I saw myself working at a bank wearing black pants, black shoes, and white socks. Do not get me wrong. Security work is an honest profession. Many of my friends work in the private security sector, but as I looked around the room, I only saw guys that either couldn't get into a police department or were retired and on Medicare and looking for part-time positions.

Feeling sorry for myself, I listened to a recruiter talking about some of the perks of working for Pinkerton and Burns. Soon the company was being bought out, and the new name was going to be Securitas. Someone asked if that meant more pay and the recruiter said no. I was close to walking out when they called my name, and asked me to go out and see another recruiter.

The new recruiter had my résumé, and asked why I was here with my qualifications. I gave him the abridged version, and he told me I had perfect timing. They had a new position at the World Bank for which they were looking for people like me. This job paid more than the normal Securitas jobs and there was always the possibility of full-time. It sounded great, even though I knew nothing about the World Bank. He told me he was going to set up an interview for me with the head of the new project. If that went well, I could start soon. I didn't know what the job was, but it still sounded interesting. Maybe it was something I would enjoy. An interview was set up the following Monday. I went home to tell everyone the exciting news and search for the World Bank on the Internet.

The World Bank provided financial and technical assistance to developing countries. They had offices all over the world. That piqued my interest. Maybe Floyd had done me a favor and I was on to bigger and better things. Even though I didn't have the job, we decided to celebrate. I even gave my dad a call. I was sure he had heard that I had lost my job from my brothers. They had told Mom. She used the situation to remind me how well John was doing at the police department. Thanks, Mom.

I called my dad. When Wendy and I got married, Dad had complained about chest pains, like he had a pulled muscle. When he got back to Texas, he found out he had lung cancer. Doctors had removed one of his lungs and taken part of the other. I remember the first time I saw Dad after the surgery. Dad had never looked his age. He always looked ten years younger than he was. While working for Templar, I had taken a trip to California that had a layover in Dallas. I remember watching for him. When I was young, I had envied how straight my dad always walked and how young he looked. The man I saw now finally looked his age; he was frail and hunched over. I felt so sorry for him. He told me that the cancer was gone. He was back to gardening and mowing the yard. His stamina and perseverance always amazed me. The big C was never going to slow him down.

After we talked for a while, I told him the reason I had called. I did not want him to worry about me losing my job because I had found another one. Wendy, Jessica, and I were doing well. Before I finished telling him that, he blurted out, "I hope you are not going to ask me for money. I have always said money and relatives never go together, so I hope you are not going to ask for any." I was stunned. Nothing was further from my mind. Hearing that just reminded me how nasty he was. I hated being around him. I was looking for a "great, good job" and only got the "don't ask for money" punch. I was so ticked that I just shut down abruptly. There was an uncomfortable silence. I just wanted to hang up. He finally told me to come see him when I could. I told him I would, and that was it. I sat looking at the phone and wondered if he would ever affirm me in any way. It dawned on me that I had never heard him express confidence in me. Why would he start now?

The World Bank was on H Street in Washington, D.C. I pulled it up on the map and saw that it was just a few blocks from the White House. I left the house almost two hours early to make sure I was on time for my interview and still wasn't. I quickly learned how to handle the crazy one-way streets. Looking for parking was impossible, so ten minutes before I was supposed to be there, I called my contact, Dave Brown. He calmly told me it was okay. He understood the downtown traffic situation. He told me to take it easy, and he would find me a parking spot at the World Bank. I was impressed with the way he handled that and hoped the rest of the interview would go so smoothly. I turned down the street he had given me, and he was standing on the corner, looking for me, and waved me into a parking spot.

Dave Brown seemed as genuine as you could get. He was retired military and respectful of my law enforcement background. Once he saw my résumé, he had been looking forward to meeting with me. He took me on a tour of the bank, and then down to the Command Center, the room with the camera system you always saw in the movies. The bank had several buildings with camera systems in each of them, so you could follow a person all around the area. To this day, it is still one of the most impressive buildings I have ever visited. Dave explained that the bank had many offices worldwide and was a 24/7 operation. If there was a plane crash in Russia, one of our jobs was to check that plane's manifest to see if any bank employees were on it. If there was an earthquake somewhere, we had to see how it affected our offices. If necessary, we would send somebody there to help. Our job was to sit in the Command Center and scan the news around the world. Sounded like a plan. However, the pay was half of what I had been making at Templar. I needed the job so I asked when I could start.

I could write a whole book on my experience at the World Bank. The building was incredible. Rich with history, it was like a mini-UN. It had its own travel agency (because everyone was going somewhere) and medical section. I never had to go there but I heard it was very comprehensive. There was an extensive cafeteria with all sorts of exotic foods. My only complaint was the pay. It was shift work. The midnight shift was interesting because the building was closed down. I would walk around with a captain of security. He had a key to every room, and even took me into the president's office. The president of the World Bank at that time was James Wolfensohn. His office was full of pictures of him with world leaders, presidents, and other VIPs. He was a big fan of U2 and had them stay at his home at times. The captain told me the president was a nice guy, but very busy. When you did get the opportunity to meet him, he was grateful for what you did and let you know it. He was also great at remembering names.

After I was there a couple of weeks, I met Gordon McIntosh, Chief of the Security Operations Section. Gordon knew the bank inside and out. He introduced me to its Executive Protection (EP) operation. I wasn't there more than three months when Gordon asked me if I wanted to join the EP team. He told me it usually took longer to get an invitation to join the team, but my police experience spoke for me. He thought I would be a good fit. It didn't change my pay. I was still working for Securitas, but if I worked hard and excelled, they might hire me full-time with the bank. Excited at the thought of advancement, I was eager to go to the EP school. They set the date for me to attend Robert Oatman's Executive Protection Training school in Baltimore, Maryland.

There was only one hiccup to EP with the bank. Gordon told me that the president of the bank loved to be on the go, so I could be traveling for more than six months out of the year. That stopped me. I didn't want to be away from home that much. I didn't want to miss Jessica growing up. I wanted her to say daddy first. When I changed her diapers, I repeated "Daddy, Daddy, Daddy" all the time. I wanted to be there to see her first steps. I didn't want to come home one day and find her all grown up. However, I needed this position to get back in the game too, so I was ready to sacrifice time with Jessica for a position that fed my ego. I didn't like myself for it though.

At home, things took a turn for the worse. Wendy wanted Megan out of the house. Even though she helped with Jessica and finances, they had begun to have issues over who was running the house. Megan felt that Wendy was taking advantage of us. She thought that the two of us were working hard and Wendy was not doing anything. I defended Wendy. Being a mother was a full-time job. The tension grew intense, and I wondered how long it would be before there was a physical fight. Megan seemed changed. She was not the same person that had charmed her way into our lives. She was short-tempered and thought she was better for me than

Wendy. I pulled her aside and questioned her about these sudden changes. She confided in me that she took medications for mood swings and anxiety, but had stopped taking them because she didn't like the way they made her feel. She was substituting the medication with alcohol, and was sorry for the way she was acting. She didn't like Wendy anymore but didn't want to lose her relationship with me and Jessica. She blamed the present hostility on Wendy, claiming she was a victim of Wendy's postpartum depression.

I spoke with Wendy. She was angry, and the more I talked to her the madder she got. I talked to her on several occasions about trusting me and letting me handle things, but in reality, I didn't have a handle on anything. I was living a lie. Every time I spoke to Megan about moving out, she demanded that I leave with her. I told her I wasn't going to leave Jessica and wasn't going to take her away from Wendy, so I guessed I was going to stay where I was. Megan finally threatened to come clean with Wendy. I told her that if she did, it was over between us. Megan backed off and made peace with Wendy. The day before I went to the executive protection school, things seemed back to normal.

Robert Oatman's Executive Protection Training was just what I needed. I used my police knowledge, and studied their way of implementing executive protection. I fell in love with their philosophy. There was a huge difference between police work and executive protection. If a police officer saw something he considered a threat, he went after it. In executive protection, if you saw anything that made you uncomfortable, you got the person you were protecting (the principle) out of harm's way. Big change and very sensible. I used what I had learned in police work, crisis negotiation, and other training and excelled in the study. I couldn't wait to get back and be part of the EP team.

Just a few months later, I was called to be part of the team on the president's next European tour. Our first stop was Oslo, Norway. From there we visited several other countries, ending in England and then home. It was a two-week trip. I would go a couple of days early and run point, which meant I would fly first class, pick up the rented vehicle, go where the president was staying, and make sure everything was in order for him. Then I would check the president's itinerary, going over the routes to his meetings. After that, I just had to wait for him and the rest of the team to get to Norway. I was excited. They were going to send me out there all alone; I was back in the game!

I went home and told everyone about the trip, making both Wendy and Megan promise they would behave. We would talk about what we did next when I got back. Acting all manly, I told them I didn't want to hear of any trouble, and both seemed to agree to the terms. That was a little scary. Before I left, Wendy told me she had demanded Megan would be gone when I got back. Megan told me she wasn't leaving, so I just hoped that they would both be alive when I got back.

Except I never went. Two days before the trip, Wolfensohn collapsed from the flu. He was rushed to the hospital and put in intensive care. The trip was scrubbed so I went back to the daily grind of being a Watch Officer, reading news reports as they came across the wire. I would walk around with the captain of the security guards listening to him talk about his home country and how much he loved America. Many that worked in security were from different countries and they all felt the same way. I met doctors, lawyers, schoolteachers, and all sorts of professionals who came from broken countries for a better life. They had all found jobs here. It was humbling to hear their stories.

The bank had its perks. For example, we had a front-row seat for the fireworks on the Fourth. It was the most spectacular display I had ever seen. I really felt better. Sure, I had a couple of issues to take care of but I was in control of my own life again, or so I thought.

My next EP assignment came in August. The president was returning from vacation and I was supposed to pick him and his wife up at an executive airport with his driver, and take them to the Silk Road: Connecting Cultures, Creating Trust Festival being held at the National Mall, one of the most visited parks in the United States. The Mall is beautiful with the U.S. Capitol Building on one end, the Lincoln Memorial on the other, and the Washington Monument in the middle. The Smithsonian Museum buildings are also there. When we worked EP for the president, we had to wear a suit, so I had on a dark blue suit and tie. The president and his wife got off the Lear jet wearing khakis. He wore a golf shirt and she was in light cotton. It felt like the temperature was over 100 degrees with 99 percent humidity. Sweat poured down every possible place you could imagine. At the festival, we met a friend of the president who had a golf cart and acted as our guide. Dust choked me as I sat in the back of the golf cart as it made its way along the dirt paths in the Mall. The guide took us from place to place where the president met with people from different countries. He was very polite, and introduced me as his personal assistant but they all knew who I was. People sometimes asked me about the bank president's identity since he had a Secret Service guy with him.

The highlight of the day was listening to the famous cellist Yo-Yo Ma jamming with other musicians. Yo-Yo Ma and the president and his wife were good friends. I was impressed that they knew him, and the next thing I knew, Yo-Yo Ma was hugging them. Once again I was introduced as his personal assistant. I would have enjoyed it more if I weren't wearing a suit and sweating my ass off. We stayed at the festival for several hours until the President's wife decided she want to get home and we called for the car. He needed to go back to the bank, so I returned there with him. Once inside, he shook my hand, told me what a great job I had done, and I was dismissed.

He walked away and I never saw him again. I stood there, dripping wet from the heat and humidity, and thought to myself, *What am I doing here? This wasn't what I had planned for my life.* Even so, I was thankful for a job. Still I knew that a couple more days like today, and the thought of being away from Jessica for half the year would be intolerable. I needed a career change. I just didn't know what it was going to be. One night on the midnight shift searching the Internet, I came across a public safety computer company in New Port Richey, Florida that was looking for help.

CHAPTER 17

I had no idea where New Port Richey was, but when I looked it up on the map, I couldn't believe it. It was an hour and a half from Sarasota. I checked out the company, CISCO Public Safety Software Company, and saw there was a contact email for the president of the company, so I sent them my résumé.

After the training I had done in Sarasota, Wendy and I had printed out a map of Florida and placed it on the fridge. We had circled Sarasota. It was our dream retirement area. When I told her about New Port Richey, she saw how close it was to Sarasota and got excited about the prospect of leaving Alexandria. She also viewed it as an opportunity to move away from Megan, and get our life in order. Megan had scored an incredible job in the area, and we knew she wouldn't want to leave it. Wendy's justifiable anger was putting a wedge between us at times. The thought crossed my mind about leaving them all, but I could not leave Jessica.

I started working on the pros and cons of making a move to Florida. I really enjoyed the executive protection work I was doing. One of our upcoming trips that year was to China. I thought about the opportunities that Jessica could have if we stayed here. I was sure I would be hired full-time at the bank soon. I was doing everything I could to better myself there. I would walk around the building after closing with some of the other full-time fire and safety people and learn everything I could about the building and its operation.

Even though I loved working *in* D.C., I didn't like living *near* D.C. A recent murder hit close to home. A couple was visiting near the area and pulled into a drugstore near where we lived. While the husband went inside to get a couple of things, his wife stayed in the van to change their daughter's diaper. When the husband came out, the van was gone. At first, he thought it was a joke, but when she didn't return in a few minutes, he knew something was wrong, so he called her cell phone. She didn't answer, so he called 9-1-1.

Meanwhile a man driving near the CVS thought he saw a large doll on the road when it moved. He stopped the car, got out, and found the daughter of the couple. When police found the van, the wife was dead. While changing her daughter, a man came up behind her, pushed her in the van, threatened to kill her and the child, and made her leave the parking lot. As they drove, the suspect threw the baby out the window and later killed the woman. The infant survived and was reunited with her father, but the story haunted me because we lived in that area and the child was Jessica's age.

The traffic around Washington was also bad. The area seemed full of rude people, and we didn't have the good support system we had in Norfolk. I was also tired of the winters. Even though I like the Metro System, it was sometimes brutal waiting on the platform for the train. Every time I went to Florida, I loved the weather and the people seemed to be nicer. I hadn't even gotten a response from CISCO, and I was already making the move in my mind. I dreamed of moving to Florida and leaving Megan behind.

I was worried about what would happen when we told Megan. I was surprised when she thought it was a great idea. This metropolitan area was no place to raise a family, she said, and she loved the Florida area. The idea of starting fresh seemed like a good one to her. We mentioned that this was a move with just Wendy and me. She said she understood, but would love to come down and visit us once we got settled. Wendy told her that would be perfect.

Of course, all of this hinged on me getting the job at CISCO. After a week with no response from them, I gave the company a call. I spoke to a human resource person who said he had never received my résumé, so I resent it. He called me back within an hour and set up an interview. They were looking for a guy like me. They needed someone who understood relational databases. They were using an outdated flat file system and wanted to make a change.

I told Wendy and Megan and Wendy quickly got online and found a house to rent in Palm Harbor. We knew nothing about the area, but the house and neighborhood looked nice. Somehow Megan talked her way into coming with us, saying she could help with Jessica and maybe even give us the chance to get out alone one night.

In less than three weeks, I was having an interview with Tom, the HR guy, and the president of the company's wife, Laura. It was a family-run business and most of Laura's siblings worked there. The interview went well. They liked my knowledge of police systems, were looking for a database manager, and I fit the bill. They would let me know their decision in two days.

We were back in Florida when they contacted us. CISCO offered me a job at the same rate of pay I was making at the World Bank. I could start working in October. Since it was the middle of June, we had a little over three months to get the house sold and find a place in Florida near New Port Richey. We decided to not tell the bank until we got closer to the moving date. We also told Megan she needed to be out of the house as soon as possible. I guess that was when reality sunk in. Wendy, Jessica, and I were moving, and Megan wasn't. Megan had decided she was going to do everything she could to break us up. Wendy put the house on the market, Megan started looking for a place to stay, and things were looking good. At the end of August, it all came crashing down.

Let me just say that I was so afraid of losing Jessica that I would lie, cheat, and steal to keep her. I was juggling, trying to keep Wendy calm. I did not want her to lose her temper and do something she would regret. I was also trying to keep Megan happy, so she wouldn't tell Wendy everything that was going on. What a mess! If I had been half the man I should have been, I would never have let this happen. Because of my weakness, I had allowed all of this. I should have told the truth.

Wendy was so angry that I didn't see us staying together. Things had changed. Lately it seemed that we were unable to communicate without getting into a fight. Nobody wanted to listen to the other. To be honest, and maybe some people would not understand this, but Megan helped us stay together because she was the mediator for the longest time. She had a knack for handling Wendy, which helped us make it through some tough times. Of course, her motive for this was so she could also have a relationship with me. And that was screwed up. In the end, if it had not been for Jessica I don't think Wendy and I would be together today. I wanted her to have a father in her life, and I was in a fight for that reality.

I knew that when Wendy and I moved to Florida, if we didn't work it out, I would fight to keep Jessica with me there. If Wendy and I split up, I would contact Megan. That was my plan. I even sent Megan an e-mail about it. In the e-mail, I talked about how I would help Wendy find a job. Once she made good money, if things still didn't work out, we would go our separate ways. I had every intention of trying to work things out with Wendy though. I didn't want Jessica to grow up in a blended family. I wanted her to have one dad and one mother. It was what I had always wanted for myself, so I was going to do everything I could to give it to her.

One night, Megan called and told me she was going to tell Wendy about us. I had had enough. I said I would meet her at the house and we could tell her together. She told me she was sorry, but she loved me too much and didn't want me moving to Florida. I had a good job at the bank. I could stay here, move in with her, and file for divorce and get custody of Jessica. She would be more than happy to testify that Wendy was not a good mother and I should have full custody. I told her that wasn't going to happen. I was not going to take Jessica away from Wendy. We were going to Florida and this needed to stop. Truthfully, Wendy was an excellent mother. Megan hung up as I got to the house.

Wendy met me in the doorway, screaming at me. Perhaps, she yelled, I was going to take her to Florida and kill her so that Megan could come down and live some perfect life with Jessica and me. I asked her where she heard this. She pointed to the e-mail I had written to Megan, open on the computer so Wendy could see it. I knew there was no arguing with Wendy about the letter and what I meant. She wasn't going to believe me. Her anger was blinding her, and the only thing I could do was say that it was over with Megan and me. My plan was to go to Florida with Wendy, not Megan, so we could start over, and see if we could make it work.

About that time Megan entered the house and Wendy went after her. She was screaming. How could this person she thought was her friend be sleeping with her husband? Jessica was sitting on the floor between them, so I picked her up, got in our car, and drove to a park near our house. I didn't know what was going to happen between the two of them, but I didn't want Jessica in the middle of it. Wendy walked out the door and down the street. I went back to the house and told Megan she needed to leave. She got some things and left. I didn't know it, but someone had called the police. When they arrived, I told them everything was okay, but they wanted to talk to Wendy. By that time, Wendy came back to the house and demanded to take Jessica. I wasn't going to argue with her. She took Jessica and walked out without saying a word.

I remember watching them drive off, thinking, I have been here before. I had lost everything before, but I always came back. I sat in the empty house. *I would overcome this somehow.* Yet for the first time in my life, I didn't know how I was going to do it. I had to figure out some way of getting Jessica and Wendy back, but I just sat there and cried. I cried the same way I did the day Doctor English died. I cried as I had when I realized I had lost Pat and the family I loved so much. I realized I wasn't crying for Wendy leaving though. I cried because she took Jessica.

I don't know how long I sat there in the house, trying to figure out what to do. How could I recover? What I was going to say to Wendy when she came back to the house? I needed some excuse, not the total truth, but something plausible. I started working on my story. The phone rang. It was Wendy. Before I could speak, she said she was going to Iowa. If I wanted the car, it was at the airport. Instead of pleading with her to come home and talk, I told her to go, and call me when she got settled. She told me she wasn't going to talk to me until Megan was completely gone. I told her I understood. She hung up and I cried some more.

Then I got mad at God again. I knew He didn't have anything to do with the situation, but somehow I was still mad at Him. I don't know why we blame God when we screw up, but we do. We think that if He really loved us, He wouldn't let these things happen. I was yelling at God for my own iniquities, but in my mind, I went back to Glen Rose: If my dad had not killed Doctor English, I wouldn't be in this situation today. Somehow, it was all God's fault. Isn't this how we are? We can't accept the responsibility for our own faults, so we blame someone else. As this played out in my mind, I made a plan. I was going to do whatever it took to be near Jessica. If I couldn't get them back to Virginia, then I was moving to Iowa. I got mad at God again just thinking of Iowa in winter.

I needed to get the car from the airport. Knowing I would need cash I walked over to the ATM, and found that Wendy had taken all the money. She had left me $20.00. Now I was really ticked off. Thinking about it later, I couldn't blame her, but that didn't matter at the time. I had to call Megan to get a ride to the airport. On the way, she just kept apologizing for the e-mail being open. She lied, saying she had been in a hurry that morning and must have forgotten to close it. The more she spoke, the more certain I was that it was intentional. She had been planning this for some time. She asked me what I was going to do. I told her I was getting our car, and going home. She needed to move out.

When I got back home I called some friends to see if I could borrow some money. Wendy had called Larry's wife and told her I was planning to kill her in Florida. They didn't want to have anything to do with me. I knew my brothers would shun me too. I didn't speak to anyone in the D.C. area. I don't know why, but I called the last person in the world I thought I would ever call when I was in trouble. Mom. I thought she would say, "I told you so," and I'd have to listen to her tell me what a sorry person I was, but I called her anyway. When I told her what was going on, she said that she and Bob would be there the next day to help out. She told me not to worry. She said she knew Wendy would come back with Jessica; she just had that feeling. I hung up and cried again.

Mom and Bob showed up the next day as promised. She loaned me some money to pay the bills, and explained she was there for support, not condemnation. Working the midnight shift at the World Bank gave me time to reflect on what had just happened, and what I needed to do to get things back on track. It also gave me time to think about how supportive Mom was being. I never found out what was going on between my mom, my dad, and Doctor English, but I am sure it was similar to what I was going through. Maybe she understood more than I gave her credit for. I will never know, but she was my savior during this time.

Wendy and I started negotiations the next week. She started going to a counselor she knew in Cedar Rapids. Megan moved out; and Mom and Bob were helping as much as they could—financially and mentally. Except for work and maybe a run, I stayed home, waiting for Wendy to call. I was desperate. Finally we came to an agreement. She would come back if I would go to counseling and never see Megan again. That was fair. I would do anything to get Jessica back. She nixed the job in Florida, so I should stay at the Bank. I didn't like that, but agreed to talk it over when she got back to Virginia. I didn't want to make a rash decision about the move. I still thought we would have a better chance of making things work in Florida with no one pointing out all our faults. Nobody would know us in Florida, and we could start over.

It took Wendy almost a month before she came back to Virginia. The first time I saw Jessica, it was like she didn't recognize me. She wouldn't come to me at first until she remembered me. Then we were back to our old selves. I was going to make this work, but didn't know how. All I knew was that the self-centered jerk that I was had been broken because of my love for this child. I couldn't live without her in my life, so I was ready to do anything. You name it: counseling, therapy, even Wendy's crap (and there was a lot of it right now). I was going to take it because of Jessica.

Then Wendy said something that made me understand we were still on the same page about taking care of Jessica. She told me that when Jessica was sixteen and asked why her mom and dad were no longer together, she could look at her and tell her it wasn't because we didn't try. I felt the same way, so I was willing to do anything to stay together. I also told her we needed to move to Florida because it would give us a fresh start. In time, Wendy conceded, and we put a plan together that would hopefully get us out of the house in one month and on our way to Florida.

We contacted a real estate agent and put the house on the market. At our second open house, a lady offered us full price (eighty thousand more than we had originally paid). We closed on the deal, so we just had to pack up our things and get on the road by

October 3rd. That would give us time to get to the house and get as unpacked as we could, before I began my new job.

Before we left, Wendy wanted us to fit in a couple of counseling sessions. During the sessions, Wendy's anger often erupted. I was afraid she was going to change her mind and not go to Florida. She would repeat her speech about working on our relationship. I could work with that.

The move was going as smoothly as possible until we realized we had more stuff than we could pack in our trailer. Once again, Mom and Bob came to the rescue. They told us not to worry; they would follow us down with another load. Two days before we were supposed to leave, Wendy told me we didn't have a place to stay. Earlier she had called the original house we were going to rent, and told them we were not coming. When she had called them back, they said it was already rented. She got on the Internet and found us a house in Trinity, Florida, a town which didn't even appear on any of our Florida maps. Looking at the pictures, the house looked better than the one we had originally picked. I looked at the address. It was also closer to my new job, less than 15 minutes away.

On October 3rd, we headed to Florida. I still wondered if I was making the right decision. Washington, D.C. was an incredible place. Even though Templar had been a hard lesson, the World Bank had been nothing but good to me. Even when I turned in my letter of resignation, nobody had been upset. They really understood. Why wouldn't someone take a job in Florida for a similar rate of pay? Besides executive protection and traveling the world was a single man's game.

But on October 3rd another reason emerged for getting out of there. On that day, I even worried about Mom and Bob. Two men, later called the Beltway snipers, killed five people randomly on the highway. None of the shootings happened near Alexandria, but several of the killings were near friends of ours.

This was the second time in my life that Florida seemed to be a safe haven. The first was in 1970 and now in 2002. This time it was me running from a problem I had created though. I was hoping for a fresh start, but every time Wendy thought about what happened, she would unload on me. Was she ever going to get over it? What would it take to work through this? How could I build trust again? To be fair, when you thought about it, this would take intense reconstruction. I hadn't just had an affair. An occasional fling. I had had a wife *and a live-in mistress* that the wife had trusted. Wendy had been completely unaware of the true nature of my relationship with Megan. And this had gone on for a long time. I needed to just be thankful Wendy and Jessica were even with me. I told myself to accept her anger as long as I could. I had to keep us together.

It took us two days to get to Trinity. We found the house and thanked our lucky stars that we had found it just two days before we had to leave. Jessica had had enough of traveling. She jumped out, and went for the yard. It was her first experience with St. Augustine grass, and she found it hard to walk on. She would take two steps, sit down, turn around, and look at us. She had never encountered such a thick carpet of green before. The house was perfect. It had a pool and a Jacuzzi and the neighborhood looked family-friendly and crime-free. We had never been in a gated community before; everyone seemed very polite.

The neighbor next to us was a Clearwater police officer. Kyle came over the first night while we were unloading and pitched right in. He spoke to me about becoming a cop here in Florida, but

I told him those days were over. I had a job that was straight days, with weekends and holidays off, and making what I did in Virginia. He joked that I would miss it, and I told him I already did.

The second day we were there the neighbor that lived across the street, Steve Plummer, walked over and introduced himself and his wife, Beth. He asked if we went to church. I quickly responded with a "No," hoping that was the end of the conversation, but I heard myself say, "I've been thinking about going back." I don't know where that statement came from, but I did intend to do whatever it took to keep Jessica and Wendy under one roof. If going to church and being a good boy would help, I was in, so the next weekend we attended First Christian Church. I enjoyed the preacher, Greg Johnson, but I still wasn't sold on the whole Christian thing. Too many previous unfavorable memories told me I didn't need religion. I still thought I could run my own life without any help from some supreme deity that judged people.

My new company was exceptionally good to Wendy, Jessica, and me. A family-run business always has its idiosyncrasies, but all in all, it was a good first four years in a new place. If it had not been for their great insurance, I don't know that we would have had my second daughter, Jaycee. However, after four years, I wasn't going anywhere in the company. It was a perfect place to start, but had no opportunity for advancement. While I worked there, Wendy and I put our lives back together.

Times were tough at home. Wendy often thought about the past and got angry which caused us to fight. It seemed like we were fighting a lot. When she would go off on me about the past, that old, familiar urge to just move on rose up within me.

I poured myself into my work, and Florida life suited me. If I moved out, it would be difficult, but I would at least have Jessica nearby so I could see her all the time. Then one night when I was running with Steve, he said something that corrected that thought. I needed a new way of thinking.

Wendy and I had one of those days and I mentioned it to Steve. Then I told him I was thinking of leaving Wendy. I still wanted to be involved in Jessica's life, but I was tired of all the fighting. His words were the best advice anyone had ever given me. Steve was divorced and had joint custody with his two children. He told me the hardest thing in his life right now was walking past their rooms when they weren't at his house, and knowing that some other man was tucking them in at night. His ex-wife had remarried, and the new husband was there with them all the time. They liked him, and Steve had no say so about it. I suddenly realized how likely this was in my case. If Wendy remarried, some other guy would be tucking my Jessica in every night too. She would not be with me anymore.

Just the thought of that broke me. I would go to hell and back for Jessica. I had to make this work—somehow, someway. I went to bed that night and couldn't sleep. I needed help. We had talked about finding a therapist down here, so the next morning I started looking and found one nearby. Sometimes Wendy and I went together, and other nights we had separate sessions. During one of my sessions, I spoke about Glen Rose. I told the therapist about the night my mother stopped a mile from the house and told me to tell my dad she wasn't coming home.

While I related about my walk home, I started to choke up. He stopped me and asked what had just happened. I told him I didn't know. I had told that story many times and never had it affect me like tonight. He explained that he felt that I had a fear of abandonment. Maybe that was why I had so many relationships and did not stick to one. I was afraid the person I was with might leave me, so I got out first—before that happened. He told me to think about it: I had been left on the side of the road by my mom. Then my dad had abandoned me when he shot and killed Doctor English. I was also abandoned by Doctor English when he died. He went on to say that I seemed to feel that God had abandoned me too. There's a saying that life flashes before our eyes when death is upon us. Well, I saw my life flash before my eyes when the therapist said all that. With this newly found information, I hoped he could help me find a way to correct this. Two visits later though, we found out he did not accept our insurance and that was the last time we saw him.

However, I pondered what he had shared. I started to search for a way to alleviate my fear of being alone. Pastor Greg Johnson preached a sermon about how God never leaves us—never. He said we are never alone. All we have to do is call upon Him, and He will come and heal us of our pain. Later as I was running, my life played out again in my mind. For the first time, I saw that God had never left me. In fact, I was where I was because of the way He never left me. I couldn't explain why some events in my life had happened, but I could see where God was in my past. He had moved me out of harm's way. It broke me. I was not god of my life. He was now and always had been with me.

Still, I was battling. I felt like I would lose myself if I surrendered everything to God, but my holding back continued to lead to bad decisions and trouble for Wendy and me. It seemed that the more I wanted to be better, the worse I got. Wendy gave me a two-strike rule. I was so close to striking out, I figured that if we had any chance of making it at all, I had to give everything to God. One night, after a very trying week of fighting, I told Him I was done. If He thought He could run my life better, it was His. I surrendered. He could do what He wanted with me. There was a lot I didn't understand though. Like grace.

I felt like I had found a place to volunteer in church. That way I could work off my sins. I did this by handling the audio/visual aspect of the church. There was a small office in the balcony area that we called the crow's nest. There we handled Pastor Greg's slides for his sermons and the cameras. When Greg stood up, we put one camera on him, and if he sat down on his stool, we put the other camera on him. This involved two switches. Nobody came into the crow's nest while the sermon was going on, so I sat up there for all three Sunday services, working off my sins.

I had joined a small men's group too, and we met at a Starbucks. Another Christian from another church brought over some Christian books that he was giving away. I don't know why but I picked up one. It was Max Lucado's *Come Thirsty: No Heart Too Dry for His Touch*. I had never heard of Max Lucado, but the title struck me. As I read it, I began to learn of God's unending love for me. I learned of his ability to take any life and heal it and make it whole again. God was that powerful! But the biggest thing I learned about was grace. His grace for me meant I didn't have to work off my sins. *They were forgiven.* All I needed to do was love Him and let Him take over. His love for me would do the rest. I had to stop wallowing in my past and start being an heir to the throne of God.

Being a Christian is not for the weak of heart. It takes courage to walk with God, to be the leader of your household and let Him lead you during the day. We have to have faith that He is going to be there for us. He gives us all the grace we can handle. I began to see that I was free from my past in God's eyes. I needed to live that way. There was no condemnation, just freedom with grace. This was a game-changer.

When we start to understand that God will keep us out of danger if we follow Him and that He gives us the tools we need in every situation, we find it easier to say, "Your will be done." As long as I let Him lead, I can be secure. I follow His power and grace. Is it easy? No, but it helps to be surrounded by Christian brothers. Being right with God was a tremendous relief. I was truly changed deep inside. Now I needed to work on my relationship with Wendy, and somehow repair our relationship.

I think she saw the change. She told the church that she believed and got baptized to publicly declare her love for God. We both worked on being more open with each other, and we started to see a difference. We put God first, family second, and then all the rest. Our choices changed. Now we weren't party animals anymore. We could see the difference in the way we handled Jessica too. Being firstborn, she did just anything she wanted. She had a take-charge attitude (a bit like me), but she would still give someone her favorite toy to make them happy.

At the beginning of 2003, I received word that my dad's cancer had returned. He would probably not survive the year. His eightieth birthday was on February 11, so Wendy and I decided to take Jessica and go celebrate what could be his last birthday. He had never met Jessica. My brother Joel came down too and so did Joy. We had a couple of days that felt like old times with Dad. Jessica followed him around like a little puppy. She handed out all his gifts at his party and wanted to sit in his lap while we played dominoes. That didn't last too long because she was a distraction and he was extremely competitive. Dad felt that dominoes should have been an Olympic sport, so there were many nights of intense games.

The day came for us to say goodbye. I was holding Jessica and told her to give Grandpa a kiss. She leaned into him and kissed him right on his lips. Dad took Jessica out of my arms and handed her over to Joy, and then grabbed me by the arm. Pulling me close, he said I should never let a child kiss an older person on the lips. What if she had a cold and killed them? At first, I wasn't sure he was serious, but then I remembered who was talking. I told him Jessica was his granddaughter, not some strange person off the street. If he was so worried about her kissing him on the lips, next time he should turn his head and let her kiss him on the cheek. However, I noticed he didn't do anything to change the position of the next kiss.

Those were the last words I spoke with him. On September 8, 2003, he passed away. He had been under hospice care for three months, just hanging on. Joy told me she thought he was hanging on because he didn't want to meet his Maker because of what he had done. Before he passed away, I wrote to him, telling him how much I loved him and how I had forgiven him for what he did. I am hoping that his wife, Winnie, read it to him and he heard my words. I am sorry to say that when he passed away I was relieved. That might sound bad, but when he passed, John, Joel, and I went to his funeral. The people that were there were saying all these really nice things that my father had done for them. John looked at Joel and me and said, "We are in the wrong funeral; this wasn't our dad." Not the one we knew anyway. Whenever we went to Texas, we were regretting it after thirty minutes with our dad. I do pray that I get to see him again when God calls me home.

I could never remember a time that Dad looked at us and told us he was proud of us while we were with him growing up. The first time he talked about all of us older boys being police officers, he had not been supportive. I didn't understand my father. He never missed an opportunity to demean us and was abusive all our lives. There had been a time that I wanted to be just like him: hardworking, dedicated to his cause, but now I just wanted to be the best son to my God and the best father and husband ever. I closed the door on my anger and hurt when they laid him to rest.

I came back to Florida with a different attitude. I had tried to live without God most of my life. I had done nothing but screw everything up over and over again. I needed to surrender everything to Him on an even deeper level. Once I truly surrendered, my life really started to change.

Eventually, we decided to build a home in the area. My job had its ups and downs, but it fit our needs. I couldn't ask for anything more. Wendy and I started volunteering at church. I coached one of the church's softball teams, really getting connected. Then I went on my first mission trip to Guatemala in May 2005 with my future boss, Mike Esposito.

Wendy went to Iowa to visit her family. One night around ten, Wendy called me, saying she had been out with friends when she started having stomach pains. She figured it was something she had eaten and went to bed. Wendy's mom called her sister, Crystal, and told her Wendy didn't look right. Crystal came, woke Wendy, and noticed she didn't have any color. She forced Wendy to go to the emergency room. She was bleeding internally. If they hadn't woken her, she would probably have died in her sleep.

Crystal's call to me came as Wendy was being taken into emergency surgery in the middle of the night. Wendy had an ectopic pregnancy. It had ruptured and taken out her left ovary. We had not even known she was pregnant. I flew to Iowa and got her back home. After that, we started seeing a specialist, but after a second and third miscarriage, we felt a second child was not in our future. The doctors found the reason for the problems. If we really wanted another child, Wendy would have to give herself an injection of a blood thinner every day during the pregnancy. Wendy was all in.

On August 8, 2006, after nine months of injections every night, we had our second daughter, Jaycee Nichole Howard. Just like Jessica, as soon as I held Jaycee, I told her I would do anything for her.

A year later, Mike Esposito offered me a job. He owned a painting company, and during this time, the painting business was good. The Pasco County area was the fastest growing county in the state of Florida. Construction was everywhere and new construction needed painters. Even though new construction was the company's main source of income, they saw a need for servicing previously painted homes too. The jobs were smaller, but they received more calls for repainting a house than they did for new construction. Mike asked me if I would come and be their salesperson for that side of the business. He needed someone who was professional and treated people well, and he saw that in me. His offer was a lower salary but a higher commission, so I could build it up based on my clients.

Wendy and I talked about it. The CISCO job was going nowhere. I hadn't received a raise in two years, so we decided to give it a try. CISCO was great to us, but we needed to move on. Wendy started a new business with loan closings; between that and my new job, we were hoping we wouldn't be broke by the end of the year. Mike estimated that I would get about ten percent of my contracts, but I was soon was getting thirty- to forty-five-percent of my closings, so my commission checks were huge. Wendy started scheduling closings all over the United States (even as far as Alaska) and her business took off. We made more money that year than we had over the last four. But in 2007, the rug was yanked right out from under us with the economic crash. New construction and loan closings came to a halt, and we were both in danger of losing our jobs.

When the new construction dried up, Mike decided to close down his painting company. If there was no new construction, there were no closings, so Wendy's business took a big hit. I spoke to Wendy about returning to law enforcement. It was a job that never shut down. In October of 2007, I attended an abbreviated two-week police academy for previous law enforcement officers and by January, I was back working as a police officer for a little town in Pinellas County. Belleair had a twelve-man police department that covered a two-mile radius of some of the most expensive homes in the area. As we drove during December, residents waved and wished us a Merry Christmas. I thought I had died and gone to heaven.

I had reservations about becoming a police officer again. I was worried about being put in a position in which I would be easily propositioned by another woman. I had not done well with that before.

I was also worried about my pride. I could do this job. I had as much experience as the Chief and the Lieutenant. I could have run the department, but if my pride got the best of me, it would cause all sorts of problems. I was intimately acquainted with my capacity to be a jerk. I turned to the Lord. There were many times I felt His presence. He moved me out of trouble on many occasions. It was great having a Father that didn't mind giving me guidance, support, and the biggest gift of all, peace.

The Town of Belleair began in 1897 as a resort town with the opening of the Belleview-Biltmore Resort and Spa. By 2008, the resort had fallen onto hard times. Even though it was still a functioning hotel and convention center, it was slated to be closed in 2009 for renovations. It never reopened.

A lot of history and great stories came from that resort. Zillow placed the median home value in Belleair at over $400,000. I was not in Norfolk anymore. The town treated the police department well. I could do this job forever, except for taking a huge financial hit, cutting our salaries to just over half of what we had been making. Even so, we knew this job wouldn't go away. I settled into working nights for the first three months, sometimes not getting a call all night long. After three months I applied and got the new detective position. I went from straight nights to days with weekends and holidays off. I thought I would be working with the Belleair Police Department for the rest of my working days, but God had other plans.

I was having an issue at church. I wanted to serve but couldn't find a place that fit me. I started out with the audio/video in its infancy. When we put a band on the stage, that process changed dramatically from a two-camera switchboard and slides on the screen to a soundboard that you needed a college degree to operate. I was not interested in learning a new trade. The manual alone was three inches thick. Wendy asked me to help Jessica and her in the children's ministry. I thought, *Why not? Jessica, my little buddy, was there. How hard could it be?* At some point, I realized I couldn't Taser little Johnny for not sitting down. I didn't have the tolerance for working in the children's ministry. I was asked about being a greeter, but I had nightmares about that. I was afraid that if a person did not acknowledge my friendly smile, I might spin them around and demand to know what their problem was. Hadn't they seen my smile?

But God has plans, plans that I didn't see coming. The church had bought property in the next county, almost twenty-nine acres of land. Because of the building fund drive, we saw large amounts of money being collected during the weekly offering, so a couple of the church leaders who knew my background in law enforcement asked me if I could make sure the money got from point A to point B.

A switch flipped. I told them that in 1999 when the Columbine school shooting happened, Norfolk had been one of the first police departments in the state to do active shooter training. I was in the D.C. area when 9/11 happened and had learned all about soft targets. Soft targets are easy-to-hit places where a shooter could inflict mass casualties without any resistance. Churches were considered soft targets. When I finished my two-minute rant, the church leaders were stunned. They looked at me and said, "Jim, we appreciate your expertise, but all we need you to do is get the money from point A to point B."

I was their guy. I could do this, and that was how our safety team got started. I asked a couple of other officers to help me. We were diligent in our watch for anything that might threaten the church while watching the money too. All that went to a whole new level when Charles Dear started coming to church.

Charles Dear was attending just so he could watch his ex-wife's movements. They had two children, but Charles had been out of the picture for a 2005 aggravated battery with a deadly weapon charge. He spent a year in jail, and then had supervised visitation, which meant he couldn't see his children unless they were at a state facility. At the church, Charles waited for his ex-wife to drop off their children at children's ministry, watched her go into service, and then took his kids out, and walked around with them until she came out. When she found out what he was doing, she was upset and went to the church leaders for assistance.

They came to me and asked me how we should handle this. I told them that if there was a court order that granted only supervised visitation, then he should not be allowed to take the kids from the children's ministry. Now that we knew about the order if something happened to the children, we would be liable too. The children were supposed to be in our care. They were our responsibility until their mother came and got them. They asked Charles's ex-wife to bring in the court order, and we would make a decision; but before she could get the papers to us, Charles gave us a reason to trespass him off the property, which meant he could not return to the church without breaking the law.

Charles's ex-in-laws were in town and came to church. They went to get the kids and met Charles at the children's ministry door. We had been following Charles. As he came out with the kids, the in-laws politely asked him for the kids. Charles threatened to beat up the grandfather right there. We quickly stepped in and escorted Charles to the edge of the courtyard. We advised him that he had to abide by the church and the state rules, and threatening ex-in-laws was against all rules. Charles had a few choice words for us, and walked off the property.

The next week a Pasco County detective showed up on our property and got the church really interested in security. Charles had killed his landlady and burned down her house to cover his crime the same weekend he had threatened his ex-father-in-law. It was almost full circle. I had been in this situation before, and I knew God had trained me in how to handle it now. The church decided we needed to look into real church security, but that didn't happen until we moved into our new facility.

Even though I had so much police experience, when the church decided that they genuinely wanted to talk about church security, I felt that I needed some guidance. I turned to the Bible and searched the subject. God led me to Nehemiah. Nehemiah was the wine taster for the Persian king, Artaxerxes I. When Nehemiah found out about the destruction of the wall of Jerusalem, he wept. Without going through the whole story, the king cared about Nehemiah to the extent that he gave him the materials to rebuild the wall, and allowed him to go there to do it. Once Nehemiah started rebuilding the wall, the local non-Jewish settlers plotted to kill all the Jewish people working there. Nehemiah asked God for guidance. I based our ministry on Nehemiah:

> Therefore I stationed some of the people behind the lowest points of the wall at the exposed places, posting them by families, with their swords, spears and bows. After I looked things over, I stood up and said to the nobles, the officials and the rest of the people, "Don't be afraid of them. Remember the Lord, who is great and awesome, and fight for your families, your sons and your daughters, your wives and your homes." When our enemies heard that we were aware of their plot and that God had frustrated it, we all returned to the wall, each to our own work. From that day on, half of my men did the work, while the other half were equipped with spears, shields, bows and armor. The officers posted themselves behind all the people of Judah who were building the wall. Those who carried materials did their work with one hand and held a weapon in the other, and each of the builders wore his sword at his side as he worked. But the man who sounded the trumpet stayed with me. *(Nehemiah 4:13-18)*

I searched for church security training online, and found several webpages with minimal information, but nothing concrete. Tina

Lewis Rowe had written a document titled "How to Assess the Safety and Security of Your Place of Worship." I began with that. Merging that with my own experience, I put together a safety plan for our church. Most of the training I found was focused on dealing with an active shooter, but after the Charles Dear incident, I realized that domestic issues were the greater challenge in churches across the country. That plus children's safety were the two top issues on my training list. Having an active shooter got the most publicity, but there was a greater chance of having a disruptive attendee than an active shooter.

In 2009 we moved into our new building and became Generations Christian Church (GCC). The leadership of GCC made safety and security a priority. With the help of strong Christian men like John Carver and Matt Pittard, we assessed our church for its strengths and weaknesses. Then we put together policies and procedures that worked for us. We put together a fire plan in case of evacuation or medical emergencies, and looked at equipment like radios and medical kits. We also wrote job descriptions for each component of the safety team and talked about who would be best for those positions. We ran into a snag here. Our church put out questionnaires asking people where they wanted to serve. If they said safety team, we had to take them. It took us four years to change that.

I went to the leaders of the church, and told them it was time to train all the volunteers, staff, and safety team members on church safety. I didn't realize what would be involved in this. Not everyone understood the importance of having a "security team" in the church. We set up two dates to do the training and had everyone sign up for the events. The first night we had 120 people. The next night we had 80. This took the church by surprise. They thought only a handful of people would show up, but the members of the church understood the importance of church safety and wanted to learn more about being aware.

We started doing yearly training and other churches started joining us too. A few churches approached me to come and assess their churches. At the time, church safety was more of a hobby than anything else. I was still also working as a policeman in Belleair and thought I would be there for the rest of my working days. In fact, for as small as the Town of Belleair was, we had some unusual cases come our way.

One burglary case started out as a real whodunit. By the time we identified the suspect, we discovered he had committed burglaries all across Florida, stealing up to half a million dollars' worth of jewelry and other items. In another case, I chased a suspect who had hacked into over 500 people's e-mails and social media accounts. That case and arrest appeared in an edition of *PC Magazine* from London. I started teaching at the police academy and used all my cases as examples on how to investigate crimes. The whole time I was in Belleair I never had to testify, but still got convictions because of my work ethic. I never went a day without asking for God's guidance, and it showed. I knew where to give credit and it was to Him.

I had a couple of opportunities come up over the years through which I could have left Belleair. I applied for a lieutenant's position in another department, but that didn't work out. Then I was offered two other positions by the Sheriff of a local county, but both interviews went poorly. This just told me God already had me where He wanted.

It wasn't all great in Belleair though. The department had lost faith in the leadership and had a vote of no confidence against the Chief of Police. I was the union representative and given the responsibility of presenting our case to the town management. I would never wish this on anyone, but God had laid it on my heart that—no matter what happened—I should stand for what the other officers as a whole saw as just. We loved the department. Since it was going down a destructive path, we had to take action. After a lengthy investigation, the Chief was asked to step down. The lieutenant became the new Chief. If I had stayed with the police department, I had the greatest chance to be the next Chief, but God had another plan for me, and it was about to unfold.

At several of my church trainings, a Pinellas County detective named Mitch Smithies told me that my training was good enough to share with others. I wasn't interested at the time. I liked my job. In August of 2015, he called again. He had retired and was living in North Carolina. Would I send him my presentation, so he could help set up a safety team for his church? I told him that if he paid for my expenses, I would come up and do the training for free. He spoke to his church and they paid for my airfare. I was going to stay with him and his wife in their beautiful house on the side of a mountain. The next thing I knew I was in Waynesville, NC doing church safety training.

When I got back, I was excited that I had been able to teach what God had given me. Wendy took me out to dinner to "have a talk." This was never good news. After I had a beer and she had a glass of wine, she told me we needed a change. She and the girls never saw me anymore. I was doing all these things for the church and also working at the department. Since the Town of Belleair was an hour from our house, I was working over fifty hours a week, and that was only when I didn't have any overtime. She had looked at the finances. We could live on my retirement from Norfolk and my estimated retirement from Belleair. Doing some part-time training at the academy would be fine, but I needed to make a choice. It either going to be full-time police detective or full-time church safety ministry. I needed to consider our family and myself as well. She told me I looked tired all the time.

I knew what I wanted to do, but I didn't know what God wanted me to do. I prayed, and went to work as usual, but everything had come to a standstill. Before this my workload had been challenging; now nothing was coming across my desk. This was probably due to the work of the great police officers in Belleair, but I also thought God might be telling me something. I continued to pray. I needed His specific guidance or I was staying with the town of Belleair.

I had a little bit of a falling out with the new Chief of Police. He had been good friends with the previous chief and had taken offense about the way he had been forced to resign. He claimed that I had lied about him in my complaint. Was this the answer God was sending me? Was this His way of showing me it was time to go? I am a little like Gideon. I want my fleece to be dry tomorrow and the ground wet, but I typed up a resignation letter, just in case.

I was at the State Attorney's office for a case I was working on. As I got back into my car, I opened up my folder and there was my resignation letter. I prayed again and asked for some sort of sign. His will be done. As I sat there looking at the letter, I got a text from a church I had worked with before. They said that last

Sunday during a sermon on why they were pro-life, a member of the church seemed to lose it, and walked out cursing at the church. People were afraid he was going to come back with a gun and open fire.

There is a joke about a town that is flooding. A farmer is sitting on his front porch watching the water rise. A big four-wheel truck drives up and tells him to hop in so they could take him to safety. He says, "Thanks anyway, but I am waiting on my Lord to rescue me." Later when the water is over the porch, a boat pulls up, and the man in the boat says, "Jump in, and let me take you to higher ground!" Still the farmer refuses, saying he is waiting on the Lord to save him. Eventually the water is up to the roof, and the farmer is on top of the house. A helicopter comes by, and yells, "Grab the line and we'll rescue you!" Once again, the farmer tells him he is waiting on the Lord. So the farmer drowns and goes to heaven. When he meets the Lord, he asks, "Lord, why didn't You rescue me?" The Lord replies, "I sent you a truck, a boat, *and* a helicopter! What else did you want?"

It was clear to me after the text that the Lord wanted me to resign, so I went into the office and turned in my letter.

In October 2015, we formed Trinity Security Allies. Two weeks later, Wendy quit her job and began helping me. It was sink or swim. Our motto is: "Our Ministry Is Your Church's Safety," and in no time, we started doing trainings in the area. We next realized that those that want to hurt the church change churches often in the same way that criminals go from area to area, so we began networking. We had found that a disruptive attendee that came to our church had talked about another church we knew. We warned that church; and when we did, we found out that a sexual offender we had asked to leave our church for preying on young teenage girls, had gone to their church and started grooming another thirteen-year-old. (That person is now serving life in a penitentiary.) In our first networking meeting, we had five churches and ten people register ahead. When we showed up for the meeting, there were ten churches and twenty people at the gathering.

My church hired me as a safety consultant. Most of the time, we asked for a prayer offering for our services. We received between $50.00 and $500.00, but we knew we couldn't maintain the ministry on that. Wendy came up with a pay structure that I felt was too high, but the churches agreed to it, and because we had put a value on the training, more churches started calling us. We also got calls from businesses to come and do "Situational Awareness" and "Threat Profiling" training for their employees. Before I knew it, we were doing trainings in North Carolina, Georgia, South Carolina, and all over Florida, and this was only through word of mouth. There had been no marketing.

I attended a Sheepdog Training Seminar. Jimmy Meeks with Sheepdog asked me to tell people about myself and what we did. From that contact, lots of churches called us. During some training in Polk County, a S.W.A.T sergeant heard me speak. The next time he went to a church and they mentioned church safety, he gave them my card. The word was spreading. I knew we were for real when we got a call from James Poucher. His church, Christ Community Church, in Zion, Illinois wanted us to come and do safety training. James had been to a church in St. Petersburg, FL and saw their safety team in action. They told James Trinity Security Allies had taught them.

We started doing Church Safety Seminars (a one-day conference). God provided us with speakers from all different types of church violence. Pastor Terry L. Howell, Sr. told of his harrowing experience when he went to terminate an employee, only to have the employee pull a weapon and shoot, and miss him, at point-blank range. Pastor Howell was armed that day and returned fire. He did not miss. The following year I met Ron Holland who had taken a youth group to Wedgwood Baptist Church in Fort Worth, Texas on September 15, 1999. While watching a play put on by the church's youth, a crazed gunman walked in and killed seven and wounded seven. Last year we had Julie Workman, a survivor in the Sutherland Springs Baptist Church shooting where twenty-six members of her church died and twenty were injured. One of her sons, Kris, was shot and is crippled from the waist down. Hearing these different testimonies brought chills, and there was never a dry eye in the house. However, every one of these stories glorified God.

Our training started with just the basics: "Putting Together a Safety Plan" and "Developing a Safety Team." When we realized there was too much emphasis on active shooters and being reactive, we developed a deeper understanding of being proactive, and put together our "Sunday Morning, What to Look For" and "Verbal De-Escalation." These trainings covered situational awareness and threat profiling, and instructed participants about how to talk to those in need. There were so many questions about weapons in the church that we created, "Carrying Weapons in Church" too. We now provide these PDFs free on our webpage at trinitysecurity-allies.com. In 2018, we were able to bring John Carver and Max

Creason in to help us with training, and to do comprehensive risk assessments that allowed pastors and staff to make critical safety decisions for their church. We thought we had covered all areas of church safety.

In 2017, we stepped up the training even more with the purchase of a firearm simulator. This placed safety team members in real-life scenarios so they could learn situational awareness and "shoot, don't shoot," which taught security team members how to judge a situation as it unfolded in front of them. In 2019, Laser Shot contacted us and asked if we would help them create church-based simulations. Working with them, we created twenty-eight real church scenarios based on real-life incidents that had occurred in churches across the country. Through this, we were now able to train safety team members in situational awareness, verbal de-escalation, and "shoot, don't shoot" *using real-life church situations.*

Every day we see God's handiwork in our journey in this ministry. There are still times I find myself questioning the past. Satan likes to get at us like that. He whispers in your ear, trying to convince you of what a loser you are.

I was getting ready to do training in Venice, Florida. Their police department invited me to speak to their churches. The night before the training, we found out that we had over 300 registered. It was the largest group I had ever directed.

The local news had found old newspaper articles about my dad's trial. It was in these articles that I discovered my dad had called my grandmother three weeks before the shooting and told her that he was going to kill Mom, all of us boys, *and* Doctor English. Even though Mom was made aware of the threat, she still allowed my dad to have custody of us. As I mentioned earlier, on the Sunday of

Mom and the Boys at Bob's funeral in 2017

The Howard Boys: John, Jim, and Joel in 2018

the shooting, my dad had taken us to a field to shoot. *He had never done that before.* Ironically, the last time we had done that was with Doctor English and some of his sons. That was the same night my dad walked out and killed Doctor English—using the same gun we had been shooting hours before. As a father, knowing that my ex-spouse had threatened to kill all of us, would I allow my children near that person? No! Why did Mom do that? That is still an unanswered question that sometimes bounces around in my head. What my father did still overwhelms me sometimes.

But during those times, I hear my heavenly Father reassure me that even though my earthly dad may have had thoughts about killing us that day, God had softened his heart. God had plans for my brothers and me. I am living proof that God has a plan for everyone. The problem with most of us is that we don't listen. Because of that, we miss the calm words of Jesus:

> "Come to me, all you who are weary and burdened, and I will give you rest." *(Matthew 11:28)*

I was extremely tired when I finally made my way back to God. Since then, He has given me an amazing degree of grace and rest. I will never know what Mom was thinking that day. She passed away before I could ask her. On December 23, 2019, Joel contacted me and told me she had been admitted to the hospital and it didn't look like she would ever leave. She went to the emergency room because she felt like she had a urinary tract infection, but when they did some bloodwork, they told her it looked like kidney failure. She was being transported to another hospital which specialized in that. Typically, she was worried about her car in the parking lot. They reassured her about it, but she insisted on driving her car home and then got an Uber back to the hospital.

She finally called Joel and told him where she was. Why hadn't she called him first? She didn't want to bother anyone. This was Mom through-and-through. She was immediately put into ICU. By the time Joel got to the hospital, her kidneys had failed, and she had severe sepsis. They asked Joel if she was a fighter; because if not, they would make her comfortable and pray for the best. Joel told them she was a fighter, but on their first attempt in getting her back to normal, she coded and her heart stopped. On Christmas Day, the doctors told my brothers that they would fight for her as long as she wanted, but everything they planned to do would cause another life-threatening problem. They needed to know if she wanted to fight or go home. Joel spoke to Mom and she wanted to go home.

On Christmas Day, Joel called me about Mom's decision. I told him I would drive to Virginia soon. She died that night before I could get there, even though the doctors had assured us there was some time. Just like that she was gone. I had to laugh. That was Mom all over. Once she had chosen her path, she had her bags packed, and was waiting for her escort to heaven. She went the way she wanted: quick and with nobody fussing over her. On her own time.

Jessica and I drove to Virginia for the funeral. It was the second Howard Boys' reunion since Bob's passing in 2017. I had a chilling thought that the next time we got together, it would probably be for one of us. Even as I write this, I know that I have to somehow correct that. I must make it a priority to see my brothers more often.

I was trying to remember the last time I had talked to Mom. She had become my windshield buddy. I often called her when I was on the road. Sometimes we would talk for hours. She and I had been through a lot together, some really bad times, but lately some really good times. I was very happy that we had let the past go and had the time to get to know each other. We had both finally accepted each other. I did not talk about politics with her, but kept the conversation on religion and family. With our dysfunctional family, there was always an interesting topic for discussion. She loved it when I told her about my men's Bible studies, and was very supportive of Trinity Security Allies.

I will never forget how mad she got when I joined the police department. I think she stopped talking to me for two years. Then just when she started inviting me back into the family, John and Joel had joined and she blamed me. Once again, she had stopped talking to me. Then she bought a police scanner; and if she heard of a shooting or of an officer involved in an accident, she would call to make sure none of us was involved.

One Christmas she found a bunch of old pictures of the three oldest Howard Boys. In every picture, there was a toy weapon. Even in diapers, we wore gun belts and had a six-shooter in our hands. She wrote me a little note once. It said: "I should have figured out that by the time you grew up, you would be outlaws or lawmen. I have never been ashamed of telling people what my sons do for a living." Even though she didn't say she was proud of me outright, I cherished that note. I will miss the many hours we used to talk when I was driving. Mom was a great windshield buddy.

When I look back at my life, I look at the major incidents. In them, I can always see God. I was the cause for all my mistakes: failed marriages, affairs, and everything else bad that happened to me once I was on my own. I can point to times when I was a victim and how those things changed my life. If God didn't have a plan for me and my brothers that September day in the field, He would have just let my dad kill us. It was because God had a specific plan for us that my dad did not. God was going to see it through, no matter how many times I messed up.

I can see His work in so many ways. Even though I did not have a good father and ran the streets with my friends, God kept me out of trouble with music. Being robbed and carjacked catapulted me into a path that I had never even imagined. He taught me through all the things I went through in the police department. As crazy as I was on the street, I survived. He put me in Crime Analysis, and then Systems Development, which could have been a dead-end for my career. Instead, God gave me a cause to fight for, and my career soared.

Then there was Templar. That company broke my pride and forced me to look for a job for which I was overqualified. Yet it was there that God taught me things I still use in church training today. In my darkest hour, He opened doors He could have closed. Even the way He found a house for us was amazing. God carefully placed us in our home in Trinity, Florida across the street from Steve Plummer, which led me to First Christian Church where I found rest. In all of my trials and tribulations, He always gave me a cause—one I could fight for with all my heart and soul.

The helpful friends He put in my life were no coincidence either. One day when I was worrying about competition, James Sutherland yelled at me, "You have no competition. You have God!" James was right. God is the greatest Authority, so if I am in His will, what do I have to worry about?

"Keep this Book of the Law always on your lips; meditate on it day and night, so that you may be careful to do everything written in it. Then you will be prosperous and successful. Have I not commanded you? Be strong and courageous. Do not be afraid; do not be discouraged, for the Lord your God will be with you wherever you go." *(Joshua 1:8-9)*

When I was invited to lead training in Zion, Illinois, I told a friend, Ken Kunsman, that I had no clue where it was. He said, "That doesn't matter. If you travel less than 100 miles, you are the guest speaker. More than 500, and you're the expert. Over 1,000 miles, you're the authority." I had never thought of myself as an authority over anything, but God has a way of putting us out there to do His work.

He brought me up out of the pit of destruction, out of the miry clay, and He set my feet upon a rock making my footsteps firm. *(Psalm 40:2 NASB)*

He has given me a mission: "Our Ministry Is Your Church's Safety" and a voice and a platform, and it goes way beyond church safety. It is all about the expansion of the kingdom of God. That is my cause and I will fight for it with all my heart and soul and strength.

JIM HOWARD

To get an idea of what was happening to churches across the world, we created several Google Alerts that provided a daily list of church-related incidents. When they are of interest to the churches in our network, we post them on our social media pages. We noticed an increase in domestic violence in the churches. We felt that our "Situational Awareness" and "Threat Profiling" training covered all the bases on how to spot a possible issue inside the church before it got violent. We teach that there are three types of people that come into your church: those that come simply to worship, which include the church shoppers (and if you live in Florida, the "snowbirds" that will be there just for the winter). These are believers that genuinely want to be part of a church family.

Then there are those that are hurting and possibly one step away from doing something they will regret for the rest of their lives. They walk into your church looking for answers. I was one of those at one time. As Christians we need to make sure that we minister to the hurting person.

The third type is the wolf in sheep's clothing. They might look like that hurting person looking for answers, but they are not. They usually come into your church with an agenda. They come to disrupt in some way—either as a prophet that doesn't agree with a church's teachings or a disgruntled person looking to make a scene.

Our ministry teaches how to spot them as they come in the door. Do they appear nervous or distant? Do they stand in a corner by themselves, watching the activities of the church? We teach how to walk up and start a conversation with an easy statement like, "Good morning! Is this your first time here?" We initiate the dialogue from there. "The friendliest church I have ever attended" is what I want to read about a church from their online reviews. People should have that kind of experience in church. The truly hurting person comes to church to receive help in their "time of need" (Hebrews 4:16) from a Christian congregation. Compassionate believers help one another. That's how real families operate.

Team members need to know how to handle every type of person. We need to be able to differentiate them when they walk in our door, or we will continue to see situations like the 2019 West Freeway Church of Christ shooting. That guy walked in with an obviously fake beard and wig, and *nobody spoke to him*. What a costly mistake. We teach that once you start a conversation with a person, you will find out in less than two minutes whether this person could be a potential threat or someone needing help. If an unknown person walks into your church dressed all in black and you are not the Church of Johnny Cash, you need to walk over and introduce yourself. We must be able to talk to anyone and not be afraid.

Over the years we have observed an increase of attacks on church facilities. Every day we seem to be reading about a vandalism attack on a church. However, the type of vandalism has changed. In the old days, it was just spray painting graffiti on the walls or knocking out a window. Today, it is total destruction. We saw food pantries wrecked, worship centers that had their pianos and other musical instruments destroyed, and pews ripped up from the floor and broken in pieces. Statues outside churches are being shattered. There is probably one fire a month in which a church is totally destroyed. This isn't vandalism. It's hate. We have received calls from churches across the country that were seeing serial attacks (multiple churches attacked with the same *modus operandi)*. Law enforcement did its best to investigate these situations, and arrests were made, but it continues.

We get most of our calls to talk to churches about security after an active shooter incident. It breaks my heart when I do an after-action critique on these shootings, and realize that if these churches had some sort of training, the incident might have been prevented or the carnage lessened. There are almost always red flags prior to an incident.

In June of 2015, there was an attack on the Emanuel African Methodist Episcopal Church in Charleston, South Carolina. It became quite clear that churches were in a spiritual battle "against the powers of this dark world and against the spiritual forces of evil in the heavenly realms" (Ephesians 6:12). That Wednesday night attack was nothing more than Satan using a demented person to carry out his plan against a welcoming church. The media emphasis on the shooting was that a white racist picked an all-black church to start a civil war, but in reality, this was Satan showing all of us in the church security business that he could send anyone into a church at any time to attack. This church had welcomed the shooter with open arms and prayed for him. During his interrogation, he admitted that he almost did not complete his plan because the members of the church had been so nice to him. However,

Satan's plan was already in play. A lot of churches woke up to how vulnerable they were when this happened.

One more thing about the Charleston shooting. I watched the shooter's video court appearance after the incident. As he stood there in front of the camera listening to the charges against him, he also heard the voices of the victims' families, telling him they forgave him and would pray for him. Satan can't win while we have the power of the Holy Spirit in us. I can tell you that I would not be able to forgive someone who had done such a thing against Christians except through the love of Jesus Christ and the power of the Holy Spirit.

I was doing training at a church of about 100 members on November 4, 2017. I clarified that we needed to be more proactive when it came to church shootings. We need to be aware of family issues going on in a church. Instead of not wanting to talk about them or feeling that they are none of our business, we need to be aware of them. Information on issues like this is not gossip. If you have a family that is going through hard times, you need to reach out to them. If there is even a hint of domestic violence, it can easily bleed into the church.

The next day while having lunch with Wendy, my phone erupted with links about a church in Sutherland Springs, Texas. As I watched the horror unfold, I knew in the back of my mind that this was a domestic issue. Later we found out that the shooter had probably gone to the First Baptist Church of Sutherland Springs to kill his mother-in-law because of her concern for her daughter's safety. The man had an extremely violent past and brought that violence into the church, killing twenty-six innocent people and wounding twenty others. Satan wanted to show that he could reach out at a moment's notice and destroy a church. He didn't succeed. One of the survivors tells us that God never left her or the church on that tragic day.

Most of our training has been about these incidents that have occurred in churches. We prepare a church for the worst. I was comfortable that we were covering all the bases with the tools we had developed. We were traveling all over the country: teaching church safety, doing quarterly networking meetings, and keeping monthly blogs and a Facebook page that was posting current events. Then Wendy talked me into doing a weekly Facebook Live segment, in which I spend thirty minutes basically ranting about things I saw churches do or not do to protect the flock.

I felt confident we were doing all we could to protect the flock and explain the kingdom of God. We regularly got calls from churches relating a scary incident, a domestic issue, or a prophet walking in and creating a scene. I thought we were right where we were supposed to be in our work for Him. As always God had a larger plan, and He expanded my vision and laid it on my heart to not only fight for churches, but for our country too.

JIM HOWARD

H ow many times have you heard that God takes a small-town farm boy from somewhere, and well, you know the rest. That's *not* what happened here. In my story, God lost one of His sheep and searched for it for years and years until He found it—broken, battered, and lost, and brought it back into His fold. He cleaned it up and gave it a mission, and uses that sheep every day for the expansion of His kingdom. I am content in my life today. Nestled between Wendy, Jessica, Jaycee, my earthly family, and my Christian family, I am right where God wanted me from birth. Right here, right now. And God had more for me still.

> Before I formed you in the womb I knew you, before you were born I set you apart; I appointed you as a prophet to the nations. *(Jeremiah 1:5)*

I always read the first part: "Before I formed you in the womb I knew you, before you were born I set you apart" and never paid much attention to the last bit of it. It wasn't until I studied that part that it hit me: "I appointed you as a prophet to the nations." That scared me. A Hartford Institute for Religion Research Statistics study done in 2005 said that 37% of the churches across the United States have 350 or less people in attendance, and almost 47% have under 100.[2] I thought our mission was to reach those

---

2   David A. Roozen, "America's Congregations 2005," faithcommunitiestoday.org, 2007, https://faithcommunitiestoday.org/wp-content/uploads/2009/10/American-Congregations-2005-pro.pdf.

two groups (the 84%), but God's vision was broader, including not only the churches but our entire nation.

There is a holy war on the horizon, and if believers don't wake up, we are going to lose this war and our religious freedoms with it. This is the message God put on my heart, and He wants me to take it to the churches across the nation. In light of Jeremiah's words, I guess I am a prophet.

When the COVID-19 pandemic hit America, all our training engagements were rescheduled. Wendy had been pushing me to do webinars, but I had been fighting that. I didn't feel comfortable speaking in front of a camera, but preferred interacting with people. However, the pandemic changed all that so I jumped into the webinar arena. Many people were doing podcasts. I had been on a few, but was terrified to do it myself. Even so, with a few glitches here and there, we started doing Thursday webinars on top of our Sunday Facebook Live segments. With this outreach, we started to get noticed and gain more members across the country. One Thursday, people from seventeen different states attended a webinar.

In May we saw a major shift in the country: Churches were being shut down, riots broke out in our cities, and it felt like our world was spinning out of control. I was praying about what to write in my next blog, and understood a deeper truth. We are at war: not a war between the races or the sexes, but a deep spiritual war against Satan. He is alive and well, my brothers and sisters, and right now he thinks he has the American people where he wants them. He thinks he is winning.

Let's think about it for a second. COVID-19 hit us hard. In March of 2020, our country came to a standstill. No more than ten people could get together at a time, and in most states, non-essential businesses were closed down. Churches fell into that category. I am sure Satan figured that if you shut down the churches, you would kill Christianity. God was ready. We often view technology as a tool Satan uses to destroy our families, yet we took that same technology and used it to expand the kingdom of God.

A lot of Christians viewed this as a wake-up call. Maybe we had made too much of a fuss over our big buildings and our grandiose services. After all, early Christianity started in small homes, caves, and anywhere two or more could get together and worship. Satan hoped we would die out, but we didn't. We flourished.

The viewing audiences for church services are growing, not shrinking. Facebook, YouTube, and Zoom have become the venues in which people come to worship. Satan didn't take us down. God united us. And many new people began tuning in as well. COVID-19 made them aware of their need, and they were looking for answers. Believers saw this as an opportunity to shine. We were the lighthouse in this storm called COVID-19.

Some in our government felt the need to make sure our churches did not open too soon, and when some churches challenged that call, issues arose. Law enforcement stepped in and arrested some pastors for holding church services, or intimidated members by writing down their license numbers at drive-in services. They even shut down churches that were giving away Easter baskets to members using CDC guidelines. Did that stop us? No.

Good sense prevailed. Discerning politicians came together and pointed out that churches were essential. With both suicide calls and domestic violence on the rise, we needed to get people back to God. Some saw the church as nearly as essential as the hospitals. Churches are in the business of helping those that are hurting. Yes, we are essential, and Satan, you lost again.

But Satan wasn't finished. We had two racial incidents that Satan knew would pit brothers and sisters against each other. On May 5, 2020, a video went viral of the February 23, 2020 incident when Ahmaud Arbery, an unarmed twenty-five-year-old African American man, was fatally shot near Brunswick, Georgia. This was a tragedy. Many people's lives have been drastically changed because of this, and it saddens me to think of all the families involved.

As the facts of the case slowly came to light, many who had been initially irate over an unarmed black male being shot and killed by an armed white male began to wonder if this was the war they wanted to invest in. I was incredibly surprised that after law enforcement arrested those involved in the death of Arbery, the case seemed to have been placed on the back burner. I will not get into it here, but no person deserves to die in what possibly could have been a property crime violation. No one. Once again, Satan was on the scene, pulling the strings and trying to split the country apart, but it didn't happen. I am not sure why, but I would like to think that it was because so many prayed for peace, comfort, and strength for all of those involved in this terrible incident.

Then on May 25, 2020, came the perfect storm. George Floyd, another African American man, died in police custody. The initial video caused everyone to blame his death on injuries inflicted by a white officer who had placed his knee on Floyd's neck.

Floyd had been arrested for passing counterfeit money. After being handcuffed, Floyd resisted arrest, and physically refused to get into the police vehicle, claiming he was claustrophobic and would not be able to breathe. Floyd was placed face down on the street, while officers tried to assess the situation and called for paramedics for fear Floyd was experiencing "excited delirium."

In a Lexipol article, the American Medical Association described excited delirium as "a widely accepted entity in forensic pathology" that is "cited by medical examiners to explain the sudden in-custody death of individuals who are combative and in a highly agitated state. Excited delirium is broadly defined as a state of agitation, excitability, paranoia, aggression, and apparent immunity to pain, often associated with stimulant use and certain psychiatric disorders."[3] Begun in 2003 by two attorneys, Lexipol serves "more than 2 million public safety and government professionals with a range of informational and technological solutions to meet the challenges facing them. Their vision is to provide a better, safer way to run a public safety agency."[4]

Floyd pleaded with the officer that he couldn't breathe, begging the officers to let him go. Witnesses who filmed the incident also urged the officer to get off Floyd's neck. After a period of time, Floyd got silent and stopped breathing. Paramedics arrived on the scene, and took him to the hospital where he was pronounced dead. The initial perspective was that an unarmed black man had been killed by a white police officer.

---

3 ·   Lexipol Team, "Understanding Excited Delirium: 4 Takeaways for Law Enforcement," Lexipol (Lexipol, January 20, 2020), https://www.lexipol.com/resources/blog/understanding-excited-delirium-4-takeaways-for-law-enforcement-officers/.

4   Lexipol Team, "Learn About Us - Lexipol Policy & Training Solutions," Lexipol, October 26, 2020, https://www.lexipol.com/about/.

Satan scored big on this one. The video was damaging. Everyone jumped on the bandwagon and felt that this was an atrocity. Including me. This was race against race, police against civilians; and even today, riots continue to threaten cities across the United States. Sadly, this case is far from over, and every time a new court decision comes out about it, there is going to be more pain and violence in this country.

Both of these deaths were tragedies. Right, left, black, white, male, and female: all can agree on that point. We all agree that we have the right to peaceful protest and some changes need to be made. However, we don't seem to recognize that riots that destroy our cities, and the lives and businesses of those that live in them, are not peaceful protests. They are extremist acts against the very fiber of our country.

So, let's recap what we have been through since March of 2020. As of June 2, 2020, the Center for Disease Control and Prevention (CDC) reported 105,157 COVID-19 deaths in the United States. (By November that number would more than double.) We were shut down and stuck at home for over a month and we are now in the slow process of opening up again. Churches are still working on getting back into their buildings because of all the CDC requirements. They want to make sure they do not cause another outbreak. If that wasn't enough, American cities are being torn apart from riots over the deaths of Ahmaud Arbery and George Floyd.

In light of all that, I started reading a book called *Trumpocalypse*. This jumped out at me:

> While a simply conservative revolution can never succeed, a revolution inspired by Christianity certainly can, because it draws its energies from the existence of the biblical God, the reality of the resurrection of Jesus Christ and His second

coming, the truth of the Word of God, and the power of the Holy Spirit. It's these factors, and these alone, that ignited the American Revolution. A true "Christian Revolution" can never happen unless the church, individual Christians, and Christian leaders really believe what they are teaching and then act upon it. Only a holy fire can ignite the hearts of men and women. Mere intellectual acknowledgment of the truth of the gospel will never release the explosive energies of heaven. The human heart, mind, and will must be absolutely gripped with the truthfulness of God's existence and His purpose for their lives and the destiny of mankind. When, and only when, this happens will the Christian Revolution occur and radically change our world.[5]

We need a revolution. You read that right. We need a revolution inspired by Christianity. If you didn't fully take in that excerpt, take the time to read it again. This is it. We need a Christian Revolution. This Christian Revolution is not against the races, the sexes, the first responders, the American citizens, the conservatives, or the liberals; it is against a much more powerful foe.

For our struggle is not against flesh and blood, but against the rulers, against the authorities, against the powers of this dark world and against the spiritual forces of evil in the heavenly realms. *(Ephesians 6:12)*

Brothers and sisters, our war is not against each other. Our war is against the spiritual forces of evil in the heavenly realms that are tearing us apart. We need to wake up—and take up—the full armor of God, and get in the streets and take our country back.

Man has been trying to run this country without God for almost a century, and where has it gotten us? We have cities in poverty, brothers fighting brothers, a criminal system that needs to be

5   Paul McGuire and Troy Anderson, *Trumpocalypse: The End-Times President, a Battle Against the Globalist Elite, and the Countdown to Armageddon,* Nashville: Hachette Book Group, 2018.

revamped. Clearly taking God out of everything was not a good idea. Satan has thrown down the gauntlet. How will we respond? Sit back and let him tear our country apart? Or stand up for what is right and share Christ's teachings and His love with everyone we meet? What are you going to do?

I don't know about you, but I am tired of hearing that Christians are weak. We are not. I am tired of Satan attacking this country and taunting us like Goliath did Israel. We need to suit up.

> Therefore put on the full armor of God, so that when the day of evil comes, you may be able to stand your ground, and after you have done everything, to stand. Stand firm then, with the belt of truth buckled around your waist, with the breastplate of righteousness in place, and with your feet fitted with the readiness that comes from the gospel of peace. In addition to all this, take up the shield of faith, with which you can extinguish all the flaming arrows of the evil one. Take the helmet of salvation and the sword of the Spirit, which is the word of God. And pray in the Spirit on all occasions with all kinds of prayers and requests. With this in mind, be alert and always keep on praying for all the Lord's people. *(Ephesians 6:13-18)*

We need to get organized. I know some networkers, so I am going to find out how we can get this started. I am tired of hearing about things that are going wrong while we do nothing. We really do need a Christian Revolution.

Theodore Roosevelt once said, "Complaining about a problem without posing a solution is called whining." (Thank you, Greg Heckroth, for telling me about this quote.) I am tired of the whining. It is time to put together a Christian solution. Please join me as we take our nation back for God.

Epilogue

When Jessica was invited to go to Embry-Riddle Aeronautical University, Wendy and I were ecstatic. Neither one of us ever finished college, so to see our oldest get to this point in life made both of us very proud. Here was my little buddy, who loved to go shooting with me, got her black belt in karate at a very early age, and had been around the world before she was eighteen, majoring in Homeland Security and following in her dad's footsteps.

I owe a lot to Jessica and who she is because of her walk with Christ. When she was seven, she went to a Vacation Bible School. On the last night, they baptized everyone that had accepted Christ. She told Wendy she was ready, but I doubted it because she was so young. I thought she was only doing it because everyone else was doing it. The night of the baptism, I pulled her aside and told her she wasn't ready. She looked at me and told me she wanted Jesus in her heart. She knew He loved her, and she wanted to follow Him for the rest of her life. I sat back and told the Lord that she was His daughter. I committed to watch over her, protect her, love her, and give her guidance while she was in our home. With tears of joy in my eyes, I let her go and get baptized. To this day she still follows Christ, and at times, is a better Christian than I am.

Dropping her off at college hit me hard. She was leaving the nest. I was both excited and hurting because I knew things would never be the same. A part of my life had gone on. Jessica had become her own person and the world was hers for the taking.

One the way back from Daytona, I reflected on how we had gotten this far. I realized that as parents, we believed in Jessica. We believed in Jaycee too. Wendy and I always told them they could be whatever they wanted to be. We supported and encouraged them to go after their dreams. Even during hard times, we stuck by them. This kind of support was something Wendy and I never really had.

Jessica is following in her dad's footsteps, but Jaycee is more like me when I was young. She doesn't know what she wants to do with her life yet; she wants to enjoy it and grow up. She is the dreamer, the artist, and the one with the quick humor. Jaycee also has my discernment and sometimes, can read people better than I can. I am happy she is still trying to figure out what she wants to be when she grows up. I was eighteen before I knew my mission in life.

Wendy and I have tried our best to give the girls the life neither one of us had with the love and support of *both* parents. We are not perfect, but following God is our focus. With Him leading, we know we are following His unseen plan, and all is well.

Author's Note

This September will mark the fiftieth anniversary of the shooting in Glen Rose, Texas. Because of the anniversary and the completion of this book, Wendy, Jessica, Jaycee, and I are leaving for Texas in a few days. We are stopping in Sutherland Springs for a fundraiser for Kris Workman, Julie Workman's son, who was paralyzed from the waist down in the shooting there. They want to raise enough money to build him a house; I pray that they do. We are also going to Glen Rose, so I can show my family where it all began. I hope to see some of the English family that I have not seen in fifty years.

The only reason I am here today is because of the love of Jesus Christ. After his conversion, Jesus told Paul this:

> Now get up and stand on your feet. I have appeared to you to appoint you as a servant and as a witness of what you have seen and will see of me. *(Acts 26:16)*

When I turned my life over to Christ, I saw how He had been everywhere in my life. He had never left me. He was always there; and because of His love, I am His servant today. He has blessed me and continues to bless me. If it were taken away tomorrow, I would still have my memories of all that He has given me and I would live in those memories and continue to serve Him until He comes or takes me home. Then I will at last rest from fighting for the safety of His bride.

To my family and friends who keep asking me when I am going to really retire, I answer, "I did pray to God about that one night and I felt His answer was, 'Find retirement in the Bible, then we can talk about it.'" I still haven't found it. I know He has a special place for all of us who are out here taking our "stand against the devil's schemes" (Ephesians 6:11). We will continue to be true to our callings.

> Be shepherds of God's flock that is under your care, watching over them—not because you must, but because you are willing, as God wants you to be; not pursuing dishonest gain, but eager to serve; not lording it over those entrusted to you, but being examples to the flock. And when the Chief Shepherd appears, you will receive the crown of glory that will never fade away. *(1 Peter 5:2-4)*

I look forward to that banquet in my heavenly Father's house.

Me and Jean and Jane English – Texas, July 2020 – 50th year after incident